Victoria Crosses of the Gurkha and Indian Regiments

Victoria Crosses of the Gurkha and Indian Regiments

Kevin Brazier

Pen & Sword
MILITARY

First published in Great Britain in 2023 by
Pen & Sword Military
An imprint of
Pen & Sword Books Ltd
Yorkshire – Philadelphia

Copyright © Kevin Brazier 2023

ISBN 978 1 39906 749 2

The right of Kevin Brazier to be identified as Author of this work has been asserted by him in accordance with the Copyright, Designs and Patents Act 1988.

A CIP catalogue record for this book is
available from the British Library.

All rights reserved. No part of this book may be reproduced or transmitted in any form or by any means, electronic or mechanical including photocopying, recording or by any information storage and retrieval system, without permission from the Publisher in writing.

Typeset by Mac Style
Printed in the UK by CPI Group (UK) Ltd, Croydon, CR0 4YY.

Pen & Sword Books Limited incorporates the imprints of Atlas, Archaeology, Aviation, Discovery, Family History, Fiction, History, Maritime, Military, Military Classics, Politics, Select, Transport, True Crime, Air World, Frontline Publishing, Leo Cooper, Remember When, Seaforth Publishing, The Praetorian Press, Wharncliffe Local History, Wharncliffe Transport, Wharncliffe True Crime, White Owl and After the Battle.

For a complete list of Pen & Sword titles please contact

PEN & SWORD BOOKS LIMITED
47 Church Street, Barnsley, South Yorkshire, S70 2AS, England
E-mail: enquiries@pen-and-sword.co.uk
Website: www.pen-and-sword.co.uk

Or

PEN AND SWORD BOOKS
1950 Lawrence Rd, Havertown, PA 19083, USA
E-mail: Uspen-and-sword@casematepublishers.com
Website: www.penandswordbooks.com

For Queen Elizabeth II
Duty done
RIP

Contents

Acknowledgements ix
Introduction x

Part 1: The Gurkha Regiment VCs 1

Chapter 1
Indian Mutiny, 1857–59 3
Lushai Expedition, India, 1871–72 5
Perak War, 1875–76 6
Second Afghan War, 1878–80 8
Second Naga Hills Expedition, 1879–80 9
Manipur Expedition, 1891 10
Hunza-Nagar Campaign India, 1891 12

Chapter 2
Third Somaliland Expedition, 1903–04 15
Armed Mission to Tibet, 1903–04 16
First World War, 1914–18 18
Second World War, 1939–45 21
Malaysia-Indonesia Confrontation, 1963–66 37

Part 2: The Indian Regiment VCs 43

Chapter 3
Persian War, 1856–57 45
Indian Mutiny, 1857–59 48

Chapter 4
Third China War, 1860–62 131
Umbeyla Campaign, 1863 132

Second Maori (Waikato-Haubau) War, 1863–66   134
Bhutan War, 1864–65   136

Chapter 5
Third Ashanti War, 1873–74   140
Baluchistan, 1877   141
Second Afghan War, 1878–80   142
Karen-Ni Expedition, 1888–89   154

Chapter 6
Hunza-Nagar Campaign, India 1891–92   156
North-West Frontier, 1895   157
Malakand Frontier War, 1897–98   159
Tirah Campaign, 1897–98   160
Mohmand Campaign India 1897–98   164

Chapter 7
Second Boer War, 1899–02   167
Fifth Ashanti War 1900–01   169
Second Somaliland Expedition, 1902   171
Third Somaliland Expedition, 1903–04   172
Fourth Somaliland Expedition, 1903–04   174
First World War, 1914–18   175
Waziristan Campaign, 1919–20   193
Second Mohmand Campaign, 1935   197
Second World War, 1939–45   198

Glossary   222
Acronyms and Abbreviations   224
Indian Army Ranks   225
Bibliography   226
Alphabetical List   227

Acknowledgements

I would like to thank a few people for their help in bringing this book to publication. Firstly, Amy Jordan, for commissioning me to write it. Jill Sugden and Sofia Brusling, for their many hours of proofreading. Mark Green, for his continued support and research, and for access to his excellent website and photo archive, which can be found at www.victoriacrossonline.co.uk. All grave photos are from the author's collection.

I must also mention the Victoria Cross Trust for their continued support. They do amazing work caring for VC graves that do not come under the CWGC. Check out their website at: www.victoriacrosstrust.org.

Introduction

This book tells the stories of the men who were awarded the Victoria Cross while serving in the Gurkha and Indian regiments of the Indian Army; this also includes British soldiers serving in these regiments. The Indian Army have been involved in wars all over Europe, Africa, the Middle East and Far East, in many campaigns. However, although the VC has been awarded for valour 'in the presence of the enemy' since 1857, native Gurkhas and Indians only became eligible for the medal from 1912 onwards. It was not until 1914 that the VC was awarded for the first time to a native Indian, and then in 1915 to a Gurkha. Prior to this, awarding of the VC was only to British soldiers serving in the Indian Army.

I have divided this book into two parts. Part 1 tells the stories of the men who were serving in the Gurkha regiments at the time of their VC actions. Of the twenty-six Gurkha regiment VCs, half were awarded to native-born Gurkhas and half to British officers. Part 2 tells the stories of the men who were serving in Indian regiments at the time of their VC actions. Of the 135 VCs awarded to Indian regiments, only twenty-eight were given to native Indians.

I was lucky enough to hold all of the VCs held by the National Army Museum in London when I worked there as a volunteer.

Part 1

The Gurkha Regiment VCs

Chapter 1

Indian Mutiny, 1857–59

The Indian, or Sepoy, Mutiny began in Meerut on 10 May 1857, and although it was ultimately unsuccessful, it tested Britain's military resources to the limit. There had been unrest among the Indian population for several years. The infamous 'greased cartridges' incident was the flashpoint for the mutiny. Loading the new Enfield rifle required tearing open the greased cartridge and many sepoys believed the cartridges were greased with cow or pig fat, thereby offending both Muslims and Hindus. Soon the sepoys at the Delhi garrison joined the Meerut rebels and the mutiny quickly spread across northern India.

John Adam TYTLER, Choorpoorah, 10 February 1858

John Tytler was born on 29 October 1825 in Monghyr, India, the third son of John Tytler, surgeon in the Honourable East India Company (HEIC), and Anne (née Gillies). When he was 5 years old, young John was sent home to England and did not see his parents for the next five years. The family lived for a year in Jersey, but when his father died in 1837, John and his mother moved to Edinburgh. In 1843, he was commissioned as ensign into the HEIC, being posted to the 66th Bengal Native Infantry Regiment.

John Adam Tytler.

Tytler took part in the Second Sikh War in 1848–49, involvement in which was regarded by the sepoys as foreign service. When the Punjab was annexed and foreign duty pay was discontinued, the 66th mutinied. The rebellion was put down and the regiment marched to Umbeyla, where it was disbanded in February 1850. Its weapons and colours were handed over to the 1st Nasiri Battalion, which assumed the title of the 66th Goorkha Regiment of Native Infantry (later 1st Gurkha Rifles).

When, in May 1857, the sepoys mutinied at Meerut, Tytler (by now a lieutenant) and his men were at the hill station of Haldwani. In September that year, 1,000 rebels attacked Haldwani, and with just seventy men, Tytler played a major part in defending it.

The rebels hid in the Kumaon Hills area and awaited reinforcements. On 9 February 1858, the 66th, commanded by Captain Ross and with 200 cavalry and two guns, surprised a rebel force of 4,000 to 5,000 infantry, 1,000 cavalry and four guns at the village of Charpura.

The next day at Choorpoorah, Ross led two companies of the 66th against the rebel right flank. When the men began to waver under grapeshot and musketry, Tytler rushed forward alone on horseback and engaged the enemy gunners in hand-to-hand combat, during which he was shot through the left arm and speared in the chest. When his men caught up with him, the position was taken.

For this action, Tytler was recommended for the Victoria Cross. When the recommendation reached the Duke of Cambridge's desk, he was not keen to see it as a VC action. However, approval was granted on 24 August 1858, and, like many of the mutiny VCs, Tytler's medal was sent to him in the post.

After a period of rest, Tytler re-joined his regiment and in a six-week period was involved in four battles in the Kumaon Hills. As part of Brigadier General Throup's force, the 66th won victories at Pusayan on 17 February 1848 and Mittowlee on 9 November 1848.

Tytler next saw action during the Black Mountain and Lushai campaigns in the Second Afghan War. As a brigadier general, he commanded the 2nd Infantry Brigade of the Peshawar Valley Field Force under General Sam Browne, vc.

After a year of hard fighting, Tytler succumbed to pneumonia on 14 February 1880. He was buried in Kohat Cemetery, India (now Pakistan). His VC is held by The Gurkha Museum, Peninsula Barracks, Winchester, Hampshire.

Lushai Expedition, India, 1871–72

From 1850, the Lushai, or Looshai, tribesmen had gradually migrated from the Chin Hills into Assam, subjugating the local people to their own rule. They remained untouched by foreign influence until Britain annexed Assam in 1862. The Lushai were furious at this foreign intrusion and started raids into British territory, to which Britain responded with punitive expeditions. When, in 1872, the Lushai kidnapped a girl, Mary Winchester, a field force was sent out to save her and to punish the kidnappers, and this was called the Lushai Expedition. Mary Winchester was indeed rescued, and lived until 1955.

Donald MACINTYRE, Lalgnoora, 4 January 1872

Donald Macintyre.

Donald Macintyre was born on 12 September 1831 in Kincraig, Ross-shire, Scotland, the son of Donald and Margaret (née Mackenzie) Macintyre. He was educated at Addiscombe Military Seminary, near Croydon, Surrey, and entered the army in June 1850. Macintyre served with the 66th Goorkha Regiment of Native Infantry (later 1st Gurkha Rifles) against the hill tribes of the Peshawar Frontier, including the destruction of the fort and village of Prangbur and the action at Ishkakot during 1852 under Sir Colin Campbell. A year later, he was engaged with the expedition against the Boree Afridis.

In 1856, by now a lieutenant, Macintyre served under Sir Neville Chamberlin in the expedition to the Kurram Valley in Afghanistan. During 1857–58, he raised what was to become the 4th Gurkha Regiment, which on a number of occasions was employed in protecting the hill tribes on the Kale Kumaon Frontier and maintaining order in the area. Macintyre was promoted to captain in June 1862, and in 1864 served in the Doaba Field Force in the Peshawar Valley.

On 4 January 1872, while serving in the Bengal Staff Corps and during the assault on Lalgnoora, Macintyre (now a major) was the first man to reach the 9-foot high stockade. After climbing over it, he ran into the flames of the burning village. His men were following behind, and they stormed the village.

Macintyre's VC, gazetted on 27 September 1872, was presented to him later that year, after he had been promoted to lieutenant colonel. In 1877, he was promoted to full colonel. His last active service was as commander of the 2nd Gurkhas in the Second Anglo-Afghan War. He retired from the Bengal Staff Corps in December 1880 with the rank of major general. He is author of *Hindu-Koh: Wanderings and Wild Sport on and Beyond the Himalayas 1853–1854* (White Lotus Press, Edinburgh, 1889).

Macintyre died on 15 April 1903 and was buried in his family plot at Rosmarkie Churchyard, near Fortrose, Highland. His VC is held by The Gurkha Museum, Peninsula Barracks, Winchester, Hampshire.

Perak War, 1875–76

Britain, which had occupied Singapore since 1819, had exercised a policy of not getting involved in local upheavals in the Malay states to the north. However, when civil war broke out in nearby Selangor in 1871, Britain intervened, annexing the region. The next year, trouble flared up in Perak and threatened to spread to Singapore, so the British also annexed Perak. These areas proved difficult to control, with the British administrator James Birch's measures to keep law and order bringing him into direct conflict with the local Malay leaders.

In July 1875, seeing their power and revenue seriously threatened, the Malay chiefs had Birch murdered. He was stabbed to death while in the bathhouse of his boat. Britain replied with a punitive expedition to find the assassins.

George Nicolas CHANNER, Perak, 20 December 1875

George Channer was born on 7 January 1843 in Allahabad, India, the son of Colonel George Girdwood Channer and his wife Susan (née Kendall). He was educated in England at Truro Grammar School and Cheltenham

College. Channer entered the Bengal Infantry with the rank of ensign in June 1859 and was promoted to lieutenant in 1861. He served with the 89th and 95th regiments until 1866. He took part in the Umbeyla Campaign on the North-West Frontier of India in 1863–64 and the Lushai Expedition in 1871–72.

In 1872, he married Annie Isabella and they had six sons (two of whom died young) and four daughters. On 20 December 1875, by now a captain in the Bengal Staff Corps, Indian Army and 1st Gurkha Rifles, Channer was tasked with gathering intelligence on the enemy's strength. He crept up so close to the stockade that he could hear them talking and, seeing there was no watch, he signalled to his men to attack. He shot the first man dead himself and was the first man to enter the stockade, which was taken before the enemy could react effectively. His action undoubtedly saved a great many lives, as it would otherwise have been necessary to resort to the bayonet.

George Nicolas Channer.

Channer's VC was gazetted on 12 April 1876 and presented to him later that year, although it is not known by whom. He served in the Jowaki Afridi Expedition of 1877–78. During the Second Afghan War, he was present at the capture of Peiwar Kotal in 1878, and was mentioned in despatches and promoted to brevet lieutenant colonel. Channer commanded the 1st Brigade during the Black Mountain Expedition in 1888 and was mentioned in despatches again. In the Chitral Campaign of 1895, he commanded the reserve brigade, having by then been promoted to major general. His final rank was general.

Channer died on 13 December 1905 and was buried in East-the-Water Cemetery; Section C, Grave 505, Bideford, Devon. His VC was sold at auction in 2016 for a hammer price of £200,000 and is now in the Lord Ashcroft Gallery, Imperial War Museum, London.

Second Afghan War, 1878–80

Britain had been keeping an eye on this important buffer to the north-west of India as part of a 'masterly inactivity' policy. In 1866, the Emir Sher Ali came to power. He was well disposed to Britain and feared Russian intrusion as much as he feared the British. In 1872, Britain and Russia signed an agreement stating that Russia would respect Afghanistan's northern border, and that there would be no need for the British Government to give any promises of support to Afghanistan. Alarm bells sounded when, in 1876, the Emir reluctantly allowed a Russian mission to Kabul, and then refused to admit the British envoy. This intrusion was too close to British-ruled India to go unopposed. Sher Ali had to go; an ultimatum was sent demanding that a British envoy be admitted, and when this was ignored, three columns of British soldiers moved in.

John COOK, Peiwar Kotal, 2 December 1878

John Cook was born on 28 August 1843 in Edinburgh, the second son of Alexander Shank Cook, Advocate Sheriff of Ross & Cromarty. John was educated at Edinburgh Academy, followed by the Scottish Naval and Military Academy. At 11, he was nominated to attend the Addiscombe Military Seminary, near Croydon, Surrey.

At 17, he was posted to India and joined the 3rd Sikh Regiment as an ensign, and served with them during the Umbeyla Campaign, on the North-West

John Cook.

Frontier. He was mentioned in despatches for his gallantry in leading a bayonet charge. He also took part in the Hazara Expedition of 1888 and, after ten years' service, decided to take a year off and return home.

Cook returned to India in 1871, was promoted to captain in 1872 and transferred to the 5th Gukha Rifles. When the Afghan War broke out, the 5th Gurkhas joined the Kurram Field Force under Lord Roberts, vc.

On 2 December 1878 at Peiwar Kotal, Cook led a charge out of the trenches with such intensity that the enemy broke and fled. During the fight, Cook went to the assistance of Major Galbraith, who was in imminent danger of being killed by an Afghan. Cook parried the Afghan's bayonet and they wrestled for some time until the man bit into his sword arm. Cook hurled him over and charged his bayonet to give the final blow, but at this point, the Afghan was shot in the head.

Cook's VC, gazetted on 18 March 1879, was presented to him on 24 May that year by Lord Roberts, vc, in Kabul. He would only wear it for seven months.

Promoted to major in November 1879 (gazetted on 16 January 1880), Cook next saw action on 11 December at Argundeh, where the British were compelled back by a large force of the enemy. Cook and his brother Walter distinguished themselves by covering the retreat and saving the baggage. Walter received a chest wound and John a head wound. Major Cook was still able to get about and the next day took part in the attack on the That-i-Shah peak. During this action, he was wounded in the left leg.

Unfortunately, Cook's wound became affected with gangrene and he died on 19 December 1879. He was buried in Sherpur Cantonment Cemetery, C of E Section, Kabul, Afghanistan. His VC is in the Lord Ashcroft Gallery, Imperial War Museum, London.

Second Naga Hills Expedition, 1879–80

Although Britain controlled most of India, the tribal Naga people in the north were turbulent and resisted British rule. In 1879, they murdered a British Commissioner and besieged the garrison at Kohima. A punitive expedition under Brigadier General J. Nation was sent to restore order.

Richard Kirby RIDGEWAY, Konoma, 22 November 1879

Richard Ridgeway was born on 18 August 1848 in Oldcastle, County Meath, Ireland, the second son of Richard and Annette (née Adams). He was educated privately and later at the Royal Military Academy Sandhurst. Ridgeway entered the 96th Regiment of Foot as an ensign in January 1868 and was promoted to lieutenant in February 1870.

In 1871, he married Emily Maria (whom he called Amy). The following year he transferred into the Bengal Staff Corps and from 1874 was adjutant of the 44th Gurkha Rifles (later 8th Gurkha Rifles). Ridgeway took part in the First Naga Hills Expedition of 1875, during which he was mentioned in despatches.

On 22 November 1879, at Konoma, a small village near to Kohima, a strongly fortified series of trenches, each with stone walls and towers, the outer fortifications were taken by the 44th Gurkhas. During the final assault, Ridgeway charged up to a barricade and attempted to tear down the surrounding planking to enable him to effect an entrance. Under very heavy fire the whole time, he sustained a severe wound to his shoulder.

Richard Kirby Ridgeway.

Ridgeway's VC, gazetted on 11 May 1880, was posted to him in Ireland as his wounds prevented him from travelling to receive it. In 1883, he graduated from the Staff College, and became a Deputy Assistant Quartermaster General the following year. He was promoted to major in 1888 and commanded the 44th Gurkha Rifles from 1891 to 1895. During this time, he took part in the Manipur Expedition (1891), and in 1894 was promoted to lieutenant colonel. He also served in the Tirah Campaign of 1897–98. After retiring from the army in 1906, he lived in Harrogate, Yorkshire, where he died from pneumonia on 11 October 1924. He was cremated at Lawnswood Crematorium, Leeds, and his ashes were scattered in the cemetery copse, near the Columbarium. His VC is not publicly held.

Manipur Expedition, 1891

Manipur is a small hill state lying between Assam and Burma on India's north-eastern border. In September 1890, the Maharaja of Manipur was ousted in a palace coup during which several British officers were murdered and others imprisoned. In March 1891, the British government in India, the British Raj, sent an expedition to crush the rebellion.

Charles James William GRANT, Thobal, 21 March–9 April 1891

Charles Grant was born on 14 October 1861 in Bourtie, Aberdeenshire, to Lieutenant General P.C.S. St John Grant and Helen, daughter of Colonel William Birset. He was educated privately and later at the Royal Military Academy Sandhurst. Grant joined the Suffolk Regiment in May 1882 and the Madras Staff Corps in May 1884, and took part in the Burma Expedition of 1885–87.

When the Manipur rebellion started, Lieutenant Grant was serving in the Indian Staff Corps and commanded a detachment of the 43rd Gurkha Rifles (later the 8th Gurkha Rifles) stationed on

Charles James William Grant.

the border post of Tamu, some 55 miles from Manipur. On hearing of the rebellion, he volunteered to attempt the relief of the British captives, with just eighty native troops. They reached Thobal, 15 miles from Manipur, on 21 March 1891, stormed the village, and entrenched themselves there. The next day, the enemy advanced in great numbers, but without waiting for their attack, Grant went out to meet them with forty of his men, formed up and opened fire. For the following nine days, they fought off repeated attacks. Grant kept the initiative by sallying out whenever possible to attack the Manipurs, inflicting heavy casualties on the enemy and demoralising them. A relief force arrived on 9 April. Grant had lost one man killed and four were wounded, including himself, twice.

For this action he was awarded the VC, which was gazetted on 26 May 1891 and presented to him on 6 July that year by the Governor of Madras, Lord Wenlock, at Ootacamund, India. Grant

Grant's grave, Sidmouth Cemetery.

was then appointed Aide-de-Camp (ADC) to Lieutenant General Sir J.C. Dormer, Commander-in-Chief, Madras.

Grant also got married in 1891. He eventually retired from the army in 1913, with the rank of brevet colonel. He died on 23 November 1932, aged 71, and was buried in Sidmouth Cemetery, Devon, Section 0, Grave 40. His VC was sold at auction in 2011 for £230,000 and is not publicly held.

Hunza-Nagar Campaign India, 1891

In 1891, following tribal unrest in the Hunza-Nagar District, an expedition was sent to the mountain region to storm the fort at Nilt.

Guy Hudleston BOISRAGON, Nilt Fort, 2 December 1891

Guy Boisragon was born on 5 November 1864 in Kohat, India (now Pakistan), the eldest son of Major General Henry M. Boisragon and Anna (née Hudleston). He was sent to England for his education at Charterhouse School in Surrey, and later at the Royal Military Academy Sandhurst.

Guy Hudleston Boisragon.

Boisragon gazetted to the 10th Regiment of Foot (later the Lincolnshire Regiment) in 1885, but transferred as a lieutenant into the 1st Battalion, 5th Gurkha Rifles in 1887. His first combat experience was during the Second Black Mountain Expedition of 1888. He then took part in both the Hazara Expeditions of 1888 and 1891. He also served in both the Miranzai Expeditions of 1891, in the first of these as orderly officer to the general officer commanding (GOC).

On 2 December 1891, Boisragon led the assault on the outer gate at the Nilt Fort but, finding his force insufficient, he went back, under heavy crossfire, to get more men to relieve the first party. He then fought his way to the inner gate, which was forced open by Captain Fenton Aylmer of the Corps of Royal Engineers, using guncotton. Captain Aylmer, who was badly wounded, was awarded the VC for this deed. It was largely due to the actions of these men that the fort was taken.

Boisragon's VC, gazetted on 12 July 1892, was presented to him later the same year, while he was still in India. He next saw service in the Waziristan Campaign of 1894–95 under Major General Sir William Lockhart, and then was ADC to the Lieutenant General of the Punjab Command. In 1896, he was promoted to captain, and in 1897 and 1898 took part in operations in the Samana and Kurram valleys. His last service of the nineteenth century was in the 1897–98 Tirah Campaign. Promoted to major in 1903, he was a brevet colonel and later colonel of the Frontier Force. Boisragon also served in the First World War and was wounded at Gallipoli. Following the war, he retired to the South of France with the rank of brigadier.

Boisragon's headstone, Kensal Green Cemetery, London.

Boisragon died on 14 July 1931 and was buried Kensal Green Cemetery, London, Square 119, Row 2, Grave 18585. His VC is not publicly held.

John MANNERS SMITH, Nilt Fort, 20 December 1891

John Manners Smith was born on 30 August 1864 in Lahore, India (now Pakistan), the fifth son of Charles Manners Smith, Fellow of the Royal College of Surgeons and Surgeon General of the Indian Medical Service. He was educated at Trinity College, Stratford-upon-Avon, King Edward VI School, Norwich, and the Royal Military Academy Sandhurst.

On passing out as a lieutenant in 1883, Manners Smith was posted to the

John Manners Smith.

Norfolk Regiment. In 1885, he joined the Indian Staff Corps and served with the 2nd Sikh Infantry before being attached to the 5th Gurkha Rifles. Two years later, he was appointed Military Attaché to the Foreign Office, Government of India, and admitted to the Political Department. He then accompanied Sir Mortimer Durand on his mission to Sikkim in 1888, and again in 1893.

Manners Smith's grave, Kensal Green Cemetery, London.

The 5th Gurkhas joined the Hunza-Nagar Field Force and Lieutenant Manners Smith accompanied them as a political officer. The field force reached Nilt on 2 December 1891, and for seventeen days was unable to progress. Then, on 20 December, Manners Smith led a small party of men up a steep cliff in an attack on the strong enemy position that had barred their advance. Avoiding rocks that were being dropped from above, he was the first man to reach the summit. He then charged his men at the enemy, shooting the first tribesman himself, and they took the position.

Manners Smith's VC, gazetted on 12 July 1892, was presented to him later the same year. In 1896, he married Bertha Mabel, eldest daughter of Philip Arderne Latham. From 1889 to 1919, Manners Smith held political appointments in Kashmir, Bundelkhand, Balochistan, Rajputana (where he was badly mauled by a panther while out hunting), Central India and Nepal. He served in the Tirah Expedition of 1897–98, following which he became Political Resident of the Political Department, Government of India, and agent to the Governor General in Rajputana in 1917. After the First World War, he retired to London.

Manners Smith died from a wasting disease on 6 January 1920 and was buried in Kensal Green Cemetery, London, Square 187, Row 4, Grave 46720. His VC is held by The Gurkha Museum, Peninsula Barracks, Winchester, Hampshire.

Chapter 2

Third Somaliland Expedition, 1903–04

Most of the tribes in this region had accepted British protection, but the Mullah, Mohammed bin Abdullah (the Mad Mullah), raised an army of 15,000 dervishes and began attacking pro-British tribes. These tribes turned to the British for help. Colonel E.J. Swayne raised a force of Somali levies (enlisted troops) to take on the dervish rebels. As the Mullah retreated, it became apparent that the Somali levies were not seasoned enough to deal with the threat he posed, so a much bigger force was sent to the region.

William George WALKER, Daratoleh, 22 April 1903

William George Walker was born on 28 May 1863 in Nainital, India, the son of Deputy Surgeon General William Walker of the Indian Medical Service. He was educated at Haileybury College, Hertfordshire, and St John's, Oxford. In August 1885, he joined the Suffolk Regiment, and in May 1887 became a lieutenant in the Indian Staff Corps. He served in the Second Miranzai Expedition of 1891 and in the Waziristan Campaign in 1895. Walker was promoted to captain in 1896.

William George Walker.

On 22 April 1903 at Daratoleh, while serving in the 4th Gurkha Rifles, he, Captain Rolland and four others were in the rearguard under heavy fire from the pursuing enemy, when

Captain Bruce was shot through the body. Rolland ran 500 yards to fetch help, while Walker kept up a desperate fire to hold the enemy at bay. When Rolland returned with Major John Gough (of the Rifle Brigade), the column commander, he helped lift Bruce onto a camel. The enemy remained in close pursuit for a further three hours, during which time Bruce died. Walker, Rolland (*see* Chapter 7) and Gough were awarded the VC for this action.

Walker's VC was gazetted on 7 August 1903 and was presented to him by Major General William Manning while he was still in Somaliland. He was promoted to major at the same time, and to lieutenant colonel in January 1904. In 1907, Walker married Alice Molesworth and they had two children. He was given command of the 4th Gurkhas in 1910, and promoted to colonel in 1911.

Walker served during the First World War from 1914–17, being mentioned in despatches three times. He ended his career with the rank of colonel.

He died on 16 February 1936 and was cremated at Woodvale Crematorium, Brighton, Sussex. His VC is held by the National Army Museum, London.

Armed Mission to Tibet, 1903–04

Although notionally under Chinese rule, Tibet had never subscribed to the trade regulations and border demarcations agreed by China and Britain. This led to considerable unrest. Word had reached the British Government that China was engaged in secret talks with Russia to give up her interest in Tibet to them. This would provide Russia with a base from which to threaten India's north-eastern frontiers. Britain sent a mission to talk with the Chinese and Tibetans, but the Tibetans refused to negotiate.

John Duncan GRANT, Gyantse Jong, 6 July 1904

John Grant was born on 28 December 1877 in Roorkee, Uttarakhand, India, the eldest son of Colonel Suene Grant of the Royal Engineers. Young John was educated at Manor House School, Hastings, Cheltenham College and the Royal Military Academy Sandhurst. He entered the army in January 1898 as a second lieutenant and the following year joined the Indian Staff Corps and was promoted to lieutenant in 1900.

On 6 July 1904 at the Gyantse Jong, Grant was serving in the 8th Gurkha Rifles when he led a storming party up a precipitous rock face in single file, crawling on hands and knees and under heavy fire. Grant and a havildar (equivalent of sergeant) attempted to scale the final defence but, on reaching the top, they were both wounded and hurled back. They made another attempt and this time they were successful, Grant being the first man into the fort. Once inside, the Gurkhas quickly routed the enemy.

John Duncan Grant.

Grant's VC was gazetted on 24 January 1905 and presented to him on 24 July that year by Edward VII (the last investiture he carried out). Grant married Kathleen Mary Freyer, daughter of Lieutenant Colonel P.J. Freyer, in January 1907 and they had two children. He was promoted to captain the same year. He continued to serve in India and New Zealand until the outbreak of the First World War. By now a major, he fought in the Persian Gulf in 1915–16, where he was wounded, and was mentioned in despatches in France and Belgium in 1917, and Mesopotamia in 1918.

After the war, Grant served in the Third Afghan War in 1919, being mentioned in despatches, and then as a lieutenant colonel in the Waziristan Campaign of 1919–20, again being mentioned in despatches, and was awarded the DSO. From 1915 to 1928, he was Assistant Adjutant General, Amy HQ, India, and promoted to colonel in September 1926. Grant retired in 1929 but was made an honorary colonel of the 10th Gurkha Rifles in 1934. During the Second World War, he served in the Home Guard.

Grant died on 20 February 1967 and his ashes were scattered in the Garden of Remembrance at Tunbridge Wells Crematorium, Kent. In 2014, his VC was sold at auction for £340,000 and is now in the Lord Ashcroft Gallery, Imperial War Museum, London.

First World War, 1914–18

The causes of the First World War are well known, the tipping point being the assassination of the Austro-Hungarian Archduke Ferdinand on 28 June 1914 in Serbia. Austria-Hungary turned to Germany, who, on 6 July, confirmed that it would back Austria-Hungary in reprisals against the Serbs. The war might have ended as a local Balkan war if it were not for a series of complex treaties that locked countries together.

On 30 July, Austria-Hungary declared war on Serbia. Then, Russia and France, linked by treaty, began to mobilise. Germany presented ultimatums to Russia and France, threatening war if they did not demobilise. On 1 August, Germany declared war on Russia and the next day entered Luxembourg. On 3 August, Germany declared war on France and a day later, German troops entered neutral Belgium. Britain, who had promised to protect Belgium's neutrality, declared war on Germany; Austria-Hungary declared war on Russia the same day. Five days later, France declared war on Austria-Hungary.

KULBIR THAPA, Fauquissart, France 25–26 September 1915

Kulbir Thapa was born on 15 December 1888 (or 1889) in Nigalpani, Palpa District, Nepal, the son of Haria Gulte. Very little is known about Kulbir Thapa's early life other than he was married and had at least one son. He enlisted into the 1st Battalion, the 3rd Queen's Alexandra's Own Gurkha Rifles in December 1907, becoming 2129 Rifleman Kulbir Thapa. He transferred to the 2nd Battalion on the outbreak of war and arrived in France in September 1914, seeing action at Givenchy and Neuve-Chapelle, and at Festubert in 1915.

Kulbir Thapa.

Then, on 25 September 1915 at Fauquissart, Rifleman Kulbir Thapa, despite himself being wounded, found a badly injured man of the

Leicestershire Regiment behind the first line of the German trench and remained with him all day and night, although he was urged by the soldier to save himself. The next morning, he brought the injured man through the German wire and placed him in a shell hole. Then he returned to the German wire and brought back two wounded Gurkhas to the British lines. He then went back and carried the first wounded man in, being under fire most of the way. Kulbir Thapa was subsequently admitted to hospital for his wounds.

His VC was gazetted on 18 November 1915 (making him the first Nepalese-born Gurkha to be awarded the medal), but there does not seem to have been an investiture. In January 1916, he reported back to his battalion in Egypt. He was promoted to naik (equivalent to corporal) on the same day, and later to havildar. Kulbir Thapa served in Palestine with Rifleman Karanbahadur Rana, vc, and they were photographed together at the Gurkha Memorial in Gorakhpur, India, in 1937.

Kulbir died on 3 October 1956 and was buried in Nigalpani Cemetery (exact location unknown), Palpa District, Nepal. His VC is held by The Gurkha Museum, Peninsula Barracks, Winchester, Hampshire.

George Campbell WHEELER, River Tigris, Shumran, Mesopotamia, 23 February 1917

George Wheeler was born on 7 April 1880 in Yokohama, Japan, where his father, Dr Edwin Wheeler, was practising medicine. He was educated in England at Bedford School from 1893 to 1897, and played cricket and rugby for the school. He was fluent in French, German, Japanese and Hindustani.

After Sandhurst, Wheeler was commissioned as a second lieutenant into the East Yorkshire Regiment in January 1900, and joined the Indian Army in April 1901. In early 1902, he joined the 2nd Battalion, 9th Gurkha Rifles, with a

George Campbell Wheeler.

promotion to lieutenant. He was further promoted to captain in 1909, and major in 1915.

In 1916, he was posted to Mesopotamia, where, on 23 February 1917 at the Tigris River, along with one Gurkha officer and eight men, he crossed the river and rushed the enemy's trench in the face of very heavy fire. Having got a footing on the bank, he was counter-attacked almost immediately by enemy bomb throwers. Wheeler at once led a counter-charge, receiving in the process a severe bayonet wound to the head. In spite of this, he managed to disperse the enemy and consolidate the position.

Wheeler's grave, St Mary Magdalene Church, New Milton.

His VC was gazetted on 8 June 1917 and was presented to him on 26 July 1919 by George V at Buckingham Palace. Wheeler was promoted to Acting Lieutenant Colonel of the 1st Battalion, 9th Gurkha Rifles, in December 1921, when they were posted to Malabar in southern India for active service against the Moplahs. He held this rank until January 1922, and ended his career as Commandant of Military Police at Port Blair, in the Andaman Islands.

George Wheeler died from pneumonia following an operation on 26 August 1938 and was buried in St Mary Magdalene Churchyard, New Milton, Hampshire. His VC is held by the National Army Museum, London.

KARANBAHADUR RANA, El Kefr, Palestine, 10 April 1918

Karanbahadur Rana was born on 21 December 1898 in Mangalthan, Gulmi, Nepal. He was a Rana of the Magar clan. He joined the 2nd Battalion, 3rd Queen Alexandra's Own Gurkha Rifles in 1914 at 16 years old.

In April 1918, the British XXI Corps was on the coastal sector of Palestine, just north of Jaffa, with the 75th Division on the right of the corps. The 75th Division launched a preliminary attack at 05:10 hours on 9 April, which met with fierce resistance. On the following day, Rifleman Karanbahadur Rana and a few others crept forward with a Lewis gun under intense fire to engage an enemy machine gun. When the leader of the gun team was killed, he took over and quickly knocked out the enemy gun, then silenced enemy bombers and infantry to his front. Later, he assisted with covering fire in the withdrawal, waiting until the enemy were almost upon him before retiring. In silencing the enemy position, Rifleman Karanbahadur Rana enabled his company commander, Lieutenant Frederick Barter, vc, to withdraw from a position within 30 yards of the machine gun, where he had been pinned down for five and a half hours.

Karanbahadur Rana.

His VC was gazetted on 21 June 1918 and was presented to him on 2 August 1919 by George V at Buckingham Palace. While in London for the investiture, he took part in a parade of Indian troops through the city. He left the army in the mid-1930s and almost nothing is known about his life after that.

Karanbahadur Rana died on 25 July 1973 and was buried at Bharse, Gulmi, Litung, Nepal. His VC is held by The Gurkha Museum, Peninsula Barracks, Winchester, Hampshire.

Second World War, 1939–45

The causes of the Second World War are well known: Hitler's rise to power in 1933, reoccupying the Rhineland, annexing of Austria and taking over the Sudetenland of Czechoslovakia. Next was the demand for Poland to allow access to the city of Danzig. When this was refused, Germany attacked Poland. Britain and France had guaranteed Poland's sovereignty and so declared war on 3 September 1939. The conflict truly became a world war when Japan attacked the USA on 7 December 1941. The Second World War was the most destructive conflict the world had ever known, resulting in the deaths of 60 million people worldwide.

LALBAHADUR THAPA, Rass-es-Zouai, Tunisia, 5/6 April 1943

Lalbahadur Thapa was born on 1 February 1906 in Thant Hup village, Parbat District, Nepal. Almost nothing is known about his early life prior to him enlisting into the 1st Battalion, 2nd King Edward VII's Own Gurkha Rifles in 1925. He served on the North-West Frontier of India in 1936–37, being commissioned in 1937.

In 1941, his battalion sailed for the Middle East and in 1942 was part of the 6th Indian Brigade of the 4th Indian Division. In Tunisia during 1943, the division was tasked with taking the Fatnassa heights in a flanking movement around Rommel's forces.

Lalbahadur Thapa.

On the night of 5/6 April 1943, during a silent attack, Subedar Lalbahadur Thapa was second in command of D Company. The CO of No. 16 Platoon was detached with one section to secure an isolated position on the left of the company's objective. Lalbahadur Thapa took the remaining two sections and led them towards the main objective. First contact was made at the foot of a pathway winding up a narrow cleft. This position was well defended with a series of enemy posts. The men in the outer posts were all killed by the bayonet or kukri (an Indian machete or Gurkha knife) in the first rush, and then the enemy opened a very heavy fire straight down the narrow pathway. However, Lalbahadur Thapa led his men on and fought his way up to the enemy position under heavy machine-gun fire, killing two with his revolver and two more with his kukri. Upon reaching the crest, with just two other men, he killed another two men with his kukri and the rest fled. He then covered his company's advance up to the crest. Thus secured, advance by the whole division was possible.

Lalbahadur Thapa's VC was gazetted on 15 June 1943. He would later reach the rank of subedar major. He fought on in North Africa and Italy. In September 1945, he was mentioned in despatches for action in Burma.

He retired in 1948 when his battalion moved to Malaya to become part of the British Army. Four of his sons also served in Gurkha regiments.

Lalbahadur Thapa died on 20 October 1968 and was buried in an unmarked grave in Paklihawa Camp Cemetery (outside the north perimeter fence; the exact location was not recorded), Nepal. His VC is held by The Gurkha Museum, Peninsula Barracks, Winchester, Hampshire.

GAJE GHALE, Chin Hills, Burma, 24–27 May 1943

Gaje Ghale.

Gaje Ghale was born on 1 July 1922 in the village of Barpak, Gorkha District, Nepal. (He gave his date of birth as 1 July 1918 when he joined the army.) He was a Gurung of the Ghale tribe. He enlisted into the 2nd Battalion, 5th Royal Gurkha Rifles in 1934 as a boy recruit. He served in Waziristan, and from 1939–42 was an instructor at the Regimental Centre in Abbottabad.

On 24 May 1943, a large Japanese force launched an assault into the Chin Hills, where Havildar Gaje Ghale's battalion was stationed. The Japanese occupied a key position on Basha East Hill, the approach to which was very narrow and easily raked with machine-gun fire. Two attempts had been repulsed. On the 25th, Gaje Ghale's platoon was given the task of taking the position. Although this was his first time in combat and his men were inexperienced, they engaged in attacking the Japanese position. Wounded in the arm, chest and leg by a grenade, he continued to lead assault after assault, encouraging his men with the Gurkha's battle cry *'Ayo Gurkha'*. Spurred on by the irresistible will of their leader, they finally stormed and captured the position, which Gaje Ghale then held and consolidated under heavy fire, refusing to go to the aid post until ordered.

His VC was gazetted on 30 September 1943 and, when it was proposed to present him with it at the Regimental Centre at Abbottabad, the regimental bahun, a respected religious adviser, announced that the date was inauspicious and should be postponed. Gaje Ghale was presented with his VC in 1944 by Lord Wavell in New Delhi, beneath the walls of the Red Fort, in the presence of a crowd of 5,000 people. He was also awarded the Star of Nepal by the prime minister of Nepal.

In 1946, Gaje Ghale attended the Second World War victory parade in London and, after Indian independence in 1947, he remained with his battalion and was promoted to subedar major. He served in the Congo in 1963 with a United Nations Force with Subedar Agansing Rai, vc. By the time of his retirement, he had reached the rank of honorary captain. Gaje Ghale was a regular attendee of VC reunions, and in 1990, he joined four of the seven living Gurkha VCs at the opening of The Gurkha Museum in Hampshire. Five years later, he was one of twenty-one VC holders present at the Royal Tournament for the fiftieth anniversary of VJ Day. He was married with eight children.

Gaje Ghale died on 28 March 2000 in New Delhi and was cremated at Dehradun, India. His VC is in the Lord Ashcroft Gallery, Imperial War Museum, London.

Michael ALLMAND, Pin Hmi Road Bridge, Burma, 11, 13 & 23 June 1944

Michael Allmand.

Michael Allmand was born on 22 August 1923 in Golders Green, London, the son of Professor Arthur John Allmand, mc, and Marguerite Marie (née Malicorne). He was educated at Ampleforth College, Yorkshire, and in 1941 went to Oriel College, Oxford, to study history. Called up for military service, he was commissioned into the Royal Armoured Corps on completing his officer training in 1943. Later, he was selected for service in the Indian Armoured Corps, and joined the 6th Duke of Connaught's Own Lancers, a cavalry regiment of the Indian Army.

When GHQ asked for volunteers for the Second Chindit Expedition, he immediately volunteered. He was posted to the 3rd Battalion, 6th Gurkha Rifles, 77th Infantry Brigade under Brigadier James (Mad Mike) Calvert. Their objective was Mogaung, surrounded by jungle and swamps, and hampered by the monsoon weather.

On 11 June 1944, Acting Captain Allmand's platoon came under very heavy machine-gun fire, halting them with severe casualties. Allmand charged on alone, throwing grenades into the enemy positions and killing three with his kukri. Inspired by his splendid example, the surviving men followed him and captured the objective. Now in command of the company, on 13 June he dashed 30 yards ahead of his men through marshy ground swept by machine-gun fire and personally killed a number of the enemy machine-gunners. He then led his men onto the high ground. On 23 June, in the final attack on a railway bridge that spanned the Mogaung River, although suffering from trench foot, he moved forward alone through deep mud and shell holes, charging an enemy machine-gun nest, but he was mortally wounded.

Michael Allmand's VC was gazetted on 26 October 1944 and was presented to his parents by George VI at Buckingham Palace. Allmand was buried in Taukkyan War Cemetery, Plot XIII, Row A, Grave 4, Rangoon, Burma. His VC is held by The Gurkha Museum, Peninsula Barracks, Winchester, Hampshire.

GANJU LAMA, Ningthoukhong, Burma, 12 June 1944

Ganju Lama was born on 22 July 1924 in Sangmo, Sikkim, India. Although he enlisted into the 7th Gurkha Rifles, he was not a native of Nepal, but at the time anyone who came from the border area was accepted. His real name was Gyantso but the recruiting officer wrote it down as Ganju, and that name he kept.

In May 1944, after training, he joined the 1st Battalion in Burma, near Imphal. During operations on the Tiddim Road, his battalion surprised a patrol of Japanese and killed several of them. For his part in this action, Ganju was awarded the MM.

By June 1944, the tide was turning in Burma but the Japanese launched a major attack on 12 June, with tanks in support. Rifleman Ganju

Lama, with complete disregard for his own safety, took a Piat anti-tank gun and crawled forward. He succeeded in bringing the gun into action within 30 yards of the enemy tanks, knocking out two of them. Despite a broken wrist and serious wounds to his hands, he moved forward again and engaged the tank crews, who were trying to escape. Not until he had accounted for all of them did he consent to having his wounds dressed.

Ganju Lama's VC was gazetted on 7 September 1944 and was presented to him by Lord Wavell, in the presence of Lord Mountbatten and General Slim, in New Delhi. He stayed on in the army after the war and when India gained its independence in 1947, he opted to remain in the Indian Army.

Ganju Lama.

In 1964, a large boil developed on his leg; when it burst, a Japanese bullet came out. He was promoted to subedar major and in 1965 was appointed ADC to the President of India. Ganju was promoted to honorary captain in 1968. On his retirement, he was appointed honorary ADC to the President of India for life.

Anecdotes that survive about him suggest he had little time for the niceties of military conduct, such as this one that dates from a few months before his VC action. On his first day as batman to Major Roy Gribble, he walked into his dugout at 04:00 with a mess tin of tea and told the major to 'Get up!' No 'Good morning' or 'Sir', but Gribble took to him at once.

Ganju Lama died on 30 June 2000 at Rabangla, Sikkim, India. His burial location is unknown and he may have been cremated. His VC is held by The Gurkha Museum, Peninsula Barracks, Winchester, Hampshire, England.

TULBAHADUR PUN, Mogaung, Burma, 23 June 1944

Tulbahadur Pun was born on 23 March 1923 in the village of Banduk, Myagdi, Nepal. He enlisted into the 3rd Battalion, 6th Gurkha Rifles for the Second Chindit Expedition, 77th Infantry Brigade under Brigadier James (Mad Mike) Calvert. Their objective was Mogaung, surrounded by jungle and swamps, and hampered by the monsoon weather.

On 23 June, in the final attack on a railway bridge that spanned the Mogaung River, Acting Captain Allmand, CO of B Company, charged an enemy machine-gun nest, but was mortally wounded (*see* entry for Michael Allmand). The enemy opened concentrated and sustained crossfire from a position known as the Red House and a bunker 200 yards to the left of it. His company were pinned down, and his section almost wiped out, with only him, the section leader, and another man remaining. The three men charged forward but the section leader was badly wounded. The other men continued the attack but his comrade was wounded and Rifleman Tulbahadur Pun seized the Bren gun, firing from the hip as he went, and continued the charge alone in the face of the most shattering concentration of machine-gun fire. He had to move 30 yards over open ground, ankle-deep in mud, to reach the Red House and close with the occupants. He killed three and put five to flight, capturing two machine guns. He then gave supporting fire to the remainder of his platoon, which enabled them to reach their objective without heavy loss. Major James Lumley (father of actor Joanna Lumley) was also involved in this action.

Tulbahadur Pun.

Tulbahadur Pun's VC was gazetted on 9 November 1944 and was presented to him on 3 March 1945 by Lord Wavell in New Delhi, beneath the walls of the Red Fort. After Indian independence in 1947, Tulbahadur Pun transferred to the British Army, seeing action in Malaya and Hong Kong. He rose to the rank of regimental sergeant major and retired with the honorary rank of lieutenant in May 1959.

He returned to his village and took up farming, but also opened two schools. In 1986, his farm was washed away by floods, but was able to resume after a benefit football match raised funds. Tulbahadur Pun came to England in 2007 and attended many of the VC/GC unions in London.

He supported many Gurkha charities and in 2009 was made a Freeman of the Borough of Hounslow.

Tulbahadur Pun died in Banduk (where he had gone to open a new school) on 20 April 2011, and his ashes were scattered in the Kali Gandaki River, Myagdi, Nepal. His VC is held by The Gurkha Museum, Peninsula Barracks, Winchester, Hampshire.

NETRABAHADUR THAPA, Bishenpur, Burma, 25–26 June 1944

Netrabahadur Thapa was born on 8 January 1916 in Rahu, Lamjung District, Nepal. He entered the army in 1934 and was posted to the 2nd Battalion, 5th Royal Gurkha Rifles after completing his training. Promoted to lance naik, then naik, he then joined the recruit training staff at the Regimental Centre in Abbottabad in 1940 with the rank of havildar. In the spring of 1942, he was posted back to his battalion as a platoon leader with the rank of jemadar (second lieutenant).

Netrabahadur Thapa.

In March 1944, his battalion was stationed in the Chin Hills near Imphal. At the beginning of June his battalion was moved to the Bishenpur area when, on 25 June 1944, Acting Subedar Netrabahadur Thapa was in command of a small isolated hill post known as 'Mortar Bluff'. This position was supported by 3-inch mortar fire from another post, but was overlooked by the 'Water Piquet' post, which had been overrun by the enemy the previous night. A small relief party had made its way into the post by 18:30 hours. An hour later, the enemy began their attack, firing a 75mm and a 37mm gun from Water Piquet. Shell after shell poured into the position and this was followed by a determined attack by at least a company of Japanese infantry. A fierce fight ensued in which Netrabahadur Thapa's men held their ground due to his leadership. Against heavy odds, the enemy were driven back with heavy loss. During his attack, Netrabahadur Thapa moved from post to post, encouraging his young men and tending the wounded. Under cover of night, the enemy moved around to the jungle, from where they launched their next attack. Still in great strength and as determined as before, the Japanese poured out from the jungle across the short space of open ground to the picquet defences under cover from small arms and field guns. For a short time, the Gurkhas held their ground, until both machine guns jammed at the same time. With much reduced firepower, the enemy forced an entrance and overran two sections, killing or wounding most of the Gurkhas. Having no reserve, Netrabahadur Thapa went forward himself and stemmed any further advance with grenades. With more than half his men casualties, ammunition low and part of his perimeter occupied, he would have been justified in withdrawing but, in his next report to his CO he stated that he intended to hold on and asked for more ammunition and men. Not another yard was gained by the enemy, despite their attempts. At 04:00 hours, a section of eight men with grenades and ammunition came to his aid but all of them became casualties. Undismayed, Netrabahadur Thapa went out and retrieved the ammunition, and then led his HQ platoon to the offensive with grenades and kukris until he was killed. His body was found the next day, kukri in hand and a dead Japanese soldier by his side.

After Netrabahadur Thapa's initial burial, his grave was lost, but his name appears on the Rangoon Memorial to the missing, Face 63. His VC was gazetted on 12 October 1944 and was presented to his widow on 23 January 1945 by Lord Wavell at a special parade of his battalion in Nowshera, India (now Pakistan). His VC is not publicly held.

AGANSING RAI, Bishenpur, Burma, 26 June 1944

Agansing Rai was born on 24 April 1920 in Amsara village, Okhaldhunga District, Nepal. He enlisted into the 2nd Battalion, 5th Gurkha Rifles in 1941 and was promoted to acting naik and given command of a rifle section in 1943. He saw action in the Chin Hills in early 1944, for which he was awarded the MM.

In June 1944, the 5th Gurkhas were holding the Bishenpur–Silehar track and were under a great deal of pressure to stem the fanatical Japanese assault on Imphal. On 26 June 1944, when the enemy had overrun two posts, known as Water Piquet and Mortar Bluff, his company was ordered to retake these positions, but on reaching a false crest they were pinned down by heavy and accurate machine-gun fire from Mortar Bluff, and a 37mm gun firing from the jungle. Appreciating that delay would result in more casualties, Agansing Rai led his section under very heavy fire at Mortar Bluff and, firing as he went, charged in, killing three of the machine-gun crew. Inspired by this act, the rest of the section surged forward and routed the garrison, this position again coming under fire from the 37mm and from Water Piquet. Agansing Rai advanced again, this time on the 37mm gun, his section following, but only four men reached the gun. Agansing Rai killed three of the crew himself. While the rest of his platoon were forming up for the final assault on Water Piquet, heavy machine-gun fire opened on them from an isolated bunker and once again he advanced alone, grenade in one hand and tommy gun in the other. Through heavy fire, he reached the bunker and killed all of the occupants. The enemy were now completely demoralised by his action and fled before the onslaught on Water Piquet.

Agansing Rai.

Agansing Rai's VC was gazetted on 5 October 1944 and was presented to him on 23 January 1945 by Lord Wavell. When asked by reporters what he had been feeling during the battle, he just smiled disarmingly and said, 'I'm sorry, I forget.' After the war, he became an instructor at the Regimental Centre in Abbottabad and took part in the Second World War victory parade in London in 1946. He served in the occupation of Japan and was promoted to subedar.

After the independence of India in 1947, Agansing Rai remained with his regiment and served in the Congo during 1962–63 with Gaje Ghale, vc, as part of the United Nations peacekeeping force. On his retirement from the army, he was given the honorary rank of lieutenant. He met the Queen in 1986 when she visited Nepal. He attended many of the VC/GC reunions in London and was known as a wise man with a good sense of humour.

Agansing Rai died on 27 May 2000 and was cremated at Dharan, Nepal. His VC is in the Lord Ashcroft Gallery, Imperial War Museum, London.

Frank Gerald BLAKER ('Jim' or 'Peter'), Taunghi, Burma, 9 July 1944

Frank Blaker was born on 8 May 1920 in Kasauli, Punjab, India, the son of Captain Blaker of the RAMC. He was educated at the American Methodist School, Mandalay, St Paul's School, Darjeeling, and the Government English High School at Maymyo. By the mid-1930s, he was an accomplished sportsman, interested in the jungle and wildlife and fond of shooting. From 1937–39, Blaker attended boarding school at Taunton before joining the Somerset Light Infantry in March 1940, and was commissioned into the Highland Light Infantry in 1941.

Frank Gerald Blaker..

At the end of 1941, Blaker left for India, and in May 1942 joined the 3rd Battalion, 9th Gurkha Rifles, which was operating in the Arakan region with the objective of preventing the Japanese from advancing into India. In July 1943, his battalion was stationed at Taung Bazaar and, now commanding C Company, he was sent to investigate Japanese activity 5 miles to the south. During the following action and at the end of a 2-mile chase, sixteen Japanese had been killed and three wounded prisoners taken, which included the first Japanese officer to be captured in the area. For this action, Captain Blaker was awarded the MC.

In July 1944, Temporary Major Blaker's battalion marched to Taunghi. Here the Japanese were determined to make a stand, and on 9 July, Blaker's company was ordered to make an encircling movement across unknown ground, through dense jungle, to attack an enemy position on the summit of a hill. As he got his company into position, it came under fire from three machine guns and their advance was halted. Blaker then advanced ahead of his men through very heavy fire and, in spite of a severe arm wound, he located the guns, charged them single-handedly, but was hit by a burst of fire to the body. He continued to cheer his men on while lying on the ground. His fearless courage so inspired his company that they captured the position, while the enemy fled into the jungle.

Blaker died from his wounds in the stomach, chest and shoulder while being evacuated, and was buried in Taukkyan War Cemetery, Rangoon, Burma, Plot VI, Row E, Grave 2. His VC was gazetted on 26 September 1944 and his medal is still held by his family. He was known as Blanket Sahib by his men.

SHERBAHADUR THAPA, San Marino, Italy, 18/19 September 1944

Sherbahadur Thapa was born on 20 November 1921 in Ghalechap, Tannu District, Nepal. He belonged to the Chettri tribe. It was one of the tribes that the 9th Gurkhas Rifles recruited from and he duly enlisted into the regiment at the outbreak of the war. After his basic training, he was posted to Italy to join the 1st Battalion.

The Germans were holding the Gothic Line stretching across northern Italy. On the night of 18/19 September 1944, near San Marino, Rifleman Sherbahadur Thapa's battalion was fighting its way forward against bitter German opposition in prepared positions dominating in the river valley. He, with his section commander, charged an enemy post, killing the machine-gunner and putting the rest to flight. Almost immediately, another party of Germans attacked the two men, and the section commander was badly wounded by a grenade. Without hesitation, Sherbahadur Thapa rushed at the attackers and, reaching the crest of the ridge, fired his Bren gun into them. He then lay in the open under a hail of bullets, firing his gun into the enemy. In this manner, he silenced several machine guns and checked a number of Germans who were trying to infiltrate the ridge. After two hours, both forward companies had exhausted their ammunition and, as they were by then practically surrounded, they were ordered to withdraw. Sherbahadur Thapa covered the withdrawal as they crossed the open ground to a position in the rear and he remained alone until his ammunition ran out. Then he dashed forward under accurate fire and rescued two wounded men lying between him and the advancing Germans. While returning the second time, he was killed by a hail of bullets.

Sherbahadur Thapa's VC was gazetted on 28 December 1944 and was presented to his mother in March 1945 by Lord Wavell at Delhi.

Sherbahadur Thapa was buried in Rimini Gurkha War Cemetery, Italy, Plot VI, Row E, Grave 7. His VC is held by the 9th Gurkha Rifles HQ, Varanasi, India.

THAMAN GURUNG, Monte San Bartolo, Italy, 10 November 1944

Thaman Gurung was born on 2 October 1924 in Singla, Gorkha District, Nepal. He enlisted into the 5th Gurkha Rifles and was posted to the 1st Battalion, then serving in Italy in September 1944.

On 10 November 1944, Rifleman Thaman Gurung's platoon was ordered to send a patrol to an objective for a future attack. Monte San Bartolo was a high bluff devoid of cover, the approach being a narrow, almost knife-edge saddle. He was acting as a scout with another man and they skilfully reached the German position undetected. Then, seeing that the enemy were preparing to fire on the

Thaman Gurung.

leading section, and knowing they would suffer heavy casualties, Thaman Gurung leapt to his feet and charged. Completely taken by surprise, the Germans surrendered without firing a shot. Then he crept forward to the summit of the position, from which he could see a well-dug-in party of Germans, preparing to throw grenades at the lead section. He moved across the summit and fired on them with his tommy gun, allowing the section to reach the summit without further loss. Due to heavy fire, the platoon was ordered to withdraw. Thaman Gurung covered the withdrawal with bursts of fire until his ammunition ran out. Then he threw the two grenades he had with him and went back for more, throwing them on his return to the summit and allowing all but the lead section to withdraw.

Now he seized a Bren gun and, shouting to the remaining section to withdraw, stood up on the summit and fired on the enemy positions. It was not until he had emptied two magazines and the remaining section was well on its way down the slope that he was killed.

Thaman Gurung's VC was gazetted on 22 February 1945 and was presented to his mother on 19 December that year by Lord Wavell at Delhi. Thaman Gurung (spelt Thamman on his headstone) was buried in Rimini Gurkha War Cemetery, Italy, Plot III, Row B, Grave 5. His VC is not publicly held.

BHANBHAGTA GURUNG, Tamandu, Burma, 5 March 1945

Bhanbhagta Gurung was born in September 1921 in Phalpu, Gorkha, Nepal. He enlisted into the 3rd Battalion, 2nd Gurkha Rifles, shortly after the outbreak of the war in 1939. In March 1943, his battalion was posted to Brigadier Wingate's Chindit Expedition in Upper Burma to cause disruption behind the Japanese lines. Bhanbhagta Gurung was promoted to lance naik and took part in the First Chindit Expedition in 1943.

In September 1944, during fighting around Arakan, Bhanbhagta Gurung was sent to picquet the top of a hill, but it turned out to be the wrong location and

Bhanbhagta Gurung.

he was reduced to the ranks for neglect of duty. However, it transpired later he had been ordered to go to the wrong location.

In February 1945, his battalion was landed at Ruywa on the coast to divert Japanese attention from General Sir William Slim's main thrust towards Mandalay. On 5 March 1945 at Tamandu, Rifleman Bhanbhagta Gurung's section was pinned down by heavy machine-gun and sniper fire. Being unable to fire from a lying position, he stood up fully exposed to the heavy fire and calmly shot the sniper. Then he dashed forward alone, killing the occupants of a foxhole with grenades and the next with the bayonet. Two further enemy foxholes were bringing fire down on his section and again he dashed forward and cleared them with grenades and the bayonet. During this time, he was under fire from a machine gun in a bunker. He went forward alone under fire and leapt onto the roof, from where he threw two smoke grenades into the slit. Two Japanese ran out and he killed them with his kukri. He then went into the bunker and killed the machine-gunner, capturing the gun. The enemy could be seen forming up for a counter-attack, so he took two riflemen and a Bren gunner and took up position in the bunker. Under his direction, the counter-attack was repelled with heavy loss to the enemy. His courageous clearing of five enemy positions single-handedly was in itself decisive in capturing the objective and an inspiring example to his company.

Bhanbhagta Gurung's VC was gazetted on 5 June 1945 and was presented to him by George VI at Buckingham Palace. He left the army in 1946 with the rank of havildar to help his young wife and elderly mother with farming.

He died as a result of asthma on 1 March 2008 and was cremated at Devghat of Chitwan, Nepal. His VC is held by The Gurkha Museum, Peninsula Barracks, Winchester, Hampshire. His three sons also served in the 2nd Gurkha Rifles.

LACHHIMAN GURUNG, Taungdaw, Burma, 12–13 May 1945

Lachhiman Gurung was born on 30 December 1917 in Dahakhani, Chitwan District, Nepal. He enlisted in December 1940 and after training was posted to the 4th Battalion, 8th Gurkha Rifles. He was only 4ft 11in and, because of his height, would not have been accepted in peacetime.

At the end of April 1945, the 89th Brigade, of which the 8th Gurkhas were part, was ordered to cross the Irrawaddy River and destroy the enemy north of the Prome–Taungup road. By 9 May, the Japanese had broken off contact and

Lachhiman Gurung.

were withdrawing towards the Taungdaw Valley. Lachhiman Gurung's company was positioned to block their route at the village of Taungdaw.

On 12 May 1945, Rifleman Lachhiman Gurung was manning the most forward post. Over 200 Japanese assaulted the position, the brunt of the attack being borne by his section. Before the assault, the enemy hurled large numbers of grenades at the position from close range. One landed on the lip of his trench and he at once grabbed it and threw it back at the enemy. Almost immediately, another fell in his trench. Again he threw it back. When a third grenade fell just in front of his trench, he picked it up but it exploded in his hand, blowing off his fingers, shattering his right arm and severely wounding him in the face, body and right leg. His two comrades were also badly wounded and lay helpless in the bottom of the trench. The enemy, screaming and shouting, now rushed forward in an attempt to take the position with sheer weight of numbers. Despite his wounds, Lachhiman Gurung loaded and fired his rifle with his left hand, maintaining a steady rate of fire. Wave after wave of attacks were thrown in by the enemy and all were repulsed with heavy losses. For four hours, he remained at his post alone, calmly waiting for each attack, which he met with point-blank fire from his rifle, determined not to give an inch of ground. His comrades could hear him shouting, 'Come and fight a Gurkha.' Of the eighty-seven enemy dead counted in the immediate area, thirty-one lay in front of him, the key to the whole position. Had the enemy taken this position, they would have completely dominated the whole of the reverse slope. By his magnificent example, Lachhiman Gurung inspired his comrades to resist the enemy to the last. Although surrounded and cut off for three days and two nights, they held on and smashed every attack. His outstanding gallantry and extreme devotion to duty in the face of such overwhelming odds were the main factors in the defeat of the enemy.

Lachhiman Gurung's grave, Chiswick New Cemetery, London.

Lachhiman Gurung's VC was gazetted on 27 July 1945 and was presented to him on 19 December that year by Lord Louis Mountbatten at the Red Fort, New Delhi. Despite losing his right hand and the sight in his right eye, he continued to serve with the 8th Gurkhas but transferred to the Indian Army after independence in 1947. He retired with the rank of havildar in the same year and married soon afterwards, having two sons and a daughter. After the death of his wife, he remarried and had two more sons.

Lachhiman Gurung became involved in the campaign to allow ex-Gurkha soldiers to settle in Britain. The government had refused entry to 2,000 Gurkhas who had retired before July 1997, the date when their base was moved to the UK from Hong Kong. Lachhiman Gurung had been told he could not settle in Britain because he had failed to 'demonstrate strong ties' to the UK. In September 2008, at the High Court, this decision was overturned. In May 2009, the government announced that all Gurkha veterans who retired before 1997 with at least four years' service would be allowed to settle in Britain. However, Lachhiman Gurung was appealing directly to the Queen and the Prime Minister for his 20-year-old granddaughter, who was facing deportation, to be allowed to stay to care for him. He said, 'I have paid a great price for Britain, but I do not complain as I love this country as much as my family. However, in my last days I ask Her Majesty the Queen to help by allowing my granddaughter to be with me and at my side.' The Home Office relented and allowed her to stay.

Lachhiman Gurung died from pneumonia on 12 December 2010 and was buried in Chiswick New Cemetery, London, Section V, Grave 59. His VC is held by the 8th Gurkha Rifles, Indian Army. I had the privilege of meeting him and of attending his funeral service.

Malaysia-Indonesia Confrontation, 1963–66

In 1963, the Federation of Malaysia was officially recognised, and it was agreed that a continued presence of British armed forces would be allowed. Indonesia saw this as a thinly disguised attempt to continue colonial rule in the area. The so-called 'Confrontation' began when, at first, small parties of Indonesians crossed into Malaysia, but by 1963, regular units were involved.

RAMBAHADUR LIMBU, Gunong Tepoi, Sarawak, November 1965

Rambahadur Limbu was born on 8 July 1939 in Chyangthapu village, Yangrop Thum, Limbuwan, in East Nepal. He belonged to the Begha clan of the Limbu nationality of Nepal. His family were farmers but Limbu did not take to this work and left home to join the army.

As an enlisted boy soldier he soon found that he would not be sent to Malaya as he had hoped and he became homesick. He and the friend he enlisted with decided to leave, so late one night they slipped away, but Rambahadur Limbu soon realised he could not return home and tell his brother, as he said in

Rambahadur Limbu.

his own words, that he had 'deserted because I was homesick'. After some time wandering about aimlessly, most of the time hungry and destitute, Limbu thought it was better to return home and face his angry brother than to roam around like a beggar.

Although angry, his brother was pleased to see him as he was needed on the farm. Unhappy as a farmer, Limbu often felt tormented for deserting and knowing he could not go back to the army for fear of being jailed. At the age of 17, Rambahadur Limbu left home again, this time with his brother's blessing and a little money from him. Travelling to Darjeeling and on to Gangtok, the capital of Sikkim, he found men from his village, whom he joined working in the jungle, cutting trees. He met a girl whom he wanted to marry but could not earn enough to support her and would not take money from her family.

Limbu's brother arrived to visit one day, wanting to take him back home, and told him it was time he settled down to marry. Limbu explained that he had met a girl but could not afford to support her. His brother persuaded him to return home for the Dashera (Dussehra) Festival. Limbu promised to return for the girl after the festival and bring her to his village.

After Dashera, Limbu's younger brother set out for Sikkim to join the army and the recruiter persuaded Limbu to accompany them part of the way, which he did. Before they reached the Jalapahar Recruiting Depot, Limbu got a little drunk and promised the recruiter he would join up with his brother. Realising he could not go back on his word, Limbu found himself back in the army and the girl was forgotten; thankfully, he was not recognised.

Limbu soon moved to Lehra and was enjoying the army life he had dreamed of. After a month, he was sent to the Barrackpore Transit Camp and set sail on board the SS *Santhia*, arriving in Rangoon in late December 1957. From here, he went by train to the training centre at Sungei Patani. After training, in October 1958 he was attached to the 2nd Battalion, 10th Gurkha Rifles (Princess Mary's). While on leave in 1961, Limbu married a girl from his village and they had two sons before she died suddenly in February 1966. Promoted to acting lance corporal in 1963, the rank was made permanent later the same year. In 1964, his battalion was sent to Borneo and was soon involved in operations against guerrillas.

On 21 November 1965, Lance Corporal Rambahadur Limbu's company was attacking a position on top of a jungle-covered hill, the only approach being along a knife-edge ridge. Leading his group, he could see the nearest trench, with a sentry and machine gun. Determined to gain first blood, he inched his way towards it until only 10 yards away, when he was seen and the machine gun opened fire, wounding the man to his right. He rushed forward and in seconds had killed the sentry, thereby gaining a foothold on the ridge. The enemy were now fully alerted and from their positions brought down heavy automatic fire on the attackers. Knowing that he could not carry out his task from this position, Limbu left the comparative safety of his trench and, with complete disregard for the hail of bullets directed at him, he led his group to a better firing position some way forward. He now attempted to indicate his intentions to his platoon commander by hand signals but could not make himself understood, so he again went out into the open and reported personally, despite the danger of being hit by both friend and foe. At this point, he saw that both men in his group had been wounded, and knew full well their only chance was to be evacuated for immediate first aid. Using what little cover he could find, he crawled forward in full view of at least two machine-gun posts, which opened fire on him. For three minutes, he continued forward but, when almost able to reach the first man, he was driven back by the intense automatic fire. After a pause, he again started to crawl forward but soon realised that only speed would give him the cover he needed. Rushing forward, he threw himself on the ground next to one of the wounded men and, calling for support from two machine-gunners who had by now come up to his right, he picked up the man and carried him down the hill to safety. Without hesitation, he immediately returned to the top of the hill, determined to complete his self-imposed task of rescuing those for whom he felt personally responsible. It was clear from the increased fire being concentrated on the approach to the remaining casualty that the enemy were doing all they could to prevent any further attempts at rescue. Despite this, he again moved out into the open and, with a series of short rushes, and being pinned down for some time by machine-gun fire, which could be seen striking the ground all around him, he eventually reached the wounded man. Picking him up and unable to seek cover, he carried him back as fast as he could, through a hail of bullets. It had taken him twenty minutes to complete this gallant action and the events leading up to it. For all but a few seconds he was moving in full view of the enemy and under continuous automatic fire.

That he was able to achieve this against such overwhelming odds without being hit was miraculous. His outstanding bravery, complete disregard for his own safety and determination to save the lives of his men set an incomparable example and inspired all who saw him. Rejoining his section on the left flank of the attack, he was able to recover the machine gun abandoned by the wounded man and with it won his revenge, being responsible for killing four of the enemy as they attempted to escape across the border. This hour-long battle, which had been fought at point-blank range and with the utmost ferocity by both sides, was won. At least twenty-four of the enemy are known to have been killed, at a cost of three killed and two wounded to the attacking force. Limbu's achievement in this engagement stands out as one of the most important of any VC actions and there is no doubt that, but for his inspired conduct at a most vital stage, much less would have been achieved and greater casualties caused.

Rambahadur Limbu's VC was gazetted on 22 April 1966 and was presented to him on 12 July that year by the Queen at Buckingham Palace.

While travelling home by train from his investiture, his VC medal was stolen from him. An official replacement was issued almost immediately.

When Rambahadur Limbu came to London for his VC investiture, he was taken to the Stock Exchange, where he was recognised, and almost to a man everyone stopped trading and applauded him for three minutes, then gave him three cheers. The chairman asked to meet him and led him onto the floor, where a path of honour was formed for him to walk through. Never before had one of the world's premier financial markets stood still for so long, and it was solely so that those there could pay tribute to an incredibly brave man.

Rambahadur Limbu retired from the army with the rank of captain in 1985. He is a regular attendee of the VC/GC Association reunions. His autobiography is called *My Life Story*. In the Gurkha Regiment, he is known as 'VC Sahib'.

I have had the privilege of meeting him a number of times and he was most surprised to see I had a copy of his book, which he happily signed for me. He is the last surviving Gurkha recipient of the VC.

Part 2

The Indian Regiment VCs

Chapter 3

Persian War, 1856–57

In the days when Britain ruled India, a major influence on British policy was the threat of incursions into this part of the Empire from Russia. It was with the Russian threat in mind that Britain helped to create the state of Afghanistan between India and Persia, as a buffer. The British supported the city of Herat's incorporation into Afghanistan. Therefore, when Persia annexed Herat in October 1856 and diplomatic measures failed, Britain declared war on 1st November.

John Augustus WOOD, Bushire, 9 December 1856

John Wood was born on 10 June 1818 in Fort William, Scotland. At 21, he joined the 20th Bombay Native Infantry (later the 120th Rajputana Infantry).

On 9 December 1856, he was 38 years old and a captain when he led the Grenadier Company at the head of the storming party of Bushire and was the first man onto the parapet of the fort, where a large number of the enemy immediately attacked him. A volley was fired at him and his men at very close range. Wood was hit by seven musket balls, but he at once threw himself upon the enemy, killing their leader. He was closely followed by the men of the company, who speedily overcame the garrison.

John Augustus Wood.

His wounds, although not life threatening, were very painful and debilitating, which forced him out of service for some time. He sailed to Bombay to recuperate, returning to Bushire in February 1857, and then spent eight uncomfortable months with the regiment. He finally left Bushire in September on the *Melbourne*, and disembarked at Bombay on 20 October 1857. Fully recovered, he took part in the Indian Mutiny of 1857–59. His VC was eventually gazetted on 3 August 1860 and was probably posted to him, as there is no record of it being presented to him.

Wood left the army with the rank of brevet colonel in February 1870 and died from concussion of the brain on 23 January 1878. He was buried under the name of Augustus John Wood, in St Mary's Churchyard, Poona, India. His VC was sold by Sotheby's in 1910 and is believed to be held by the 2nd Rajputana Rifles, in India.

John Grant MALCOLMSON, Khoosh-ab, 8 February 1857

John Malcolmson was born on 9 February 1835 in Muchrach, near Inverness, the son of James Malcolmson.

On 8 February 1857 at Khoosh-ab, he was serving as a lieutenant in the 3rd Bombay Light Cavalry when he saw Lieutenant Arthur Moore's horse fall dead and land on top of him, breaking his sword. Moore had charged into a square of 500 Persians by jumping over their bayonets and trying to fight them off with his broken sword. On seeing this, Malcolmson fought his way into the square, offered his stirrup to Moore and carried him to safety. Had it not been for Malcolmson's help, Moore almost certainly would have been killed.

John Grant Malcolmson.

Malcolmson's VC was gazetted on 3 August 1860, and was presented to him on 9 November that year by the Queen at Windsor Castle. He became a Gentleman at Arms in 1870 and lived in London.

Malcolmson's family vault, Kensal Green Cemetery, London.

Malcolmson died on 14 August 1902 and was buried in Kensal Green Cemetery, London, Square 99 – RS, family vault. His VC is held by the National Army Museum, London.

Arthur Thomas MOORE, Khoosh-ab, February 1857

Arthur Moore was born on 20 September 1830 in Carlingford, Co Louth, Ireland, the son of Edward Francis Moore, who was in the 45th Regiment of Foot. Arthur joined the 3rd Bombay Light Cavalry as a second lieutenant in July 1850, was promoted to lieutenant in August 1855, and was adjutant of his regiment.

On 8 February 1857 at Khoosh-ab, he charged into a square of 500 Persians by jumping over their bayonets. His horse fell dead and landed on top of him, breaking his sword. He tried to fight off the Persians with his broken sword. Had it not been for Lieutenant Malcolmson's help, he would almost certainly have been killed.

Arthur Thomas Moore.

Moore went on to serve in the Indian Mutiny, taking part in actions at Rathgahir, Barodia, Sangor, Garakota, Calpe, and Gwalior, and he was mentioned in despatches twice. His VC was gazetted on 3 August 1860 and was presented to him by the GOC Bombay, Lieutenant General William Mansfield. Moore was married to Annie Prentice. At his retirement in 1891, he was a brevet colonel.

Moore died from heart failure brought on by influenza on 25 April 1913 and was buried in Mount Jerome Cemetery, Dublin, Section C156, No. 14036. His VC was sold in 2014 at auction for £150,000 to a private buyer.

Indian Mutiny, 1857–59

The Indian or Sepoy Mutiny began in Meerut on 10 May 1857, and although it was ultimately unsuccessful, it tested Britain's military resources to the limit. There had been unrest among the Indian population for several years. The infamous 'greased cartridges' incident was the flashpoint for the mutiny. Soon the sepoys at the Delhi garrison joined the Meerut rebels and it quickly spread across northern India. British troops were ordered to proceed immediately to India.

Dighton MacNaghten PROBYN, 1857–58

Dighton Probyn was born on 21 January 1833 in London, the son of Captain George Probyn and Alicia (née MacNaghten). He enlisted into the Bengal Cavalry as a cornet in 1849 and from 1852–57 he served in the 2nd Punjab Cavalry under Captain Sam Browne (who would also be awarded the VC, *see* below) on the Trans-Indus Frontier and the Bozdar Hills.

When the mutiny broke out, Captain Probyn was at Jullundur (now Jalandhar) and he distinguished himself throughout the campaign. At the Battle of Agra, his squadron charged the rebel infantry;

Dighton MacNaghten Probyn.

Probyn was surrounded, and defended himself against five or six rebels, killing two before help arrived. On another occasion, he cut down a rebel who had bayoneted him in the wrist and wounded his horse, and later that day, Probyn killed an enemy standard-bearer and captured the colours. He also saw action at the siege of Delhi, the battles of Bolundshuhar, Allighur and Kanuje, the relief of Lucknow, the Battle of Cawnpore and the storming of Lucknow. He was mentioned in despatches seven times for his gallant actions during the campaign.

Worn down by a year of continuous fighting, he was sent home with the brevet rank of major in March 1858. His VC was gazetted on 18 June 1858 and was presented to him on 2 August that year by the Queen at Portsmouth. The reverse of the suspension bar is inscribed 'Capt. Dighton M. Probyn 2nd Punjab Cavalry'. However, the centre of the Cross is undated as his bravery was for so many actions over the course of a year. By 1860, he was back in India and given command of the 1st Sikh Irregular Cavalry, which became known as Probyn's Horse.

Probyn served in the Third China Campaign, and was promoted to lieutenant colonel in 1861. He took part in the Umbeyla Campaign, for which he was mentioned in despatches. In 1866, he was promoted to colonel and in 1870 to major general. He was also appointed ADC to the Viceroy of India, Lord Mayo. In 1872, he married Letitia Thellusson and they returned to England.

Probyn's grave, Kensal Green Cemetery, London.

He was appointed an equerry to the Prince of Wales and toured India with him in 1875. On his return to England, Probyn was promoted to lieutenant general. In 1877–81, he was Treasurer and Comptroller to the Prince of Wales, and was promoted to general in 1888. In 1902–10, he was Keeper of the Privy Purse and Extra Equerry to Edward VII. In 1911, Probyn was made a Knight Grand Cross of the Order of the Bath (Military Division), thus becoming the only non-royal to hold the highest grade of the Order of the Bath in both civil and military divisions.

Probyn was taken ill in June 1924 and was nursed at Sandringham in Norfolk (in a room previously used by Queen Victoria). He died there on 20 June that year, and was buried in Kensal Green Cemetery, London, Square 117-2, Grave 21487.

Probyn's VC medal (which is unusual in that it is undated) was sold in 2005 at auction for £160,000 to a private buyer.

John BUCKLEY, 11 May 1857

John Buckley was born on 24 May 1813 in Cocker Hill, Stalybridge, Cheshire, the son of Thomas (a labourer) and Sarah Buckley. As a young boy, he found work in the textile mills. When he was 18, he travelled to Manchester and joined the Bengal Artillery as a gunner and the following year he was posted to India.

In India, he met and married 14-year-old Mary Ann Broadway in 1835. They had three children, but by 1845, Mary and two of their children had died from disease. In 1846, Buckley married Esther Hunter, but tragically, the last child from his first married died in 1852, and in 1853, two sons from his second marriage also died.

John Buckley.

Four years later, he, his wife and three surviving sons moved to Delhi, where Buckley was appointed Deputy Assistant Commissary of Ordnance. He was employed at the Delhi magazine – a storehouse of guns and ammunition – under the command of Lieutenant George Willoughby.

On 11 May 1857, Lieutenant George Willoughby, John Buckley, George Forrest, William Raynor, Conductors William Shaw and John Scully, Sub-Conductor William Crow and Sergeants Bryan Edwards and Peter Stewart found themselves defending the magazine for more than five hours against a large force of mutineers. They barricaded the gates and put two 6-pounder guns loaded with grapeshot at the entrances. When the enemy started scaling the walls with ladders, the entire native garrison went over to join the mutiny. With no hope of help, they fired the magazine to stop the mutineers capturing the ammunition. Five of the defenders were killed outright and Willoughby was killed by the rebels two days later, but many of the enemy were also killed.

Buckley was captured by the enemy and soon learnt that his entire family had been ruthlessly murdered by the rebels. He begged for death from his captors but they refused to kill him on account of his bravery at the magazine. He later escaped and re-joined the army, volunteering for all manner of dangerous missions in order to taunt death. Buckley took part in operations that saw the capture of 150 rebels from the Delhi magazine incident and oversaw the executions of these men, who were strapped to the muzzles of cannons and blown apart.

Buckley was promoted to lieutenant and sent home on two years' sick leave. His VC was gazetted on 18 June 1858 and was presented to him on 2 August that year by the Queen at a parade on Southsea Common, Portsmouth. (Only the three surviving men would be awarded the VC as it was not awarded posthumously at that time. Although there is nothing in the Royal Warrant to this effect, it had been practice not to do so.)

Buckley's grave, Tower Hamlets Cemetery, London.

Buckley returned to India in 1858, now a major. He remained in the army for a few more years before retiring to England in 1861. He lived the remainder of his life in London with his third wife, Sara.

Buckley died on 14 July 1876 and was buried in Tower Hamlets Cemetery, London. His grave had remained unmarked for 136 years, when its location was discovered in 2012 by Doreen Kendall. On 14 July 2014, a headstone was unveiled by the Victoria Cross Trust in a ceremony attended by Doreen Kendall, Jim Fitzpatrick MP, members of the RLC and myself. Buckley's VC is held by the Royal Logistic Corps Museum, Worthy Down Camp, near Winchester, Hampshire.

George FORREST, 11 May 1857

George Forrest was born in 1800 in the St Michael's Parish of Dublin. Almost nothing is known about his life prior to him joining the army. By the time of the mutiny, he was a lieutenant in the Bengal Veteran Establishment.

On 11 May 1857, George Forrest, John Buckley, William Raynor and six other men found themselves defending the Delhi magazine for more than five hours against a large force of mutineers. They barricaded the gates and put two 6-pounder guns loaded with grapeshot at the entrances. When the enemy started scaling the walls with ladders, the entire native garrison went over to join the mutiny. With no hope of help, they fired the magazine to stop the mutineers capturing the ammunition. Five of the defenders were killed outright and one died of his wounds, but many of the enemy were also killed.

Forrest was captured by the rebels and only released after the mutiny was over. His VC was gazetted on 18 June 1858 and was presented to him on 2 November that year by Major Troup at Landour, India, and he was promoted to captain.

Forrest fell ill and died at Dehra Dun, India, on 3 November 1859, and was buried in a mausoleum there. His VC is not publicly held.

William RAYNOR, 11 May 1857

William Raynor was born in July 1795 in Plumtree, Nottinghamshire, the son of John Raynor and Elizabeth (née Tongue). In 1812, William enlisted into the HEIC. He arrived in India aboard the *Hugh Inglis* in February 1813. He took part in the Anglo-Nepalese War (aka the Gurkha War) of 1814–16. In October 1818, he married the widow Mary Wilkinson but unfortunately, she died within a few months of the wedding.

In 1820, Raynor was appointed a sub-conductor in the Ordnance Commissariat Department and was based at the Fort William Arsenal in Calcutta. In 1823, he was promoted to conductor and in the same year married Mary Anne Werrill, and they went on to have five children. By the time of the mutiny, he was a lieutenant in the Bengal Veteran Establishment.

On 11 May 1857, William Raynor, George Forrest, John Buckley and six other men found themselves defending the Delhi magazine for more than five hours against a large force of mutineers. They barricaded the gates and put two 6-pounder guns loaded with grapeshot at the entrances. When the enemy started scaling the walls with ladders, the entire native garrison went over to join the mutiny. With no hope of help, they fired the magazine to stop the mutineers capturing the ammunition. Five of the defenders were killed outright and one died of his wounds, but many of the enemy were also killed.

Raynor's VC was gazetted on 18 June 1858 and was presented to him that same year in India. He was also promoted to captain. At 61 years and 10 months, he is the oldest recipient of the VC.

Raynor died on 13 December 1860 and was buried in Ferozepore Civil Cemetery, Punjab, India, Plot 358. His VC is held by the Royal Logistic Corps Museum, Worthy Down Camp, near Winchester, Hampshire.

Everard Aloysius LISLE-PHILLIPPS, 30 May–18 September 1857

Everard Lisle-Phillipps was born on 28 May 1835 in Coleorton, Leicestershire, the second son (and one of nine children) of Ambrose Lise March Phillipps de Lisle and Laura Mary (née Clifford). Everard was educated at St Edmund's College, near Ware, and at Oscott College, near Birmingham. He learned to speck Hindustani in Paris and joined the HEIC, being commissioned an ensign in the 11th Bengal Native Infantry in 1855.

Lisle-Phillipps reached Meerut on 4 May 1857 and when the mutiny started on the 11th, his regiment was one of the first to revolt. When the Queen's proclamation against the insurgents came, he had to read it out as he could speak the native tongue. Riding forward while bullets whistled around him, but before he finished the first sentence, his horse was shot from under him and he fell to the ground, wounded by a stray bullet. Undeterred, he got to his feet and read through the whole proclamation from beginning to end before taking cover. On the desertion of the Bengal Infantry, who joined the rebels, he joined the 60th Rifles. He performed many gallant deeds, and he was wounded three times. At the assault on the city of Delhi, he captured the Water Bastion with a small party of men. He was killed in street fighting in the city on 18 September 1857, on the last day of the siege.

A citation stating that 'had he survived', he would have been awarded the VC was issued on 21 October 1859. The VC was not awarded posthumously at this time. (Although there is nothing in the Royal Warrant to this effect, it had been practice not to do so.)

Lisle-Phillipps was buried in an unmarked grave in Old Delhi Military Cemetery (The Nicholson Cemetery), India.

His VC was gazetted on 15 January 1907, making him the first posthumous VC by date of action. This came about due to Lord Roberts being awarded a posthumous VC in 1901, and in 1907, the King awarded a number of backdated awards to others who did not survive their VC action. His VC is in the Lord Ashcroft Gallery, Imperial War Museum, London.

Peter GILL, 4 June 1857

Peter Gill was born on 1 September 1831 in Dublin, Ireland. Little is known about him before his enlistment into the HEIC, being posted as a gunner in the Bengal Artillery. He took part in both Sikh wars (of 1845–46 and 1848–49) and transferred to the Ludhiana Regiment as a sergeant major in 1850.

On 4 June 1857 in Benares, the mutineers began burning bungalows and killing the inhabitants. Gill, with Sergeant Major Matthew Rosamond and Private John Kirk (both from the 10th Foot and also awarded the VC for this action) volunteered to go to the aid of Captain Brown, and his wife and daughter, whose bungalow had been set alight, and brought them back to the safety of the barracks. Gill also saved the life of a sergeant who had been bayonetted, by cutting off the head of his assailant. On the same evening, he faced a guard of twenty-seven mutineers, armed with only his sword. He is also said to have twice saved the life of a major who was being attacked by a group of sepoys.

Gill's VC was gazetted on 24 August 1858 and was presented to him in February 1859; where and by whom is unknown. He fought throughout the remainder of the rebellion. Gill was promoted to lieutenant in May 1866 and appointed barrack master at Lucknow, a post he held for four years.

Peter Gill was killed in action at Morar on 24 October 1868 and was buried in an unmarked grave in Artillery Lines Cemetery, Gwalior, India. His VC was sold at auction in 2017, for a hammer price of £70,000 to a private collector.

Matthew ROSAMOND, 4 June 1857

Matthew Rosamond was born on 12 July 1823 in St Neots, Cambridgeshire, the son of George and Elizabeth Rosamond. He enlisted into the HEIC in May 1841, served in both Sikh wars (of 1845–46 and 1848–49) and was promoted to sergeant major in the 37th Bengal Native Infantry.

On 4 June 1857 in Benares, he volunteered to go with Lieutenant Colonel Spottiswoode to set fire to the sepoy lines to drive them out. When the mutineers started burning bungalows and killing the inhabitants, Rosamond, along with Sergeant Peter Gill and Private John Kirk (both from the 10th Foot and would also be awarded the VC for this action), volunteered to go to the aid of Captain Brown and his wife and daughter, whose bungalow had been set alight, and brought them back to the safety of the barracks.

Matthew Rosamond.

Rosamond's VC was gazetted on 24 August 1858 and presented to him sometime in 1859, probably at the same time as Peter Gill's. Rosamond was appointed barrack master at Barrackpore, West Bengal, and Dundurn in 1863. He was promoted to lieutenant in 1864 and transferred to Fort William, Calcutta.

On 14 July 1866, while en route to England, Matthew Rosamond died and was buried in the Red Sea. His VC was sold at auction in 1903 for £54 and is not publicly held.

Thomas CADELL, 12 June 1857

Thomas Cadell was born on 5 September 1835 in Cockenzie, East Lothian, the son of Hew Francis and Janet (née Sydserff). He was educated at Edinburgh Academy and The Grange, Sunderland, before becoming a cadet in the HEIC. Cadell was commissioned into the 2nd European Bengal Fusiliers (later the Royal Munster Fusiliers) in May

1854 and promoted to lieutenant in November 1856. On the outbreak of the Indian Mutiny, he was posted to India with his regiment.

During the siege of Delhi, on 12 June 1857, the enemy attacked and the picquet line was forced back. Lieutenant Cadell saw a bugler fall wounded. Under heavy fire, he went to his assistance and carried him from among the enemy to safety. On the same evening, he went with three others towards the advancing mutineers to save the life of a wounded man who had been left behind.

Thomas Cadell.

After the mutiny, Cadell took part in the Oudh Campaign of 1858–59, and fought in Bundlekhund against the Bheels in 1959–60, being mentioned in despatches. His VC was gazetted on 29 April 1862 and was presented to him on 29 December 1862 by Brigadier General James Travers, vc, in Bhopal, India.

Cadell was promoted to captain in April 1866. The following year he married Anna Catherine Dalmahoy and they went on to have two sons. After promotion to major in April 1874, Cadell entered the Political Department and held various appointments in Central India and Rajputana. From 1879 to 1892, he held the post of Chief Commissioner of the Andaman and Nicobar Islands. Despite his contempt for the mutineers, he was a humane and considerate administrator. He retired with the rank of colonel in 1892.

Thomas Cadell died on 6 April 1919 and was buried in the family vault at Tranent Parish Churchyard, near Edinburgh. At the time of his death, aged 83, he was the oldest holder of the award. His VC is not publicly held. Cadell's cousin, Samuel Lawrence, was also awarded the VC.

John McGOVERN (aka McGOWAN), 23 June 1857

John McGovern was born on 16 May 1825 in Tullyhaw, County Cavan, Ireland. After schooling, he became a labourer. In November 1845, at the height of the Potato Famine, he enlisted for ten years' service into the HEIC and sailed for India, arriving in September 1846. McGovern was by all accounts not a model solider, often in trouble with his superiors for drinking and fighting. His first taste of battle was during the Second Anglo-Burmese War, of 1852–53.

On 23 June 1857 at Delhi, while serving in the 1st Bengal Fusiliers (later the Royal Munster Fusiliers), Private McGovern carried into camp a wounded man under heavy fire from the enemy's artillery, at the risk of his own life.

John McGovern.

Later, on 16 December, he volunteered to dislodge three sepoys who had taken refuge in a fortified tower. As McGovern started up the stairs he heard the sergeant major say, 'Never mind, Sir; he'll be no loss.' This made McGovern more determined and, as the sepoys opened fire on him, he managed to duck back and avoid being hit. He then rushed them before they could reload, shooting one and bayoneting the others.

McGovern's VC was gazetted on 21 June 1859 and was presented to him on 10 July 1860. After this, it was noted he was a changed man, giving up drinking and no longer getting into fights. He stated he did not want to disgrace the VC. After the mutiny, he remained in India but one of his wounds affected him for the rest of his life. He decided to emigrate to Canada, but very little is known about his life there.

John McGovern died on 22 November 1888 and was buried in Holy Sepulchre Cemetery, Hamilton, Ontario, Section E, Lot 53. His VC is held by the National Army Museum, London.

William George CUBITT, 30 June 1857

William Cubitt was born on 19 October 1835 in Calcutta, India, the son of Major William Cubitt of the HEIC and his wife, Harriet. He was educated privately and joined the 13th Bengal Native Infantry (later the

16th Lucknow Regiment) in 1853. He fought throughout the Santhal Rebellion of 1855–56.

During the mutiny, he saw action at the defence of the Residency, where he was wounded and was subsequently mentioned in despatches. Then, on 30 June 1857 at Chinhat, during the retreat Lieutenant Cubitt saved the lives of three men of the 32nd Regiment by taking one man on his horse behind him and holding the other two on his stirrups as they made their way back to Lucknow while being pursued by rebels.

William George Cubitt.

Cubitt's VC was gazetted on 21 June 1859 and was presented to him on 4 January 1860 by the Queen at Windsor Castle. He transferred into the 16th Native Infantry and was appointed adjutant in 1862. Promoted to captain in 1865, he served in the Duffla Expedition of 1874, being mentioned in despatches. In 1879, he was promoted to lieutenant colonel for his service in the Second Afghan War of 1878–80, but was invalided home due to blood poisoning while at Ali Musjid.

Cubitt was promoted to colonel in 1883, and served in the Akka Expedition of 1885. In the Burmese War of 1885–87, he was awarded the DSO. He married Charlotte Isabella Hills and they had five children.

William Cubitt died on 25 January 1903 and was buried in St Peter's Churchyard, Frimley, Surrey. His VC is not publicly held. His brother-in-law, James Hills-Johnes, was also awarded the VC.

Cubitt's grave, St Peter's Church, Frimley.

Robert Hope Moncrieff AITKEN, 30 June–22 November 1857

Robert Aitken was born on 6 February 1826 in Cupar, Fife, the son of John and Jane Aitken. Having qualified at Addiscombe Military Seminary, he was commissioned an ensign in the 13th Bengal Native Infantry and sent to India in 1847. He took part in the Second Sikh War of 1848–49 and, with the assistance of Lieutenant Loughnan, personally took prisoner Chief Koulea, for whom there was a reward of £5,000. However, the reward was not paid on the grounds that soldiers were not entitled to it.

Lieutenant Aitken performed various acts during the defence of the Residency at Lucknow from 30 June to 22 November 1857. On three separate occasions, Aitken went into the garden under the enemy's loopholes at the 'Captain's Bazaar' and brought in bullocks that had been left in the garden. On 3 June, along with others, he extinguished a fire at the Bhoosa Stock (broken straw and husks from the threshing floor used as horse fodder) by rushing out and cutting down all the tents in order to stop the fire reaching the nearby magazine. On 20 August, the enemy set fire to the Baillie Guard Gate. Aitken was the first man to reach the gateway and opened the gates to remove the burning wood and straw, thus saving the gates. On 25 September, along with his men, he attacked and captured two guns and thus prevented them from being used on General Henry Havelock's relief column. Having captured them, he attacked with a small force and took the Tehri Kothi, a building near the Residency. On the morning of 26 September, during an assault on a gateway at the Furreed Buksh Palace, he threw himself against the gate, preventing the enemy from closing it. As a result, his men were able to force open the door and capture the position. On 29 September, he led a sortie to capture a gun that had been harassing his position. Under great fire, he worked his way through lanes and houses, reached the gun, and held his ground until help arrived. The gun was taken into the Residency. Aitken was mentioned in despatches ten times for his actions.

Aitken's VC was gazetted on 17 April 1863, but the presentation was postponed due to the C-in-C General Sir Hugh Rose breaking his ribs in a riding accident and delaying his tour of inspection. In May 1865, a parade was ordered for the long overdue award ceremony at the Residency at Lucknow, almost on the spot where several of Aitken's VC actions had taken place, but the VC medal could not be found. It was thought to have been left behind at Simla and a replacement could not be obtained in time. The C-in-C was informed and was not best pleased. When General Rose had cooled down, Colonel Stewart suggested temporarily substituting the medal with his CB, which would look similar from a distance.

A search for Aitken's VC at Simla found that it had been lost. An official replacement was sent and Aitkin was billed for it but as it was proven it was lost before he received it, the fee was waived. He finally received his hard-won VC on 5 April 1866.

In 1876, Colonel Robert Aitkin retired from the army and returned to Scotland. He died on 18 September 1887 and was buried in the Eastern Cemetery, St Andrews, Fife. In 1900, his original VC turned up for sale at auction, having been bought in Simla in 1874. The War Office intervened and the medal was surrendered as property of the Crown. Aitken's VC is held by the National Army Museum, London. His cousin, Robert Digby-Jones, was also awarded the VC.

James TRAVERS, Indore, 1 July 1857

James Travers was born on 6 October 1820 in Cork, Ireland, the son of Major General Sir Robert Travers, of the 95th Rifles. In keeping with family tradition, he was sent to England to attend Addiscombe Military Seminary, near Croydon, Surrey, and was commissioned in June 1838. Travers joined the 2nd Bengal Native Infantry and served in the First Afghan War of 1839–42 and the First Sikh War of 1845–46. He married Mary Isabella in 1849. In 1857, he received the thanks of the Governor General of Central India for his actions against the rebel Sunker Singh.

James Travers.

Colonel Travers was 36 years old when the Indore Residency was suddenly attacked by rebel Seeta Ram Holkar's sepoys, and he led a charge against the guns with only five men supporting him. He drove the rebels from the guns and created a diversion that allowed many lives to be saved from the slaughter, and enabled the Bengal Artillery to man their guns. During the charge, his horse was hit three times and his clothes were riddled with bullets. In a letter home he wrote, 'Had I thirty or forty good sowars at the time, with their hearts in the right place, I would have captured their guns and cut their 200 infantry to pieces; but what could half a dozen do against so many.'

James Travers's VC, gazetted on 1 March 1861, was presented to him on 3 June 1862 by the C-in-C India, Sir Hugh Rose in Gwalior, India. Travers was promoted to major general 1865, lieutenant general in 1873 and general in 1877. He retired from the army in 1881 and moved to Italy.

Travers died on 1 April 1884 and was buried in the Old Cemetery at Pallanza, but was moved to the New Cemetery in around 1920, before finally being placed (in an unmarked grave) in the Municipal Ossuary in the Cimitero di Pallanza, Italy. His VC is not publicly held.

William CONNOLLY, Jhelum, 7 July 1857

William Connolly was born in May 1817 in Liverpool. Little is known of his early life, although it is thought he worked as a stableman and groom before enlisting into the HEIC at the age of 20, joining the 3rd Bengal Horse Artillery. He took part in the Second Sikh War of 1848–49, seeing action at Chillianwala and Goojerat.

When the news was received that the 14th Native Infantry had mutinied at Jhelum, Colonel Charles Ellice was ordered to take 300 men, a squadron of cavalry and three guns from the Bengal Artillery and assist in disarming the rebel sepoys. At dawn on 7 July 1857, the assault was preceded by an artillery barrage, during which Gunner Connolly was working his gun when he received a bullet wound to the left thigh. He insisted on mounting his horse and stayed with the gun as the battery moved to another position. He continued working his gun until he was hit again, in the hip. When urged by his officer to retire, he replied, 'I'll not go whilst I can work here.' Later in the afternoon, he was wounded for the third time, in the leg. Still he carried on, until he collapsed into the arms of Lieutenant Cookes, at which point he was carried from the fight.

Connolly recovered from his wounds and his VC was gazetted on 3 September 1858. He received the medal in February 1859 while still in India. Due to his wounds, he was invalided out of the army and returned to England. By 1886, he had fallen on hard times and sold his medal at auction for £10.

William Connolly died from bronchitis on 31 December 1891 and was buried in Kirkdale Cemetery, Walton, Liverpool, Section 17, Grave 220 (headstone is not on the exact place of burial). His VC is on display at the British in India Museum, Nelson, Lancashire. However, this may be a copy as his name is spelt Conolly and the auctioned VC was later declared to be a Victorian copy. It appears he may have pawned the original medal.

Connolly's grave, Kirkdale Cemetery, Walton, Liverpool.

Henry TOMBS, Delhi, 9 July 1857

Henry Tombs was born on 10 November 1825 in Calcutta, India, the seventh son of Major General John Tombs and Mary (née) Remington. He was sent to England to be educated, first at John Roysse's Free School (now Abingdon School), and then at 14 he entered the Addiscombe Military Seminary, being commissioned a second lieutenant in the Bengal Artillery in June 1841. Tombs served in the Gwalior War of 1843, both Sikh wars (of 1845–46 and 1848–49), and by the time of the Indian Mutiny had been promoted to major.

Henry Tombs.

His first action during the mutiny was at Ghazi-un-din-Nagar on 31 May. Tombs led his men across a bridge and put the rebels to flight. He had the first of five horses shot from under him during his engagement. Then, at Delhi on 9 July 1857, one of his subalterns, Lieutenant James Hills, was on picquet duty at 'The Mound' when Major Tombs heard a rumour that rebel cavalry were approaching. As he moved to a better vantage point, the rebels appeared out of nowhere. Hills charged alone at the enemy column. He cut down one and struck a second, but was thrown from his horse. Three men came at him; he wounded one with his pistol, caught the lance of another in his hand and slashed at him with his sword. The third man took Hills's sword and was about to kill him when Tombs arrived, saw what was happening, and shot the rebel at thirty paces, saving Hills's life. Tombs and Hills then went together to attend to the wounded men. Before long, they were confronted by a rebel carrying Hills's pistol and brandishing a sword. The rebel ran at Hills, cutting him about the head. Tombs rushed in and put his sword through the man, saving Hills again, but not before he too had been slashed about the head.

Tombs's VC was gazetted on 27 April 1858, but there is no record of a presentation. However, he may well have received it at the same time that James Hills received his, in December 1859 from Sir Colin Campbell. Tombs was mentioned in despatches four times during the mutiny. In 1858, he was appointed brevet lieutenant colonel; the rank was confirmed in 1861. In 1863, he was promoted to brigadier general and given command of the Gwalior District. In 1865, he commanded the right column of the Bhutan Field Force and afterwards was appointed ADC to Queen Victoria.

After his promotion to major general, Tombs returned to England and married Georgina Janet Stirling in 1869, and they had three children. This marriage made him a distant relative to Ross Mangles, vc. In 1871, he was back in India, now commanding the Allahabad Division.

In 1873, Tombs became ill and was sent home on sick leave. En route, his condition worsened while at Marseille, forcing him to undergo an operation in Paris. On reaching England, he was told his illness (probably cancer) was incurable.

Henry Tombs died on 2 August 1874 and was buried in Carisbrooke Cemetery, Newport, Isle of Wight, Section B, Grave 113. His VC is held by the Royal Artillery Museum (in storage), Larkhill, Wiltshire. His grandson, Joseph Tombs, was awarded the VC during the First World War.

James HILLS (later HILLS-JOHNES), Delhi, 9 July 1857

James Hills was born on 20 August 1833 in Neechindipur, India, the son of James and Charlotte Hills (née Moisgunge). His father was a well-known indigo planter. Young James was educated first at the Edinburgh Academy and then at the Addiscombe Military Seminary, from where he was commissioned second lieutenant in the Bengal Artillery in June 1853.

Hills fought throughout the mutiny, being in action at Hindun River on 30–31 May 1857, the battle of Budli-ki-Serai on 8 June 1857, and the occupation of the Delhi Ridge. Then, on 9 July 1857, Second Lieutenant Hills was on picquet duty at 'The Mound' when his force was suddenly attacked by rebel cavalry. Without hesitation, he rode straight at the enemy single-handedly in order to cause a delay and give the guns time to be loaded. Hills cut down two rebels before being thrown from his horse by two sowars charging together. Now on foot, he fought off two more rebels and was about to be killed by a third when Major Henry Tombs came to his assistance. Tombs and Hills then went together to attend to the wounded men. Before long, they were confronted by a rebel carrying Hills's pistol and brandishing a sword. The rebel ran at Hills, cutting him about the head. Tombs rushed in and put his sword through the man, saving Hills again, but not before he too had been slashed about the head.

James Hills.

Hills served under Major Tombs in a number of actions during the remainder of the year and was present at the capture of Lucknow in March 1858. They would become lifelong friends, Hills saying of Tombs, 'He was the best commander I served under.' After the mutiny, Hills was appointed ADC to the Governor General of India, Lord Canning. Hills's VC was gazetted on 27 April 1858 and was presented to him in December 1859 by Sir Colin Campbell.

Hills was promoted to captain in 1862 and was given the brevet rank of major the following year. He was appointed Brigade Major of the

Royal Artillery, Northern Division, Bengal from 1864 to 1869, during which time he served in the Abyssinian Expedition of 1867–68, being mentioned in despatches. He was made a brevet lieutenant colonel in 1869. Next, he took part in the Lushai Campaign, 1871–72, again being mentioned in despatches.

Hills served under Lord Roberts, vc, during the Second Afghan War of 1878–80. Following good reports from Roberts, Hills was appointed Military Governor of Kabul in October 1879, a post he held until it was abolished in January 1880.

In 1882, Hills married Elizabeth Johnes at Westminster Abbey, and added her name to his own. Hills-Johnes was promoted to lieutenant general in 1886 and retired in 1888. In a private capacity, he accompanied Lord Roberts, vc, during the Second Boar War from Kronstadt to Diamond Hill. In September 1915, he visited the Western Front, travelling as far as the front line and coming under artillery fire.

On 3 January 1919, James Hills-Johnes died from influenza (although legend has it that he was murdered by his butler because as a JP he had refused him a licence for a public house). He was buried in the vault in the parish churchyard at Caio, Dyfed. His VC is held in storage by the Royal Artillery Museum, Larkhill, Wiltshire. Both his brother-in-law, William Cubitt, and his nephew, Lewis Evans, were also awarded the VC.

Ross Lowis MANGLES, Arrah, 30 July 1857

Ross Mangles was born on 14 April 1833 in Calcutta, India, the son of Ross Donnelly Mangles of the Bengal Civil Service. Young Ross was educated at Windlesham House School, Brighton, in 1842–43, Bath Grammar School in 1843–51, and the HEIC College in Hertford Heath (later the Haileybury College) in 1851–52. He entered the Bengal Civil Service in 1853.

In 1857, he was assistant magistrate at Patna and accompanied the 45th

Ross Lowis Mangles.

(Rattray's) Sikhs in quelling a disturbance in Patna City. Fifteen Europeans and fifty of Rattray's Sikhs were holding out in Arrah against 4,000 rebels. On the night of 29 July 1857, the relief force fell into an ambush, losing some 300 men. The next day during the retreat, a wounded soldier of the 37th Regiment, Private Richard Taylor, begged not to be left to the mercy of the rebels. Mangles bound his wounds and carried him for 6 miles through swampy ground. Neither man had eaten for twenty-four hours or slept for forty-eight. They reached the safety of the river and Mangles swam to a boat with his comrade in his arms.

Taylor told the story to the surgeon who treated him, who told it to Sir James Outram, who in turn told it to Lord Canning, who wanted Mangles (and McDonell, *see* below) to be awarded the VC. However, at the time, civilians were not eligible for the award. A new amendment had to be made and this was passed on 10 August 1858. Mangles's VC was gazetted on 6 July 1859, making him the first civilian to be so awarded. His medal was presented to him on 4 January 1860, by the Queen at Windsor Castle, while he was on extended sick leave.

Mangles returned to India, where he then held a number of legal-related posts, and retired as Secretary to the Government of Bengal. He died on 28 February 1905 and was buried in Brookwood Cemetery, Woking, Surrey, Plot 31, Grave 154820. His VC is held by the National Army Museum, London. Mangles is one of only five civilians to have been awarded the VC, the others being William McDonell, Thomas Kavanagh, James Adams and George Chicken.

Mangles' grave, Brookwood Cemetery, Woking.

William Fraser McDONELL, Arrah, 30 July 1857

William McDonell was born on 17 December 1829 at Cheltenham, Gloucestershire, the son of Aeneas Ranald McDonell of the Madras Civil Service and Juliana Charlotte (née Wade). William was educated at Cheltenham College and the HEIC College in Hertford Heath (later the Haileybury College) in 1847–49. He entered the Bengal Civil Service, becoming assistant magistrate and collector in Sarun in 1852–55, and magistrate in 1855–59. On the outbreak of the mutiny, he volunteered to join the relief force to Arrah in July 1857.

On the night of 29 July 1857, the relief force fell into an ambush, losing some 300 men. The next day, during the retreat, McDonell was in a boat with thirty-five men. It was discovered that the rebels had taken the oars and bound the boat to the bank and fixed the rudder to the right. Exposed to heavy fire, McDonell climbed out of the boat and cut away the rope and then, with the help of a breeze, he took the boat halfway across the stream, from where he and all but two of the men were able to swim to safety.

William Fraser McDonell.

After the mutiny was over, McDonell was given the task of settling the confiscated estates of the rebel leader Koer Singh. His VC was gazetted on 17 February 1860 and was presented to him on 9 November that year by the Queen at Windsor Castle. McDonell returned to India in 1863 and was posted to Nadia in West Bengal, taking up the position of magistrate, collector and judge. He retired from service in 1886, returned to England and settled in Gloucestershire. He became a member of Gloucestershire council in 1890–94 and Governor of Cheltenham College. During 1893, his health began to fail and he spent the winter in Malta to recover.

William McDonell died from typhoid fever and pneumonia on 31 July 1894. He was survived by his wife of many years, Annie Louisa (née Duff). He was buried

McDonell's grave, St Peter's Church, Leckhampton.

in St Peter's Churchyard, Leckhampton, Gloucestershire. His original VC was stolen; an official replacement was issued in 1878, which is now in the Lord Ashcroft Gallery, Imperial War Museum. He is one of only five civilians to be awarded the VC, the others being Ross Lowis Mangles, Thomas Kavanagh, James Adams and George Chicken.

James BLAIR, Neemuch and Jeerum, 12 August & 23 October 1857

James Blair.

James Blair was born on 27 January 1828 at the military station of Neemuch, India, the son of Captain E.M. Blair, of the Bengal Cavalry. At 16, James was commissioned into the Bombay Army and joined the 2nd Bombay Light Cavalry.

On 12 August at Neemuch, Captain Blair volunteered to apprehend seven or eight mutineers. With sword in hand, he stormed into the house where they had taken up a defensive position. A struggle ensued, during which he was badly wounded. The rebels were forced to escape through the roof. In spite of his wounds, Blair pursued them but was unable to catch them. On 23 October 1857, during a skirmish at Jeerum, Blair was surrounded by a group of rebels. He broke his sword on the head of one, who then wounded him in the arm. He escaped to re-join his men and, with no other weapon than his broken sword, led them in pursuit of the rebels, who were eventually routed.

Blair was promoted to captain shortly afterwards. His VC was not gazetted until 25 February 1862 and was presented to him by Lieutenant Colonel Sir William Mansfield in Bombay. He was promoted three more times before reaching the rank of colonel of his regiment in 1875. He was married to Frances B.E. Halhed of Gateley Hall, Hampshire. As a brigadier general, he was Political Resident at Aden in 1882–85, and was promoted to major general in 1885. He retired with the rank of general in April 1895 and settled in Scotland.

James Blair died on 18 January 1905 and was buried in Trinity Churchyard, Melrose, Roxburghshire. His VC is not publicly held. His cousin Robert Blair was also awarded the VC during the mutiny while serving with the 2nd Dragoon Guards.

Charles John Stanley GOUGH, Khurkowdah, Shumshahbad and Meangunge, 15 & 18 August 1857, 27 January & 23 February 1858

Charles Gough was born on 28 January 1832 in Chittagong, India (now in Bangladesh), the son of Judge George Gough and Charlotte Margaret (née Becher). The young Gough was sent to England for his education. He returned to India aged 16 and was commissioned into the 8th Bengal Cavalry, just in time to take part in the Second Sikh War, of 1848–49. Gough saw action at the defeat of Ramnuggur on 22 November 1848, Chenab, Sadoolapur, Chillianwala and Goojerat.

Charles John Stanley Gough.

On the outbreak of the mutiny, now serving in the 5th Bengal European Cavalry, Charles and his brother Hugh joined the army and were sent to capture Delhi. On 15 August 1857 at Khurkowdah, near Rohtuck, Major Charles Gough saved the life of his brother, Lieutenant Hugh Gough, by killing two of his assailants. On 18 August, he led a troop of the Guide Cavalry in a charge against the rebels, killing two sowars during hand-to-hand combat. On 27 January 1858 at Shumshahbad, he tackled the leader of the enemy cavalry, running him through with his sword, which became lodged in the man's body. Gough was reduced to using his revolver, with which he shot two more men. On 23 February 1858 at Meangunge, he ran to the aid of Brevet Major O.H. St George Anson and cut down his opponent, killing another immediately after.

After the mutiny was over Charles Gough returned to England on sick leave. His VC was gazetted on 21 October 1859 and was presented to him on 4 January 1860 by the Queen at Windsor Castle. He took part in the Bhootan Expedition in 1864 but saw very little action. Gough married Harriet Anastasia de la Poer in 1869. In 1878, by now a colonel, he fought in the Second Afghan War with distinction.

Gough returned to India to command the Hyderabad Contingent and was promoted to major general in 1885, after which he commanded the Bengal District for the next five years. Following his promotion to general in 1891, Gough was placed on the retirement list in 1895. He moved to Ireland and settled in Tipperary, where he wrote about the Sikh wars.

Charles Gough died on 6 September 1912 and was buried in St Patrick's Cemetery, Clonmel, County Tipperary, Ireland. His VC is in the Lord Ashcroft Gallery, Imperial War Museum, London. His brother Hugh and his son John were also awarded the VC.

Duncan Charles HOME, Delhi Kashmir Gate, 14 September 1857

Duncan Home was born on 10 June 1828 in Jubbulpore (now Jabalpur), India, the son of Major General Richard Home of the Bengal Army. At age 8 he was sent to England for his education. He passed through the HEIC College in Hertford Heath (later the Haileybury College), graduating at the head of his class in 1846. Following further instruction with the Royal Engineers at Chatham, Home returned to India as a subaltern in the 3rd Company, Bengal Engineers. He was just in time to take part in the final battle of the Second Sikh War at Goojerat in 1849.

Duncan Charles Home.

Home spent the next five years working on the construction of canals in the Punjab, and was promoted to lieutenant in 1854. When the news arrived about the mutiny, he was ordered to select 160 of his best men and take them to Delhi. They arrived in August and Home's 'Punjab Sappers' went to work on building gun emplacements.

On 14 September 1857, Lieutenant Home led a storming party with Lieutenant Philip Salkeld, Sergeant John Smith, Sergeant Carmichael, Corporal Burgess and Bugler Robert Hawthorne of the 52nd Regiment of Foot, each carrying 25lb bags of gunpowder across the single remaining beam to the Kashmir Gate under heavy fire. As they nailed the bags to the gate, Carmichael fell dead. Having attached his own bag, Smith also nailed Carmichael's, prepared the fuse and called, 'All ready.' As Salkeld stooped down to light the fuse he was shot through the thigh. He held out the match to Burgess and fell into the ditch below. Burgess, thinking it had gone out, reached for a box of lucifers and, as he leant down, he was shot. Smith grabbed the match before he fell onto Salkeld. Smith quickly lit the fuse and jumped into the ditch. The gunpowder exploded, destroying the gate, before he reached the bottom. When the smoke cleared, he looked around and saw Burgess lying dead and Salkeld wounded with two broken arms. Home was uninjured. Hawthorne, as well as assisting the wounded, had to sound the advance three times to be heard by the waiting men. The men were now able to pour into the city. Home, Salkeld, Smith and Hawthorne were awarded the VC. Carmichael and Burgess were not because it was not awarded posthumously at this time. Although both Home and Salkeld were dead within weeks, their commanding officer had conferred their awards on the spot.

Home was appointed Chief Field Engineer in Colonel Greathed's column, which pursued the rebels. On 28 September, they caught up with a strong force of rebels at Bulundshahr and, after a short sharp fight, captured the town. From there, patrols were sent out looking for any sight of the enemy. A small deserted fort at Malagarh was found to have been used as an arsenal, and Homes was sent for to blow it up. He and his sappers spent three days seeing what could be saved and what should be blown up. On 1 October 1857, Home was accidently killed when the mine prematurely blew up. He was buried in Bulundshahr Cemetery (large tomb), near Aligarh, India.

Duncan Home's VC was gazetted on 18 June 1857 and was posted to his parents. The medal was believed to have been lost by children in the 1920s when playing 'soldiers' in a field. Despite many searches, it has never been seen again.

Philip SALKELD, Delhi Kashmir Gate, 14 September 1857

Philip Salkeld was born on 13 October 1830 in Fontmell Magna, Dorset, the fourth son of thirteen children born to the Reverend Robert Salkeld. Despite financial difficulties and the size of the family, a sponsor was found and Philip was sent to the HEIC College in Hertford Heath (later the Haileybury College), passing out with a commission with the Bengal Engineers. Like Home, Salkeld was employed in various road and canal projects while in India. Having also worked on the Grand Trunk Road in Meerut in 1853, he was sent to Delhi in 1856, where he worked as an executive engineer with the Public Works.

Philip Salkeld.

When the mutiny broke out, Salkeld narrowly avoided death in the rioting and found himself with other survivors near the Kashmir Gate. With the rebels closing in, he led the group to the top of the bastion and helped them escape. They joined up with a small number of officers, one of whom was George Forrest (*see* above); also in the party was Salkeld's wife and three daughters, the youngest of whom was nine. They made a tortuous journey through canals and rivers and were robbed by bandits along the way. Salkeld made the journey barefoot, having given his shoes to one of the girls. Eventually, they were helped by friendly villagers and rescued by Lieutenant Gough (*see* below).

After recovering from his ordeal, Salkeld joined General Archdale Wilson's Meerut Column and marched on Delhi. Salkeld's sappers built gun emplacements covering Hindoo Rao's house, a focus of heavy fighting. On 22 June, he took a party of sappers and blew up an important bridge on the Grand Trunk Road over the Najafgarh Jheel drain.

On 14 September 1857, Salkeld was second in command of a storming party with Lieutenant Duncan Home (in command), Sergeant John Smith, Sergeant Carmichael, Corporal Burgess and Bugler Robert Hawthorne, 52nd Regiment of Foot, each carrying 25lb bags of gunpowder across the single remaining beam to the Kashmir Gate under heavy fire. As they nailed the bags to the gate, Carmichael fell dead. Having attached his own bag, Smith also nailed Carmichael's, prepared the fuse and called, 'All ready.' As Lieutenant Salkeld stooped down to light the fuse, he was shot through the thigh. He held out the match to Burgess and fell into the ditch below. Burgess, thinking it had gone out, reached for a box of lucifers and, as he leant down, he was shot. Smith grabbed the match before he fell onto Salkeld. Smith quickly lit the fuse and jumped into the ditch. The gunpowder exploded before he even reached the bottom. When the smoke cleared, he looked around and saw Burgess lying dead, Salkeld wounded and with two broken arms. Home was uninjured. Hawthorne, as well as assisting the wounded, had to sound the advance three times to be heard by the waiting men. The men were now able to pour into the city. Home, Salkeld, Smith and Hawthorne were awarded the VC. Carmichael and Burgess were not because it was not awarded posthumously at that time. Although both Home and Salkeld were dead within weeks, their commanding officer had conferred their awards on the spot.

Salkeld's arm had to be amputated and he never recovered, dying on 10 October 1857. He was buried in an unmarked grave in Old Delhi Military Cemetery (The Nicholson Cemetery), India. His VC was gazetted on 18 June 1858 and was posted to his father. The medal is not publicly held.

John SMITH, Delhi Kashmir Gate, 14 September 1857

John Smith was born in February 1814 in Ticknall, Derbyshire, the sixth of eight children. Like his father and his uncle, he became a cordwainer (a maker of boots and shoes). At 22, possibly due to boredom or a family dispute, he took the shilling and was on his way to the HEIC Depot at Chatham to start eighteen months' engineering training.

In 1839, he endured the six-month sea voyage to India and on his arrival joined the 3rd Company, Bengal Sappers and Miners. Smith was soon promoted to sergeant and took part in the First Afghan War of 1839–42 and the First Sikh War of 1845–46. It was at the Battle of Goojerat during this campaign that he met Lieutenant Duncan Home. Smith remained in the Punjab for a number of years working on a variety of civil projects.

When news of the mutiny at Meerut reached them, Smith was at Roorkee, a town on the banks of the Ganges Canal in the state of Uttarakhand. Colonel Baird Smith organised boats to carry loyal sappers and infantrymen under Captain Fraser, and sailed down the canal to reach Meerut on 13 May 1857. On their arrival, the officers at Meerut insisted on disarming the native troops who had come to help them. Dismayed at this reaction, some of them killed Fraser and fled to join the mutineers. All that remained were John Smith, forty-five NCOs and enlisted men, and 124 Indian sappers.

Two weeks later, Smith's party joined General Archdale Wilson's column on its way to join the Delhi Field Force. On 14 September 1857, Smith was in a party with Lieutenant Duncan Home, Lieutenant Philip Salkeld, Sergeant Carmichael, Corporal Burgess and Bugler Robert Hawthorne, each carrying 25lb bags of gunpowder across the single remaining beam to the Kashmir Gate under heavy fire. Smith's job was to bring up the rear and see that no one was left behind. Four of the natives refused to go through the gate and Smith was about to shoot them, as ordered by Salkeld, but two of them went on and Salkeld said, 'OK, don't shoot; it will be enough.' As they nailed the bags to the gate, Carmichael fell dead. Having attached his own bag, Smith also nailed Carmichael's, prepared the fuse and called, 'All ready.' As Salkeld stooped down to light the fuse he was shot through the thigh. He held out the match to Burgess and fell into the ditch below. Burgess, thinking it had gone out, reached for a box of lucifers and, as he leant down, he was shot. Smith grabbed the match before he fell onto Salkeld. Smith quickly lit the fuse and jumped into the ditch. The gunpowder exploded before he even reached the bottom. When the smoke cleared, he looked around and saw Burgess lying dead and Salkeld wounded with two broken arms. Home was uninjured. Hawthorne, as well as assisting the wounded, had to sound the advance three times to be heard by the waiting men. The men were now able to pour into the city. Home, Salkeld, Smith and Hawthorne were awarded the VC. Carmichael and Burgess were not because it was not awarded posthumously at that time. Although both Home and Salkeld were dead within weeks, their commanding officer had conferred their awards on the spot.

After the capture of Delhi, Smith joined Brigadier George Barker's flying column, which was on the march for eighteen months. Smith's VC was gazetted on 27 April 1858, but there is no record of a presentation and it may have been posted to him.

Smith married an English widow, Mary Anne, and they had four daughters. He died from dysentery on 26 June 1864 and was buried with full military honours in Artillery Cemetery, Jullundur (now Jalandhar), India. He left his VC to his wife and it later passed to his nephew's widow and was subsequently lost. It turned up at auction at Sotheby's in 1989 and is now in private hands.

James McGUIRE, Delhi Kabul Gate, 14 September 1857

James McGuire was born in 1827 in Enniskillen, County Fermanagh, Ireland. He was a labourer before enlisting into the HEIC's 1st Bengal European Fusiliers at 18, and served in the Burma War of 1852–53. Promoted to sergeant, McGuire took part in the siege of Delhi.

On 14 September 1857, at the Kabul Gate, McGuire, with Drummer Miles Ryan, were awaiting orders and refilling their ammunition patches when the reserve ammunition was being carried up onto the ramparts to be put into a magazine, and five boxes caught fire. Three of them exploded. Sergeant McGuire and Drummer Miles Ryan dashed for the two remaining boxes and threw them over the parapet into the water-filled ditch below. Confused, many men began running while others stood about dazed, so by their actions, McGuire and Ryan saved many lives.

McGuire's VC was gazetted on 24 December 1858. He took his discharge from the army in May 1859 and was presented with his medal on 4 January 1860 by the Queen at Windsor Castle. Sadly, his life took a downturn when he was accused of stealing a cow belonging to his uncle. At his trial in July 1862, McGuire claimed he had taken it in lieu of an unpaid debt, but he was found guilty and sentenced to nine months. Because of this, he was the subject of a forfeiture warrant and his name was struck off the list of VC recipients on 22 December 1862.

On his release in March 1863, he petitioned (under the name MaGuire) to have his VC and annuity restored. His petition was supported by the magistrates involved in his case but not by the judge who sentenced him.

The Secretary of State at the War Office therefore would not submit the case to the Queen and it seems that McGuire gave up trying.

McGuire's date of death is something of a mystery. It has been stated that he died on 22 December 1862 (the same day he was struck off the VC register) but this is not possible as it was after this date that he petitioned to have his VC restored. It is believed he was buried (under his wife's maiden name of Patrick Joseph Donnelly) in an unmarked grave in Donagh Cemetery, near Lisnaskea, County Fermanagh. His VC is held by the National Army Museum, London.

Miles RYAN, Delhi Kabul Gate, 14 September 1857

Miles Ryan was born in 1826 in Derry, Ireland. Apart from him being a blacksmith, little is known of his early life. He enlisted into the HEIC in September 1848 for ten years' service. He sailed for India aboard the troopship *Ellenborough* and arrived in October 1849. He fought in the Burma War of 1852–53, receiving the medal and clasp for the Battle of Pegu.

On 14 September 1857, at the Kabul Gate, he and Sergeant James McGuire were awaiting orders and refilling their ammunition patches when the reserve ammunition was being carried up onto the ramparts to be put into a magazine, and five boxes caught fire. Three of them exploded. Sergeant McGuire and Drummer Miles Ryan dashed for the two remaining boxes and threw them over the parapet into the water-filled ditch below. Confused, many men began running while others stood about dazed, so by Ryan and McGuire's actions they saved many lives.

Ryan's VC was gazetted on 24 December 1858, but there is no record of it being presented and it may have been posted to him. Ryan was discharged in May 1859 with a pension of 1 shilling a day. He is believed to have remained in India, and died in January 1887 in Bengal, but he has no known grave. His VC is not publicly held.

George Alexander RENNY, Delhi Magazine, 16 September 1857

George Renny was born on 12 May 1825 in Riga, Russian Empire (now Latvia). His father died shortly after his birth and his mother took their children to Scotland, from where she came. George was educated at Addiscombe Military Seminary before being commissioned into the Bengal Horse Artillery of the HEIC's army. He took part in the Sutlej Campaign of 1846, got married to Flora Hastings MacWhirter in 1849 and, by the time of the mutiny, commanded the 5th Native Troop of the 1st Brigade.

George Alexander Renny.

Renny first saw action at Jalandhar on 7 June 1857 and by 23 June was at siege of Delhi. During the assault, he commanded No. 4 Siege Battery and, when the infantry stormed the defences, he took some gunners and 12-pounder mortars to shell the houses in front of the attack. During the attack on the Kashmir Bastion, he turned a captured gun on the enemy.

On 16 September 1857, after the capture of the Delhi Magazine, the enemy made vigorous attacks on the post. The rebels threw shells with lighted fuses onto the thatched roof. Lieutenant Renny leapt onto the wall above the magazine and flung several shells, which were handed to him with their fuses already lit, while Lieutenant Thackeray extinguished the fires. The rebels almost at once withdrew and Renny turned his mortars on the trouble spots.

Renny continued to serve during the mutiny and was promoted to brevet major. His VC was gazetted on 12 April 1859 and was presented to him, as eleven other recipients were receiving theirs, on

Renny's grave, Locksbrook Cemetery, Bath.

9 November 1860 by the Queen at Windsor Castle. He took part in the Hazara Campaign of 1868, when his mountain battery was carried by elephants. He retired from the army with the rank of major general in December 1878 and settled in the West Country.

George Renny died on 5 January 1887 and was buried in Locksbrook Cemetery, Bath, Somerset, Section FJ, Grave 864. His VC was stolen in 1978 and was subsequently found by a man using a metal detector on Sheen Common, Richmond, London, in 1983 and returned to the family. It is now in the Lord Ashcroft Gallery, Imperial War Museum, London.

Edward Talbot THACKERAY, Delhi Magazine, 16 September 1857

Edward Talbot Thackeray.

Edward Thackeray was born on 19 October 1836 in Broxbourne, Hertfordshire, the son of the Reverend Francis Thackeray and Mary Anne (née Shakespear). He was educated at Marlborough College and then at Addiscombe Military Seminary, being commissioned a second lieutenant in the Bengal Engineers in 1857, just weeks before the outbreak of the mutiny. Thackeray joined the Delhi column that fought engagements at Hindun and Budli-ki-Serai.

On 16 September 1857, Second Lieutenant Thackeray was in the Delhi Magazine when the rebels attacked and threw shells with lighted fuses onto the thatched roof. While George Renny leapt onto the wall above the magazine and flung several shells, which were handed to him with their fuses already lit, Thackeray extinguished the fires on the magazine roof, under close and heavy fire from the enemy and at the risk of his own life from the explosion of large amounts of ammunition in the magazine.

In his own account of the incident, Thackeray plays down his part in the action: 'We had got up on the roof with leather bags of water and put it out while they threw stones at us ... I had the narrowest escape of any ...'

After Delhi, Thackeray fought in many actions during 1858–59 and thought no more of his part in the Delhi Magazine fight. It was only a year later that the Bengal Engineers learned of Renny's VC award and believed that Thackeray deserved it too. Colonel Baird Smith, Chief Engineer, petitioned the War Office, who despite the five-year gap, finally agreed and Thackeray's VC was gazetted on 29 April 1862. It was presented to him in July of the same year by General A.A. Dalzell in Dover.

Thackeray went on to serve in the Second Afghan War of 1878–80 and was made Commandant of the Bengal Sappers and Miners before retiring from the army in 1888. He became an active member of the Red Cross and was Chief Commissioner of the order of St John of Jerusalem. He settled in Italy and during the First World War was Commissioner of the Bordighera branch of the British Red Cross. For his service, he was mentioned in despatches and received the British War Medal and the Victory Medal.

Edward Thackeray died on 3 September 1927 and was buried in the English Cemetery, Bordighera, Italy, Grave 228. His VC is held by the National Museum of Military History, Johannesburg, South Africa.

William OLPHERTS, Lucknow, 25 September 1857

William Olpherts was born on 8 March 1882 in Dartry, County Armagh, Ireland. He was educated at the Royal School Dungannon and in 1837 received a nomination to attend the HEIC's Addiscombe Military Seminary. On passing out in 1839 he joined the Bengal Artillery. Olpherts saw a great deal of active service during the 1840s, in Burma, Saugor, and Gwalior, as well as during the First Sikh War of 1844–45 and on the North-West Frontier in 1851.

William Olpherts.

During the Crimean War, Olpherts saw active service in the Caucasus with General Sir Fenwick Williams in the defence of Kars and Erzeroum, after which he was sent to Crimea itself, where he commanded a brigade of bashi-bazouks in the Turkish contingent.

When the mutiny started, Olpherts was disarming mutineers in Benares, and later joined General Henry Havelock's column at Allahabad. Known as Hell Fire Jack, Olpherts described himself as 'an old smooth-bore muzzle-loader, hopelessly behind the times'. On 25 September 1857, when the troops penetrated into the city, Captain Olpherts charged across the Char Bagh Bridge on horseback with the 90th Regiment as they captured two guns in the face of very heavy canister fire, after which he returned under severe fire to bring up limbers and horses to carry off the guns.

When the Residency was reached, he acted as brigadier of artillery and, after Sir Colin Campbell's column relived Lucknow, Olpherts left to defend the Alambagh as the British advanced position. For his action at the Char Bagh Bridge and many others, the officers of his regiment elected Olpherts for the award of the VC. This was gazetted on 18 June 1858 and presented to him on 4 May 1859 by Major General Sir Sidney Cotton at Lucknow.

In 1859–60, he served as a volunteer under Brigadier Neville Bowles Chamberlain in an expedition on the North-West Frontier of the Punjab against the Waziris, thus completing twenty continuous years' active service in the artillery. Olpherts married Alice Cautley in 1861 and they had one son and three daughters. In 1861–68 he commanded the artillery in the frontier stations of Peshawar, after which he returned home on leave. Olpherts returned to India in 1872, commanding the Gwalior, Umbelya and Lucknow brigades, finally leaving India for good in 1875 with the rank of major general. He was promoted to lieutenant general in October 1877, general in March 1883 and became colonel commandant of the Royal Artillery in 1888.

Olpherts died on 30 April 1902 and was buried in Richmond Cemetery, Richmond-upon-Thames, Surrey, Section N, Grave 1953. His VC is on loan (in storage) to the Royal Artillery Museum, Larkhill, Wiltshire.

Olpherts's grave, Richmond Cemetery, Richmond-upon-Thames.

Thomas DUFFY, Lucknow, 26 September 1857

Thomas Duffy was born in 1806 in Athlone, Ireland. Almost nothing is known of his life other than his service in the mutiny. At 52 at the time of this action, he must have been one of the oldest privates in the army.

Duffy was serving in the 1st Madras Fusiliers (later the Royal Dublin Fusiliers) when, on 26 September 1857, Captain Olpherts saw that a 24-pounder gun that had been used against the enemy the previous day was in danger of being captured by the rebels. It was in a very exposed position and any attempt to reach it would be met with heavy fire. Olpherts, Lieutenant C.W. Crump (of the Madras Artillery) and Private Duffy made an attempt to reach it. With a combination of daring and guile, Duffy managed to reach the gun and fasten a rope to the tail, and it was then pulled back to their position. Olpherts recommended Duffy for the VC, which was gazetted on 18 June 1858 and presented to him in 1859 by Lieutenant General Marcus Beresford at Mysore, India.

Thomas Duffy died on 24 December 1868 and was buried in Glasnevin Cemetery, Dublin, Section Z-B, Grave 8 1/2. His VC is held by the National Army Museum, London.

John RYAN, Lucknow, 26 September 1857

John Ryan was born in 1823 in Kilkenny, Ireland. He enlisted into the 1st Madras Fusiliers (later the Royal Dublin Fusiliers), and was in India with his regiment when the mutiny broke out.

On 26 September 1857, when the British were forcing their way into the Residency at Lucknow, Private Ryan was with a party of wounded men left behind in the streets. Under heavy fire, and with the help of Surgeon Anthony Home, Assistant Surgeon William Bradshaw (both of the 90th Regiment), Private Peter McManus (5th Regiment) and Private James Hollowell (of the 78th Regiment), got the wounded into a house. The two privates kept up a steady fire, shooting rebel after rebel, all the time shouting in chorus to make the enemy think they were more numerous. At one point, the two privates dashed out into the open to bring back Lieutenant Arnold, who was injured. Meanwhile, the two surgeons tended to the wounded, and Home even found time to help in shooting at the rebels. After half an hour, the house was set on fire and they had to flee to a nearby shed with the wounded. They held this position for twenty-two hours. The rebels climbed onto the roof and the defenders had to shoot them from the rooms below. Soon after dawn, when the group had given up hope of survival, they were rescued. All five men were awarded the VC.

Ryan was promoted to sergeant and presented with his VC by General Sir James Outram, although it was not officially gazetted until 18 June 1858 (after Ryan's death).

John Ryan was killed in action at Cawnpore on 4 March 1858 and was buried in an unmarked grave in Old British Cemetery, Cawnpore, India. His VC is held by the National Army Museum, London.

Jacob THOMAS, Lucknow, 27 September 1857

Jacob Thomas was born in February 1833 in Llanwinio, Carmarthenshire, the son of a farmer. At 20 years old, he decided farming was not for him and in July 1853 enlisted into the Bengal Artillery and was soon posted to India.

On 27 September 1857, Bombardier Thomas was part of a sortie sent out to destroy enemy guns. The most effective way to do this was by ramming gunpounder down the barrel and filling it with clay, rendering the gun unusable. Unfortunately, due to the very hot sun, the men had drunk all of their water and could not moisten the clay. The guns were abandoned and the men started their way back, when a soldier of the Madras Fusiliers was wounded and in danger of being captured by the enemy. Thomas picked him up and carried him over his shoulder, under heavy fire, back to safety.

Thomas stayed on the barricades until the siege was lifted in November. His VC was gazetted on 24 December 1858 and was presented to him on 4 January 1860 by the Queen at Windsor Castle. Thomas transferred to the Royal Artillery but elected to stay on in India and was later promoted to quartermaster sergeant. He was medically discharged in 1866 due to injuries sustained after being fallen on by a horse.

Jacob Thomas died on 24 April 1896 (although some sources say 3 March 1911) and was buried in an unmarked grave in Bandel Churchyard, Hooghly, near Darjeeling, India. His VC is held (in storage) by the Royal Artillery Museum, Larkhill, Wiltshire.

Bernard DIAMOND, Bulundshahr, 28 September 1857

Bernard Diamond was born in January 1827 in Portglenone, County Antrim, Ireland. He worked as a labourer until 1847, when, at the age of 20, he enlisted into the Bengal Horse Artillery and was posted to India. Diamond took part in the Second Sikh War, of 1848–49. In 1854, he was promoted to sergeant and married a widow, Mary Collins.

During the mutiny at Bulundshahr, on 28 September 1857, when the enemy attacked with determination, Sergeant Diamond and Gunner Fitzgerald worked their gun under very heavy fire after all the other crew had been killed or wounded. Between them, they cleared the enemy from the road.

Bernard Diamond.

Both men's VCs were gazetted on 24 April 1858, but there is no recorded presentation and the medals may have been posted to them. Diamond went on to fight at Agra, Cawnpore and the relief of Lucknow, during which time he was wounded three times; one injury was to the head and left him blind in one eye. Because of this, he was medically discharged in 1861. In 1875, he and his family emigrated to New Zealand and settled in Masterton, on the North Island.

Bernard Diamond died on 25 January 1892 and was buried in Masterton Cemetery, Greater Wellington, New Zealand, Block P, Row 3. His VC is held by the National Army Museum, Waiouru, New Zealand.

Richard FITZGERALD, Bulundshahr, 28 September 1857

Richard Fitzgerald was born in December 1831 in Cork, Ireland. Almost nothing is known of his early life, other than he enlisted into the Bengal Horse Artillery in December 1851 and was posted to India.

During the mutiny at Bulundshahr, on 28 September 1857, when the enemy attacked with determination, Gunner Fitzgerald and Sergeant

Diamond worked their gun under very heavy fire after all the other crew had been killed or wounded. Between them, they cleared the enemy from the road.

Both men's VCs were gazetted on 24 April 1858, but there is no recorded presentation and the medals may have been posted to them. After the mutiny, Fitzgerald transferred to the Royal Artillery as 'Local in India' and was pensioned off in 1872.

Richard Fitzgerald may have died in 1884, as this is the year he stopped drawing his pension, possibly in Ghaziabad, India, but he has no known grave. His VC is held by the Bristol Museum & Art Gallery, Somerset.

John Charles Campbell DAUNT, Chota and Gopalganj, 2 October & 2 November 1857

John Daunt was born on 8 November 1832 in Avranches, Normandy, France. He attended the Addiscombe Military Seminary and was commissioned as an ensign into the 70th Bengal Native Infantry in July 1852, and promoted to lieutenant in July 1857. Daunt transferred into the Bengal Military Police in July 1857.

John Charles Campbell Daunt.

On 2 October 1857 at Chota (Chuttra), Lieutenant Daunt with Corporal Denis Dynon (of the 53rd Regiment) charged the guns of the Ramgurh Battalion. They captured two guns, killing the gunners (who had shot down a third of their detachment) with their pistols, and turned the guns on the rebels. On 2 November at Gopalganj in Bihar, Daunt chased mutineers of the 32nd Bengal Native Infantry across a plain into a rice cultivation, into which he followed them with a few of Rattray's Sikhs. During an attempt to drive out a large body of these rebels from an enclosure, he was seriously wounded.

Daunt re-joined the 70th Bengal Native Infantry in April 1858 in Canton, China, where he fought in the Third China War, of 1860–62.

His VC was gazetted on 25 February 1862 (the same day as Dynon's, whose medal was presented to him while in hospital in Ireland), and his VC was sent to him by registered post. He wrote to the War Office claiming he should have received the VC and Bar as his citation was for two separate actions. The War Office replied saying his claim did not come within the rules as he would have had to have already been awarded the VC for a Bar to be awarded.

Daunt's grave, Redland Green Chapel graveyard, Bristol.

In April 1862, Daunt entered civil employment as a district superintendent in the Bengal Police. He received the brevet rank of captain in July 1864, which was confirmed in September 1966. He was promoted to major in 1872, lieutenant colonel in July 1878 and brevet colonel in 1882, retiring to Bristol the same year.

John Daunt died on 15 April 1886 and was buried in Redland Green Chapel Graveyard. Bristol, Somerset. His VC is in the Lord Ashcroft Gallery, Imperial War Museum.

James William MILLER, Futtehpore, 28 October 1857

James Miller was born on 5 May 1820 in Glasgow. A candle maker, he enlisted into the HEIC's Bengal Artillery in June 1841 and was posted to Chatham Dockyard in Kent. He was promoted to sergeant in 1846 and by the time of the mutiny, he was serving in the Bengal Ordnance Department as a conductor at Agra.

On 28 October 1857 at Futtehpore, Lieutenant Glubb was severely wounded and lying in an exposed position. Without hesitation and at great personal

James William Miller.

risk, Miller rushed out to his aid and carried him to safety. Miller was wounded during his action.

Miller's VC was not gazetted until 25 February 1862 because Colonel Cotton, who recommended Miller for the award, had died. Miller's medal was presented to him later the same year in India. He rose to the rank of honourable captain and deputy commissary in 1879, and retired in 1882.

James Miller died from pneumonia on 12 June 1892 and was buried in an unmarked grave in Simla Churchyard, Himachal Pradesh, India. It is thought his VC was stolen and its location is unknown.

Thomas Henry KAVANAGH, Lucknow, 9/10 November 1857

Thomas Kavanagh was born on 15 July 1821 in Mullingar, County Westmeath, Ireland. His father was the bandmaster of the 3rd (Buffs) Regiment, and his family moved to India when the regiment was posted in 1833. When he was old enough, the young Kavanagh worked as a clerk, until 1839, when he took up employment in a counting house at Mussoree. In 1843, he became head clerk to the Government Treasury at Umbelya. Later, he was appointed head clerk at the Board of Administration at Lahore and then assistant magistrate at Jullundur (now Jalandhar). Despite

Thomas Henry Kavanagh.

his advancement up the civil service ladder, Kavanagh was struggling financially. He then transferred to Mooltan, but was almost fired for his mounting debts. He was saved by Lord Dalhousie, who secured him the position of Superintendent of the Office of the Chief Commissioner in Lucknow.

When the siege of Lucknow began, Kavanagh had his wife, Agnes, and four of his ten children with him. He was put in charge of the male civilians and set about arming them to help with the defence, although some thought this was not a good idea as they could be more of a danger to themselves than the enemy were. Kavanagh tried to introduce military style training but some of the men found his methods too much and openly questioned his authority.

By the end of July 1857, the bigger threat to the defenders was disease: cholera, fever and smallpox were rife. One of Kavanagh's sons was lost to sickness, and he feared the same fate awaited the rest of his family. He would rather they play outside and risk the fire of the enemy than die from disease. During August, there were many rumours of a relief column but each time, there was no sign of it. When Hancock's relief column finally reached the Residency, there were too few to achieve a relief, but they did boost the defenders' numbers.

Kavanagh was determined to play a prominent role and use the situation to pull himself out of the poverty trap. In October, he was appointed assistant field engineer. By now, the rebels were digging tunnels under the perimeter of the Residency in order to lay explosives. Kavanagh dug counter-tunnels, and he found and killed a number of enemy rebels. On one occasion, after shooting a rebel he crawled along to recover the sepoy's tools. Unable to find them, he went further into the tunnel, realising he had gone too far when he could hear voices. Another sepoy appeared and he shot him, but having only one round left, he moved back. Boldly, Kavanagh called out that he would retrieve their tools, to which the reply came that he could have them if he could take them. Kavanagh started telling the rebels of the excellent state of their provisions and the fast approaching British Army, and distracted the sepoys for long enough for him to grab the tools and leave. The loyal Sikh soldiers called him Burra Surungwalla – the Great Miner.

Kavanagh learned that an Indian messenger, Kanauji Lal, had managed to get into the Residency carrying a despatch from Sir Colin Campbell, who would be able to lift the siege within a week. Senior officers had drawn up a plan to assist Campbell, outlining the best route through the city. Kavanagh knew that the plan on its own was of little use without someone to explain it, or give directions of what to do if the route was blocked. He volunteered to go with Kanauji Lal disguised as a native. Colonel Robert Napier was not keen on the idea as Kavanagh was an unlikely candidate, being 6 feet tall with blue eyes and red hair. However, he was impressed by Kavanagh's courage and consulted with Sir James Outram, who also thought Kavanagh was not a suitable candidate. But

Kavanagh would not give up easily. Uppermost in his mind were his strong sense of duty and the fate of his family, but also that this could be a chance to further his advancement.

To prove to Napier and Outram that he could fool the rebels, Kavanagh donned his disguise and entered the house of the Europeans and took a seat without permission (something natives would not be allowed to do). Kavanagh was well known by the staff but no one recognised him, and they were outraged that a native had been so impudent. Sir James was called in to put his insolent native in his place. When Sir James entered the room, he also failed to recognise Kavanagh. Kavanagh had passed his test.

At 8 pm on the night of 9/10 November 1857, Kavanagh and Kanauji Lal made their way through the city in disguise. They were stopped four times and questioned by rebels, but each time managed to talk their way through and reached the British camp of the relieving force at 5 am.

Kavanagh accompanied the relief column and gave advice on the route to be taken. When the Residency was in sight, he decided to try to reach Sir James alone. He ran through the streets haphazardly until he found his way through. He was taken to Sir James, who gave out cries of 'It is Kavanagh! Three cheers to him! He is the first to relieve us!'

The Indian government awarded Kavanagh £2,000, which he thought a miserly sum considering that his actions had saved the public treasure, which was an estimated £300,000. This would remain a sore point for him for the rest of his life. His recommendation for the VC was at first turned down, as he was a civilian. However, Sir Colin Campbell sent a tribute, and after much lobbying, a new amendment had to be made allowing civilian awards, which was passed on 6 July 1858. However, Kanauji Lal missed out, as native Indians were still not eligible for the award. Instead, he was given land as a reward.

Kavanagh fought on until the end of the mutiny and returned to England with his family in May 1859. His VC was gazetted on 8 July 1859 and was presented to him on 4 January 1860 by the Queen at Windsor Castle, the same day that Ross Mangels received his. Despite the honour and public adulation, Kavanagh's impression was that the award was begrudgingly given, something he never really got over.

On his return to India, Kavanagh believed he would be serving a government that thought him undeserving of the award. While he was there, he wrote a book entitled *How I won the Victoria Cross*, for which he was much criticised by many for profiting from his deed and for his self-promotion. Whatever he thought about the dismissive attitude of many, the British public and press regarded him as one of the greatest heroes of the age.

In 1882, at the invitation of the Governor of Gibraltar, General Sir Robert Napier, Kavanagh sailed on the P&O ship *Khedive* but was taken ill while on board. On his arrival, he was taken to hospital, where he died on 13 November that year.

Thomas Kavanagh was buried with full military honours in North Front Cemetery, Gibraltar, Spain, Grave 4567. His VC is held by the National Army Museum, London. He is one of only five civilians to be awarded the VC, the others being Ross Mangles, William McDonell, James Adams and George Chicken.

Hugh Henry GOUGH, Alambagh and Jellalabad, 12 November 1857 & 25 February 1858

Hugh Gough was born on 14 November 1833 in Calcutta, India, the son of Judge George Gough and Charlotte Margaret (née Becher). He was educated at East India College in Hertford Heath (later Haileybury College). On passing out in September 1853, he was commissioned a cornet in the 3rd Bengal Light Cavalry. It was among the 3rd Bengal Light Cavalry that the mutiny broke out in Meerut, in May 1857.

Gough, by now serving with the 1st Bengal European Light Cavalry, was among those sent to the Delhi Ridge. He was appointed adjutant of Hodson's Horse, named after Lieutenant William Hodson, the head of the Intelligence Department. After the fall of Delhi, Gough was attached to Colonel Greathed's flying column and was involved in the battles of

Hugh Henry Gough.

Bulundshahr and Agra while it was on its way to Cawnpore, where it was absorbed into Sir Colin Campbell's force.

On 12 November 1857 at Alambagh, Lieutenant Gough led a charge across a swamp and captured two guns defended by a vastly superior force. His horse, Tearaway, was twice wounded and Gough's turban was cut.

Three months later, on 25 February 1858 at Jellalabad, Gough was ordered to charge the enemy guns, engaging in several single combats. Gough charged on alone and attacked two sepoys with fixed bayonets, one of whom shot him in the thigh. During this charge, Gough had two horses (including his beloved Tearaway) shot from under him and another musket ball passed through his sun helmet and scabbard.

Gough's grave, Kensal Green Cemetery, London.

Gough was mentioned five times in despatches and his VC was gazetted on 24 December 1858. There is no record of an investiture, so the medal was probably sent to him by post. After the mutiny, he was given command of the 12th Regiment of Bengal Cavalry and took part in the 1868 expedition to Abyssinia. During the Second Afghan War, Gough was on the staff of General Frederick Sleigh Roberts, VC.

Hugh Gough retired with the rank of general and was further honoured when he was appointed Keeper of the Crown Jewels at the Tower of London from 1898 until his death on 12 May 1909. He is author of *Old Memories*. He was buried in Kensal Green Cemetery, London, Square 175, PS-42112. Among his pall-bearers were fellow mutiny VCs, Earl Roberts and Sir James Hill-Johnes. Gough's VC is not publicly held. His brother, Charles, and his uncle, John Gough, were also awarded the VC.

John WATSON, La Martinière, 14 November 1857

John Watson was born on 6 September 1829 in Chigwell, Essex, the son of William George Watson. At 19 he joined the HEIC's 1st Bombay European Fusiliers as an officer and was posted to Madras, serving in the

Second Sikh War, of 1848–49. After two short-lived postings to other infantry regiments, he began a career with the 1st Punjab Cavalry, becoming adjutant.

Watson was present at the siege of Delhi and accompanied Colonel Greathed's flying column, where at Agra he captured a gun. On 14 November 1857, during the approach to Lucknow, the rebels were driven out of La Martinière and Lieutenant Watson found himself ahead of his men. Suddenly, he came across a squadron of rebel cavalry. Realising if he returned to his men they might misunderstand his movement and probably flee, he charged at the rebels' leader (a risaldar) and fired at him from only a yard away. It seemed he would be killed, but the shot missed, and Watson then ran his opponent through with his sword. Watson was then set upon by several more rebels, who slashed at him with tulwars. His head, arms and legs were cut and bullets passed through his coat. He was able to defend himself until his own men and others led by Dighton Probyn (who was also awarded the VC during the mutiny) joined in the mêlée and utterly routed the enemy.

John Watson.

Watson took part in further action around Cawnpore and during the relief of Lucknow. He also raised the 4th Sikh Irregular Cavalry, which later became the 6th Duke of Connaught's Own Lancers (Watson's Own). His VC was gazetted on 18 June 1858 but it was presented to him eight days earlier by the Queen at Buckingham Palace.

In 1864, Watson was promoted to major and by 1873, he was lieutenant colonel of the Central India Horse. During the Second Afghan War, he was a brigadier commanding the Kurram Field Force. He retired with the rank of colonel in 1891 and settled in Finchampstead, Berkshire.

He died on 23 January 1919 and was buried in St James' Churchyard, Finchampstead. His VC is in the Lord Ashcroft Gallery, Imperial War Museum. Watson's son-in-law, Alfred Stowell, was also awarded the VC.

Hastings Edward HARINGTON, Lucknow, 14–22 November 1857

Hastings Harington was born on 9 November 1832 in St Peter Port, Guernsey (although some sources say Hinton Parva, Wiltshire), the son of the Reverend John Harington and Anne Spencer (née Young). He was educated at Reading School before entering the Addiscombe Military Seminary when he turned 17. In the autumn of 1852, he proceeded to India as a second lieutenant in the Bengal Artillery.

Harington's regiment was in the Punjab when the mutiny broke out. He was able to join Brigadier General John Nicholson's column in its march and the

Hastings Edward Harington.

subsequent assault on Delhi, having just recovered from a severe foot wound received at Trimmoo Ghat. Lieutenant Harington took part in the battles at Bulundshahr and Agra as part of Colonel Greathed's flying column, before joining Sir Colin Campbell's flying column. He was present throughout the relief of Lucknow from 14 to 22 November 1857, during which he acted with immense bravery in helping to protect the force left at the Secundra Bagh to keep open the crossing of the River Gomti. He was elected for the award by the officers of his regiment under Rule 13 of the Royal Warrant, which states that if a number of men have acted equally bravely, then a ballot should be held where officers would vote for officers, NCOs for NCOs and privates for privates.

Later, Harington took part in Brigadier Walpole's disastrous assault on Fort Reyah on 15 April 1858, where he was severely injured in the left thigh. His wound was so bad he had to return to England to recover. His VC was gazetted on 24 December 1858 and was presented to him on 8 June 1859 by the Queen at Buckingham Palace.

Hastings Harington returned to India in 1861 to take up the post of adjutant of his regiment. However, he contracted cholera and died on 20 July that year. He was buried in Agra Cemetery, Uttar Pradesh, India. His VC is not publicly held.

Edmond (Edward) JENNINGS, Lucknow, 14–22 November 1857

Edmond Jennings (his name was misspelt Edward on his VC citation and he seems to have used this thereafter) was born in 1820 (although some sources say 1815) in Ballinrobe, County Mayo, Ireland. He enlisted into the Bengal Artillery in 1836, at 16 years of age, and fought in the First Afghan War of 1839–42 and the First Sikh War of 1845–46.

At Lucknow, from 14 to 22 November 1857, he acted with the most conspicuous gallantry. On one occasion, although not officially mentioned in his citation, Rough Rider Jennings and two companions were returning to headquarters having delivered

Edmond (Edward) Jennings.

a message when he heard a cry for help. Telling his two companions to keep a lookout, he urged his horse to jump over a high wall and found himself in a narrow street at the end of which was a British officer under attack from a group of natives. Without hesitation, Jennings galloped forward and hacked at the assailants until they fled. He then helped the officer onto his horse and carried him to the medical tent. A few days later, Jennings was summoned to the hospital and the officer rewarded him with 1,000 rupees. Unfortunately, the officer was never identified. Although a rough rider is normally regarded as a private, Jennings was elected for the award by the NCOs of his regiment under Rule 13 of the Royal Warrant.

Jennings's VC was gazetted on 24 December 1858 and he was due to be presented with it at Windsor Castle on 9 October 1860, having been pensioned in 1859 at the age of 39. However, his departure was delayed and he missed the investiture. It is not known when he was presented with it; it may have been posted to him.

Edward Jennings was employed as a road sweeper for most of the rest of his life, but he fell on hard times and was forced to sell his medal to a private collector. He died in poverty on 10 May 1889 and was buried in the RC Section at Preston Cemetery, North Shields, Northumberland, Block J, Grave 328. His grave remained unmarked until 1997. His VC is held (in storage) by the Royal Artillery Museum, Larkhill, Wiltshire.

Thomas LAUGHNAN, Lucknow, 14–22 November 1857

Thomas Laughnan was born in August 1824 in Kilmadaugh, County Galway, Ireland. Very little is known about his life prior to enlisting into the Bengal Artillery on 14 July 1844.

At Lucknow, from 14 to 22 November 1857, Gunner Laughnan acted with the most conspicuous gallantry. Unfortunately, there are no further details of his actions. Laughnan was elected for the award by the gunners of the regiment under Rule 13 of the Royal Warrant.

His VC was gazetted on 24 December 1858 and it is believed his medal was posted to him while still in India. When Laughnan was pensioned from the army, he returned to Ireland.

Thomas Laughnan died on 23 July 1864 in County Galway, but his burial location is unknown. His VC is held (in storage) by the Royal Artillery Museum, Larkhill, Wiltshire.

Hugh McINNES (spelt McINNIS in cemetery register), Lucknow, 14–22 November 1857

Hugh McInnes was born on 16 January 1816 in Glasgow. He worked as a cotton spinner before enlisting into the Bengal Artillery.

At Lucknow, from 14 to 22 November 1857, Gunner McInnes acted with conspicuous gallantry. Unfortunately, there are no further details of his actions. He was elected for the award by the gunners of the regiment under Rule 13 of the Royal Warrant.

His VC was gazetted on 24 December 1859 and sent to him by post after his discharge from the army. He returned to Scotland and took up work as an engineering labourer.

Hugh McInnes died from paralysis and debility on 7 December 1879 and was buried in Dalbeth Cemetery (formerly St Peters RC Cemetery), London Road, Glasgow. His grave remained unmarked until 2004. McInnes's VC is not publicly held.

James PARK, Lucknow, 14–22 November 1857

James Park was born in 1835 in Glasgow. Almost nothing is known about him prior to enlisting into the Bengal Artillery in 1855.

At Lucknow, from 14 to 22 November 1857, Gunner Park acted with conspicuous gallantry. Unfortunately, there are no further details of his actions. He was elected for the award by the gunners of the regiment under Rule 13 of the Royal Warrant. Like Jennings, Laughnan and McInnes, his citation is just a copy of Rule 13 of the Royal Warrant.

James Park died from cholera at Lucknow on 14 June 1858 and he has no known grave. His VC was gazetted on 24 December 1858 and sent to his family. His medal was sold to a private collector in 2017 for £70,000.

Francis David Millet BROWN, Narrioul, 16 November 1857

Francis Brown was born on 7 August 1837 in Bhagalpur, Bihar, India. As a young boy, he was sent to England to be educated at Wellington College. He enlisted into the 1st European Bengal Fusiliers (later the Royal Muster Fusiliers) in December 1855.

On 16 November 1857 at Narrioul, near Delhi, Lieutenant Brown saw a soldier from his regiment lying wounded in the open. At the risk of his own life he rushed to the assistance of the man, whom he carried off under heavy fire from the enemy, whose cavalry were only 40 or 50 yards away.

Francis David Millet Brown.

His VC was gazetted on 17 February 1860 and was presented to him in December 1860 by the C-in-C India, Sir Hugh Rose, at Mooltan. Brown stayed on in India and in 1864 joined the Bengal Staff Corps. The remainder of his career was uneventful as he climbed the promotion ladder to reach the rank of colonel before his retirement. On his return to England, he settled on the Isle of Wight.

Francis Brown died on 21 November 1895 and was buried in West Hill Cemetery,

Brown's grave, Westhill Cemetery, Winchester.

St James' Lane, Winchester, Hampshire. His VC is held by Wellington College, Crowthorne, Berkshire.

John Thomas SMITH, Lucknow, 16 November 1857

John Smith was born in July 1822 in London. Very little is known about him prior to his enlistment into the 1st Madras Fusiliers (later the Royal Dublin Fusiliers) in 1841. He took part in some of the early events of the mutiny while under the command of Colonel Neill.

At Lucknow on 16 November 1857, Private Smith was one of the first men to enter the north gateway during the attack on Secundra Bagh. He was instantly surrounded by rebels but, despite receiving a sword cut to the head, a bayonet wound to the side and a contusion from a rifle butt to his right shoulder, he fought his way out and continued to perform his duties for the rest of the day. He was elected for the award by the privates of his regiment.

His VC, gazetted on 24 December 1858, was presented to him in 1859 but it is not known where or by whom. Smith was discharged from the army with a pension in 1861 and decided to stay on in India.

John Smith died from asphyxia on 6 May 1866 and was buried in an unmarked grave, Tanjore Cemetery, Tamil Nadu, India. His VC was sold at auction in 2016 to an unknown bidder for £88,000.

Harry North Dalrymple PRENDERGAST, Mundisore, 21 November 1857

Harry Prendergast was born on 15 October 1834 in Madras, India, the son of Thomas Prendergast and Caroline Lucy (née Dalrymple). Harry was sent home to England for his education, first at Cheam School, then Brighton College before entering the Addiscombe Military Seminary. On passing out in 1854, Prendergast was commissioned into the Royal Engineers as a second lieutenant. He served in Persia with B Company, Madras Sappers and Miners under Major (later Colonel) Archibald John Maddy Boileau, before returning to India in July 1857.

On 21 November 1857 at Mundisore, Lieutenant Prendergast, now ADC to Colonel Durand, was reconnoitring in advance of the column with strict orders not to engage the enemy. Suddenly, rebels (Afghan mercenaries) appeared and opened fire upon them and the small British force were left with little choice but to charge. At this point, Prendergast noticed a rebel taking aim at Lieutenant George Dew of the 14th Light Dragoons, so he charged the rebel who then turned and fired a bullet into Prendergast's ribs, close to the heart. The mutineer was then cut down by Major Sutherland Orr.

Harry North Dalrymple Prendergast.

Prendergast's wound was not healing well and, after a number of surgeons examined him, William MacKenzie, an expert military surgeon, cut the bullet from him just in time to prevent the onset of gangrene.

At Jhansi in January 1858, Prendergast was wounded by a sword cut to his left arm, rendering it almost useless. At Ratghur, his horse was shot from under him and he was shot in the arm. Following this, he was invalided home on sick leave. His VC was gazetted on 21 October 1859 and was presented to him on 4 January 1860 by the Queen at Windsor Castle. In Prendergast's words: 'It was a foggy, gloomy day and Horse Guards and Foot Guards were drawn up on parade. … The recipients had to advance a few steps in line towards Her Majesty which we did in a slovenly style, and then each in succession stepped forward, and the decoration was attached to our breasts.'

After the mutiny, he was promoted to major and took part in the Umbeyla Campaign of 1863. He married Emilie Simpson and they had eight children. Then he served in the Abyssinian Campaign of 1868, where he was mentioned in despatches. His last field command was the Burma Field Force in 1885–86. Prendergast retired as a

Prendergast's grave, Richmond Cemetery, Richmond-upon-Thames.

lieutenant general in 1892 and took up a seat on the organising committee for the Golden Commemoration of the Indian Mutiny veterans held at the Albert Hall in December 1907. Two hundred and fifty of the surviving officers and 950 other ranks attended. Prendergast also played a leading part in funding allowances for veterans, which enabled eighty-three to leave the workhouse and relieved 243 from living on Poor Law doles.

Harry Prendergast died on 24 July 1913 after catching a chill and was buried in Richmond Cemetery, Richmond-upon-Thames, Surrey, Section M, Grave 1502. His VC is held by the Royal Engineers Museum, Gillingham, Kent.

Arthur MAYO, Dacca, 22 November 1857

Arthur Mayo was born on 18 May 1840 in Oxford, England. He was educated at Berkhampsted School, Hertfordshire, following which he enlisted into the Royal Navy in 1855. Mayo sailed to India aboard HMS *Wellesley* and on his arrival in February 1857, transferred to the Indian Navy. Mayo served on the steam frigate *Punjab* ferrying the 64th Regiment from Bombay to Calcutta.

In June 1857, the officers and men of the *Punjab* were formed into No. 4 Detachment of the Naval Brigade and sent to Dacca. On 22 November 1857, led by Lieutenant T.E. Lewis, five officers and eighty-five men stormed the Treasury. They then went on to the Lall Bagh, a large enclosure where they found 300–400 sepoys drawn up in line in front of the magazine, with two 6-pounder guns in the centre. The Naval Brigade formed into line as the enemy opened fire with muskets and canisters. The sailors replied with a volley before charging up the hill and into the barracks. Many sepoys were killed in hand-to-hand fighting and the remainder fled. The sailors now charged down the hill into the remaining sepoys. It was during this action that the 17-year-

Arthur Mayo.

old Midshipman Mayo placed himself 20 yards in front of his men and led the charge with a great cheer, and captured one of the 6-pounder guns.

Mayo remained in the Naval Brigade and was mentioned in despatches during the Arbor Hills Expedition in February 1859. He was wounded in the hand by a poisonous arrow and was invalided home. His VC was gazetted on 25 February 1862 and was sent to him by registered post, although one source claims it was presented to him in June 1864 by the Prince of Wales. Both seem odd as he was in England when it was gazetted, so why post it? If he was presented with it by the Prince of Wales, why so long after it was gazetted?

Mayo's grave, East Cemetery, Boscombe.

Mayo studied Theology at Magdalene Hall, Oxford, and passed out with a BA in June 1865. The following year he was ordained Deacon at Salisbury and served as assistant curate at Plymouth for twenty months. In November 1867, he joined the Catholic Church and lived in Torquay and Malta. In 1901, Mayo moved to Bournemouth to live with his younger sister.

Arthur Mayo died on 18 May (his birthday) 1920 and was buried in East Cemetery, Boscombe, Bournemouth, Dorset, Plot 4 Row K, Grave 207. His VC was thought to have been sold by his sister to the Museum of Bombay, India, but this is not the case and its whereabouts are unknown.

Frederick Sleigh ROBERTS, 'Bobs', Khodagunge, 2 January 1858

Frederick Roberts was born on 30 September 1832 in Cawnpore, Uttar Pradesh, India, the second son of General Sir Abraham Roberts and Isabella (née) Bunbury. As an infant, the young Roberts lost an eye due to a 'brain fever' (meningitis). At 2 years old, he was sent to England to be educated at Eton, Sandhurst and the Addiscombe Military Seminary. On entering Sandhurst at 16, his father thought the 5ft 3in tall one-eyed lad would not be able to cope with a military life and persuaded him to join the Indian Army, most likely because he also knew he would not be able to support himself on a soldier's pay in the British Army. Roberts was commissioned a second lieutenant in the Bengal Artillery in December 1851.

He became ADC to his father in 1852, but transferred into the Bengal Horse Artillery in 1854. He was promoted to lieutenant in May 1857. During the mutiny, he saw action at the siege and capture of Delhi, where he was slightly wounded. Then, as deputy assistant quartermaster general attached to the staff of Sir Colin Campbell, C-in-C India, he took part in the relief of Lucknow.

Frederick Sleigh Roberts.

On 2 January 1857, at Khodagunge during the enemy retreat, Lieutenant Roberts saw two rebels making off with a standard. He charged ahead of his men, cut one rebel down and snatched the standard. The other rebel fired directly at him but his musket misfired. Later the same day, Roberts rode to the aid of a sowar who was being attacked by a rebel. He killed the assailant with one slash of his sword.

When Roberts returned to Cawnpore, he dined with William Peel, VC, who was sadly struck down with smallpox and died that evening, 21 April 1858. Roberts returned to England in June 1858, where he was married. His VC was gazetted on 24 December 1858 and was presented to him on 8 June 1859 by the Queen at Buckingham Palace.

Promoted to captain in November 1860, Roberts returned to India, and in 1861 transferred to the British Army. He took part in the Umbeyla and Abyssinia campaigns during the 1860s. He took part in the Lushai Campaign, of 1871–72. In 1878, he commanded the Kurram Filed Force and distinguished himself in the Second Afghan War. In 1880, commanding the Kabul Field Force, he took 10,000 men on his celebrated march through Afghanistan to relieve Kandahar.

In 1889, he was given overall command of all British forces in the Second Boar War, but not before his own son had been killed at Colenso trying to save the guns. Roberts retired from active service soon after the end of the Second Boar War. He was promoted to field marshal in May 1895. He superintended the funeral arrangements of both Queen Victoria and Edward VII. His autobiography, published in 1897, is called *Forty-One Years in India: from Subaltern to Commander-in-Chief.*

Frederick Roberts died from pneumonia on 14 November 1914 while visiting troops at the front. He was given a state funeral, with his coffin being conveyed to St Paul's Cathedral in London by the very gun carriage that his son died trying to save. He was buried in the cathedral's crypt. His VC is held by the National Army Museum, London. His son, Frederick Hugh Sherston Roberts, was also awarded the VC.

Roberts's grave, St Paul's Cathedral crypt, London.

James John McLeod INNES, Sultanpore, 23 February 1858

James Innes was born on 5 February 1830 in Bhagalpur, India, the son of Surgeon James Innes of the HEIC's Civil Service and Bengal Army, and Jane (née McLeod). Sent to England, he was educated at Edinburgh University, where he distinguished himself in mathematics. He then went on to the Addiscombe Seminary, from where he graduated in 1848 and joined the Bengal Engineers.

In 1851, Innes transferred to the Public Works Department in Bengal, and a succession of civil engineering projects occupied him until he was promoted to lieutenant in 1854. He married Lacy Jane

James John McLeod Innes.

McPherson in 1855 and they went on to have four children. When the mutiny broke out Innes was at Lucknow and he was given the task of blowing up the old fortress of Macchi Bhawan. He spent much of the siege employed in mining.

Following the evacuation of the Residency, he was posted to General Sir Thomas Franks's Field Force during the advance through Oudh. On 23 February 1858, at Sultanpore, Franks's force of 5,700 men came up against a rebel army of 25,000, including cavalry and artillery. Despite this, the rebels were routed and Innes, who was far in advance of the leading skirmishers, was the first to secure a gun that the enemy were abandoning. The rebels rallied around another gun from which the shot would have ploughed through the Field Force's advancing columns. Innes rode up to them, unsupported, and shot the gunner. He remained at his gun under heavy fire, keeping the enemy at bay until assistance reached him.

Innes's grave, City Cemetery, Cambridge.

On 4 March 1858, Innes was badly wounded at Dhaurahra, near Lucknow. He was promoted to captain in August and brevet major shortly afterwards. He was mentioned in despatches three times and his VC was gazetted on 24 December 1858. It was presented to him by the Viceroy, Lord Canning. After the mutiny, Innes returned to civil engineering, and was, in turn, Accountant General, Public Works Department Commissioner, and Inspector General of Military Works. He also served on the India defence committee inquiry. He retired in 1886 with the rank of lieutenant general. He is author of *Lucknow and Oude*, published in 1895.

Innes died on 13 December 1907 and was buried in City Cemetery (aka Newmarket Road Cemetery), Cambridge, Section 8, Grave 3704. His VC is held by the Royal Engineers Museum, Gillingham, Kent.

Frederick Robertson AIKMAN, Amethi, 1 March 1858

Frederick Aikman was born on 6 February 1828 in Ross, South Lanarkshire, the son of Captain George Robertson Aikman. He was commissioned into the Bengal Army in January 1845, joining the 4th Bengal Native Infantry. He took part in the Sikh wars of 1845–46 and 1848–49.

When the Mutiny broke out Aikman's regiment mutinied and he raised the Jalandhar Cavalry (later the 3rd Sikh Irregular Cavalry). He took part in the siege of Delhi and the capture of Lucknow. He forced marched from Jalandhar to join General Franks's Field Force.

Frederick Robertson Aikman.

On 1 March 1858, at Amethi, Uttar Pradesh, Lieutenant Aikman was commanding 100 men of the 3rd Sikh Irregular Cavalry when he was informed that the enemy were advancing with 500 men, 200 horses and two guns. Aikman attacked this force at once and utterly routed them, killing more than 100 men, capturing the two guns, and driving the survivors over the Goomtee River. During this skirmish, he was cut about the face with a sabre.

Aikman was promoted to captain and in May returned to England because of his wounds. His VC was gazetted on 3 September 1858 and was presented to him by the Queen at Buckingham Palace.

Aikman's mausoleum, Kensal Green Cemetery, London.

Due to his injuries he was forced to retire from the army in 1860 on half pay. In May 1865, Victoria appointed him a member of The Honourable Corps of Gentlemen at Arms, the monarch's official body guard.

In 1877, while still a member of the Queen's guard, Aikman and some friends and servants were returning from the Epsom races when he was arrested and charged with being drunk and disorderly while responsible for four horses and a coach. At the time, he was also commander of the Royal East Middlesex Militia and retired as honorary colonel in 1887.

Frederick Aikman died on 5 October 1888 and was buried in a large mausoleum in Kensal Green Cemetery, London, Square 76/RS, Grave 4627. His VC is not publicly held.

Thomas Adair BUTLER, Lucknow, 9 March 1858

Thomas Butler was born on 12 February 1836 in Soberton, Hampshire, the son of the Reverend Stephen Butler and Mary Ann (née Thistlethwayte). He was commissioned into the 1st Bengal European Fusiliers (later the Royal Munster Fusiliers) in 1854. Promoted to lieutenant in November 1856, he became an instructor of musketry to his regiment.

On 9 March 1858 near Lucknow, his regiment was linking up with Sir Colin Campbell's assault on the Martinière. The Bengal Fusiliers were covering the heavy guns of Sir James Outram as they fired across the Goomtee River into

Thomas Adair Butler.

the enemy's outer line of field works. It appeared that the position was unmanned and it was necessary to get word to 79th Highlanders, who had just captured the Martinière.

Lieutenant Butler and four others volunteered to go to the water's edge but were unable to attract the attention of the 79th. Butler then swam across the deep, fast-flowing river and entered the enemy position from the rear. He climbed onto the parapet and was under heavy fire from the enemy for some time before he managed to attract the attention of an officer of the 79th. As a result of his action, the position was quickly occupied.

After the mutiny, Butler's regiment was transferred to the British Crown and he became a captain in the 101st (Bengal Fusiliers) Regiment. His VC was gazetted on 6 May 1859 and was presented to him on 8 June 1859 by the Queen at Buckingham Palace. Butler saw service in the Umbeyla Campaign of 1863 and on the North-West Frontier before retiring as an honorary major in 1874.

Thomas Butler died on 17 May 1901 and was buried in St Michael's Churchyard, Camberley, Surrey. His VC is held by the Royal Military Academy Sandhurst.

Butler's grave, St Michael's Church, Camberley.

Richard Harte KEATINGE, Chundairee, 17 March 1858

Richard Keatinge was born on 17 June 1825 in Dublin, the youngest son of barrister Richard Keatinge and Harriet Augusta (née Joseph). He was commissioned, and joined the Bombay Artillery in November 1843. In 1851, he was employed in the Political Department, Government of India, as assistant superintendent and then as political agent. Keatinge was also appointed commandant of the Nimaur Police Corps. In December 1857, he was captain and political agent to General Rose's column.

Richard Harte Keatinge.

By March 1858, the column had reached the fort at Chundairee, a large, and heavily defended fort that was difficult to attack. The walls were so thick it took a number of days to make a breach big enough for the assault. On the night before the assault,

Captain Keatinge discovered a small path leading across the ditch towards the fort. The next morning, 17 March, he led his men forward along the path. Having just cleared the breach, he was severely wounded, but struggled to his feet and led his men into the fort, where he was wounded again.

Keatinge went on to command the irregular troops in the Sathpoora Hills against Seeta Ram Holkar and service in the pursuit of Tantia Topi in November 1858. Although recommended for the VC by the C-in-C India, it was not gazetted until 25 February 1862 and was presented to him by the Queen on Horse Guards Parade.

Keatinge's grave, Hills Cemetery, Horsham.

Keatinge was awarded the CSI and was promoted to lieutenant colonel in 1866. He was appointed chief commissioner of the Central Provinces in 1870–72 and Assam in 1875. He retired with the rank of lieutenant general in 1887.

Richard Keatinge died on 24 May 1904 and was buried in Hills Cemetery, Horsham, Sussex, Section H. His VC is not publicly held.

Joseph Charles BRENNAN, Jhansi, 3 April 1858

Joseph Brennan was born in August 1818 in St Probus, Cornwall. Very little is known about his life before he enlisted into the Royal Artillery in December 1855, giving his occupation as a clerk. His regiment joined Sir Hugh Rose's Central India Field Force at Mhow, Madhya Pradesh, in January 1858. Brennan was despatched with a number of men to fight Tantia Topi at the Betwa River.

Then, on his return, on 3 April 1858 Bombardier Brennan joined in the bombardment of the fort at Jhansi. He brought up two guns of the Hyderabad contingent, manned by natives, and got them into position

Joseph Charles Brennan.

Brennan's grave, Shorncliffe Military Cemetery, Folkestone.

under a heavy fire, and directed their fire so accurately that the enemy were compelled to abandon their battery.

Brennan's VC was gazetted on 11 November 1859 and was presented to him on 20 April 1860 at Gwalior, and he was promoted to quartermaster sergeant. In October 1863, while stationed at Delhi with the 22nd Brigade Royal Artillery, he was court-martialled for not attending a commanding officer's parade. He was found guilty and was reduced to the ranks.

He took part in the Bhutan War of 1864–65, after which he returned to England. He regained his sergeant's stripe and went on to marry the daughter of a Royal Artillery pensioner in 1870. They had two children, born in 1871 and 1872.

Joseph Brennan died from pneumonia on 24 September 1872 and was buried in Shorncliffe Military Cemetery (aka Garrison Cemetery), Folkestone, Kent, Section F. His VC is not publicly held.

Frederick WHIRLPOOL (born Humphrey CONKER, later changed to JAMES), Jhansi and Lohari, 3 April & 6 May 1858

There is much confusion about Frederick Whirlpool's family name, date and place of birth. He was thought to have been born *c.*1829–31 in Dundalk, Ireland (although some sources state that he was born in County Carlow). Alan Leek provides evidence in his 2018 book *Frederick Whirlpool VC* that his date of birth is 17 July 1831. Whirlpool's parents are listed as either Major and Mrs Conker or Humphrey and Lavinia James. What is known is that he grew up in Ireland and received a good education at the Dundalk Institute (now Dundalk Grammar School).

On his enlistment into the 3rd Bombay European Regiment (later the Prince of Wales's Leinster Regiment) in October 1854, he used the name Whirlpool and gave his place of birth as Liverpool. It is thought the name was derived from his tempestuous relationship with his father.

At Jhansi on 3 April 1858, Private Whirlpool was among the storming party and at 3 am they charged the heavily defended walls of the fort. Using ladders, they managed to force a way in despite facing musket fire and being pelted with boulders. During the assault, Whirlpool was seen to carry two wounded men under heavy fire and bring them to safety. Then, on 6 May (incorrectly stated 2 May on his citation) at Lohari, he went under heavy fire to the rescue of Lieutenant Donne of the same regiment, who was severely wounded. Whirlpool was wounded seventeen times during this rescue and it was reported that his head was almost severed from his body. This was almost certainly an exaggeration.

So bad were Whirlpool's wounds that he spent five months recovering in hospital and he was medically discharged from the army in February 1859. With no work, he emigrated to Australia, where he changed his name to Frederick Humphrey James. He enlisted into the locally raised Hawthorn and Kew Rifle Volunteers. His VC was gazetted on 21 October 1859 and was presented to him by Lady Barkly, the wife of the colony's governor, Sir Henry Barkly, on 20 June 1861 in Albany Park, Melbourne. Whirlpool's was the first public presentation of the VC in Australia.

Whirlpool obtained work as a schoolteacher with the New South Wales Board of National Education and took charge of a school near Wiseman's Ferry, on the Hawkesbury River, north of Sydney. However, his temper got the better of him and he had a serious falling out with the school secretary, who alleged improprieties on his part. The parents supported Whirlpool but the allegations were accepted, and in 1867, the Board dismissed him. Unable to find work after this he became a recluse living in a slab hut near Windsor, New South Wales, his only friend, a Scotsman named Smith.

Frederick Whirlpool was found dead (from heart disease) on 24 June 1899 by Smith and was buried in an unmarked grave in the General Presbyterian Cemetery, McGrath's Hill, New South Wales. His friend Smith was the only person to attend the funeral. Whirlpool's VC is held by the Australian War Memorial, Canberra.

William Martin CAFE, Fort Ruhya, 15 April 1858

William Martin Cafe.

Cafe's grave, Brompton Cemetery, London.

William Cafe was born on 26 March 1826 in London. Not much is known about his life other than that he entered the Addiscombe Military Seminary as a young boy. In June 1842, he was commissioned as an ensign in the 56th Bengal Native Infantry. He took part in the Gwalior Campaign of 1843 and the Second Sikh War of 1848–49.

When his regiment joined the mutiny, Cafe was appointed captain in the 4th Punjab Infantry. On 15 April 1858, during the assault on Fort Ruhya, casualties began to mount up in the ditch in front of the fort. Cafe, along with Private Alexander Thompson and Private Edward Spence (both of the 42nd Foot), went to the assistance of Lieutenant Willoughby (brother of Captain Willoughby, one of the nine who blew up the Delhi Magazine in May 1857). On seeing that he was dead, they removed his body under heavy fire to prevent its mutilation by the enemy. Spence was badly wounded during this action and they returned to rescue him also. Thompson and Spence were also awarded the VC for this action.

Cafe's VC was gazetted on 17 February 1860 and it was probably posted to him later the same year. Also that year, he was appointed to the adjutant general's department and spent the remainder of his career on the staff, retiring with the rank of colonel in 1894.

William Cafe died on 6 August 1906 and was buried in Brompton Cemetery, London, Compartment 5 East, 31' x 6'. His VC is held by the National Army Museum, London.

Harry Hammon LYSTER, Calpee, 23 May 1858

Harry Hammon Lyster.

Harry Lyster was born on 24 (some say the 25) December 1830 in Blackrock, Dublin. He was a special constable and served in the Chartist Riots in London in 1847. He was commissioned into the HEIC's army the following year. Before he set sail his father took him to Wilkinson's in London to buy a sword, but unable to make up his mind which one to buy, a gentleman came forward and offered to help as he was a good judge of swords. They took the one suggested by the stranger, who turned out to be the Prince Napoleon (later Napoleon III).

Lyster arrived in India in November 1848 and was posted to the 48th Native

Infantry. After a few months, he was appointed to the 72nd Bengal Native Infantry, just in time to take part in the siege of Multan in the Punjab War.

He served as ADC on Sir Hugh Rose's Staff in the Central India Field Force and during the action at Baroda, he was ordered to lead a troop of the Hyderabad cavalry against the retreating enemy. Calling out for the native sowars to follow him, he found that as he clashed with the rebels, the only man to join him was a native officer who was soon killed. However, Lyster charged in among them, killing three and scattering the remainder. Seeing the enemy cavalry, he stopped and the rebel commander advanced. Lyster took this to be a personal challenge and spurred his horse forward. The two men met head-on and Lyster ran his sword through his opponent but was wounded in the process. The rest of the enemy cavalry turned and fled.

On 23 May 1858, at Calpee, Lieutenant Lyster was sent with an order for the cavalry to charge the remnants of the rebels. Seeing that some of them had rallied and formed a square, he charged alone into their midst, broke up the formation and killed two or three of the sepoys. He escaped without a wound. He was mentioned in despatches five times.

Lyster's VC was gazetted on 21 October 1859 and was presented to him in 1860 in Calcutta. He was elevated to ADC to the C-in-C. He was then promoted to major in 1864 and married Caroline Matilda Davies that year. During the Afghan War of 1878–79, he commanded the 3rd (Queen Alexander's Own) Gurkhas and was present at the Battle of Ahmed Khel on 19 April 1880.

Harry Lyster retired with the rank of lieutenant general. After the death of his first wife, he remarried in 1901 to Ada Emily Cole. He died on 1 February 1922 and was buried in St James the Less Churchyard, Stubbing, near Maidenhead, Berkshire. His VC is in the Lord Ashcroft Gallery, Imperial War Museum, London. His nephew, Hamilton Reed, was also awarded the VC.

Lyster's grave, St James the Less Church, Stubbing.

William Francis Frederick WALLER, Gwalior, 20 June 1858

William Waller was born on 20 August 1839 in Dapoolee, India, the son of Thomas Waller, a HEIC employee, and Alicia Ann (née Gilbert). Waller was commissioned an ensign in the 25th Bombay Native Infantry and joined General Rose's Central India Field Force in February 1858.

On 20 June 1858, newly promoted Lieutenant Waller and Lieutenant Wellington Rose (a relation of General Rose) were on picquet duty near the main gate of the fort at Gwalior. Hearing gunfire from inside, they decided, without orders, to attack the fort with only a handful of men. They climbed onto the roof of a house and shot the gunners opposing them, and then entered the fort, killing every rebel inside. Rose was killed by a rebel who shot him and then rushed him with a tulwar, slashing his wrist and leg. Waller killed the rebel but was too late to save Rose. Had Rose survived he most likely would have been awarded the VC for this encounter.

Waller's VC was gazetted on 25 February 1862 and was presented to him later that year by GOC Bombay, Lieutenant General Sir William Mansfield. Promotion came rather slowly for Waller; it was 1869 when he was elevated to captain, and 1877 to major. He retired from the Bombay Staff Corps with the rank of colonel and returned to England.

William Francis Frederick Waller.

Waller's grave, Locksbrook Cemetery, Bath.

William Waller died on 29 January 1885 and was buried in Locksbrook Cemetery, Bath, Somerset, Section H-A, Grave 111. His VC is in the Lord Ashcroft Gallery, Imperial War Museum, London.

Samuel James BROWNE, Seerporah, 31 August 1858

Samuel Browne was born on 3 October 1824 in Barrackpore, West Bengal (although his obituary says Alnwick, Northumberland, which is most probably an error), the son of Dr John Browne of the Bengal Medical Service and Charlotte (née Swinton). He joined the HEIC's Army in 1840 at just 16 years of age, serving with the 46th Bengal Native Infantry during the Second Sikh War of 1848–49. In 1849, he transferred to the 2nd Punjab Irregular Cavalry (later the 22nd Sam Browne's Cavalry, named in his honour), which he also commanded.

Brevet Major Browne was commanding a complete field force when, on 31 August 1858, near Seerporah while advancing on a force led by Khan Allie Khan, Browne pushed forward with a sowar. He then charged a 9-pounder gun to prevent it from firing on the infantry who were advancing to the attack. He cut down several of the gunners but received a cut across the left knee and another that severed his left arm at the shoulder.

Samuel James Browne.

With wounds so severe, he was lucky to have survived infection or being invalided out of the army. Before the mutiny, he had experimented with a more efficient way of wearing a sword, which entailed using a belt and cross belt over the shoulder. It was most fortunate as that now suited his special need and it soon became known as the Sam Browne Belt.

Browne's VC was not gazetted until 1 March 1861; it was presented to him in December 1862 by Major General Sir Sydney Cotton at Peshawar. Browne commanded the Peshawar Field Force during the Second Afghan War and retired with the rank of general in 1888.

Samuel Browne died on 14 March 1901 and his ashes are interred in Town Cemetery, Ryde, Isle of Wight. His VC is held by the National Army Museum, London.

Charles George BAKER, Suhejnee, 27 September 1858

Charles Baker was born on 8 December 1830 in Noacolly, Bengal, India, the son of Dr John Baker of the HEIC's Medical Service and his wife Lydia. Charles led an adventurous life, starting at sea with the P&O Company. He was serving on board the SS *Douro* when she was wrecked on a shoal off the Paracel Island in the South China Sea on 26 May 1854. Baker, with six volunteers, made a 500-mile perilous voyage in an open boat to find help. Short of food and water, they had to contend with heavy seas and the threat of Chinese pirates, eventually arriving in Hong Kong on 3 June.

Charles George Baker.

Baker was commissioned into the Bengal Military Police in 1856 and was involved in mopping-up operations in West Behar, where he led a mixed force of cavalry and mounted police, including George Chicken, a civilian. On 27 September 1858, at Suhejnee, the rebels advanced with a strength estimated at 900–1,000 infantry and fifty cavalry. Lieutenant Baker retired slowly as the enemy advanced towards him then, suddenly, he wheeled his divisions about and led them into the charge, routing the attackers.

His action was later described by Sir Colin Campbell as 'having been as gallant

Baker's grave, Christchurch Cemetery, Southbourne.

as any during the war'. His VC was gazetted on 25 February 1862 and sent to him by registered post. He was promoted to Deputy Inspecting General of Police but, due to bad health, he retired in 1863. In 1877, he joined the Turkish Imperial Ottoman Gendarmerie and was captured by the Russians. In 1882, he transferred to the Egyptian Police Force, as Chief of Security with the Ministry of the Interior, and retired with the rank of major general in 1885.

Charles Baker returned to England and settled in Hampshire. He died on 19 February 1906 and was buried in Christchurch Cemetery, Southbourne, Dorset, Section H, Grave 84. His VC is not publicly held.

George Bell CHICKEN, Suhejnee, 27 September 1858

George Chicken was born on 2 March 1833 in Wallsend, Northumberland (although one source says 6 March 1838 in County Down, Ireland). He was the son of George Chicken and Elizabeth (née Bell). At 20 years old, he started a career as a master mariner; strictly speaking, he was not in the navy but a volunteer for the Indian Navy Brigade, and was appointed into the service in July 1853.

On 27 September 1858 at Suhejnee, he joined a fixed force of cavalry and mounted police led by Lieutenant Charles Baker, where Chicken was involved in mopping-up operations in West Behar. The rebels advanced with a strength estimated at 900–1,000 infantry and fifty cavalry. Baker retired slowly as the enemy advanced towards him then, suddenly, he wheeled his divisions about and led them into the charge, utterly routing the rebels. In the pursuit that followed, Chicken rode recklessly forward. Catching up to twenty armed rebels, he killed five with his sword but was knocked from his horse and about to be butchered when four troopers came to his rescue.

Chicken returned to Calcutta in November 1859 and in March the following year was given command of the schooner HMS *Emily*, which was lost with all hands in a violent squall off Sandheads in the Bay of Bengal in May 1860.

Chicken's VC was gazetted on 27 April 1860 and was posted to India. He never knew of the award and was never able to wear the medal. It should have been returned to England following news of his drowning, but it went missing. An official replacement was presented to his father in March 1862. The original missing medal came up for sale in 2006, was purchased by Lord Ashcroft and is now in the Lord Ashcroft Gallery, Imperial War Museum, London. The whereabouts of the official replacement is unknown.

George Chicken is one of only five civilians to have been awarded the VC, the others being Ross Mangles, William McDonell, James Adams and Thomas Kavanagh. His action is often described as 'the only naval VC to be won on horseback'.

Patrick RODDY, Kuthirga, 27 September 1858

Patrick Roddy was born on 17 March 1827 in Elphin, County Roscommon, Ireland. The Irish Potato Famine of 1845–49 forced him to look for work in Liverpool. There he enlisted into the Royal Artillery but soon transferred into the Bengal Artillery, where the pay was higher and the promotion prospects were better. Posted to India, his conduct was so good that he was commissioned an ensign in February 1858. He was one of those left with Sir James Outram to hold the Alambagh until Sir Colin Campbell's force relieved them at Lucknow in March 1858. In May, he was attached to the Oudh Military Police Cavalry.

Patrick Roddy.

On 27 September 1858, at Kuthirga, when engaged with the enemy he charged a rebel armed with a musket when the cavalry were afraid to approach as, each time they attempted to do so, the rebel knelt and took aim at his assailant. This did not deter Ensign Roddy, who went in at him. The rebel shot Roddy's horse from under him and then came at him with his sword. Roddy seized the mutineer until he could get at his own sword and ran him through with it.

His VC was gazetted on 12 April 1859 and it was presented to him at a parade on 5 September 1861 by Colonel Schopp at Ferozepore. Roddy was promoted to captain the following year. In 1868, Roddy took part in General Napier's Abyssinian Campaign, was mentioned in despatches and given a brevet majority. He was confirmed major in 1876 and appointed station staff officer at Roorkee.

In 1878, he served in the First Afghan War, being attached to the 20th Punjab Native Infantry, part of General Sir Sam Browne's 1st Division Peshawar Field Force. The 20th were involved in the difficult flanking operations over the precipitous heights on 22 November, which forced the Afghans to abandon their mountaintop fort. Roddy was again mentioned in despatches and was breveted lieutenant colonel, which was confirmed in 1886. The following year, Roddy retired as a full colonel, having served for thirty-nine years in the Bengal Army.

Roddy died from bronchitis and cardiac disease on 21 November 1895 and was buried in Mont à l'Abbé Cemetery, St Helier, Jersey. His VC is held by his family. He was offered a Bar to his VC but chose promotion and higher pay instead. He would have been the first VC and Bar.

Hanson Chambers Taylor JARRETT, Baroun, 14 October 1858

Hanson Jarrett was born on 22 March 1839 (some say 1837) in Madras, India, the son of an employee of the HEIC. As such, he was entered into the Addiscombe Military Seminary and was commissioned in June 1854 as an ensign with the 26th Bengal Native Infantry at 15 years of age.

His regiment mutinied in July 1858 and fled Lahore, later surrendering at Amritsar in the belief they would get a fair trial. Instead, 282 sepoys were summarily executed. Jarrett, now promoted to lieutenant, was appointed to the Ferozepore Regiment (later the 2nd Punjab Infantry).

Hanson Chambers Taylor Jarrett.

On 14 October 1858, at Baroun, seventy rebels had fortified themselves in a brick building; the only way into it was from a narrow alley under constant fire. Lieutenant Jarrett called for volunteers to storm the house but only four men responded. Undeterred, he led these men through the alley to the house and forced his way in, fending off the enemy bayonets with his sword. However, being so feebly supported, he was forced to abandon the attack and return under fire.

His VC was gazetted on 21 June 1859, but there is no record of an investiture, so the medal was probably posted to him.

Despite his VC, Jarrett's post-war career rise was rather slow. He enjoyed big game hunting and sought civil employment as deputy conservator of forests in Saugor, which enabled him to indulge in his passion for hunting. He retired in 1890 as a colonel, aged 51.

Hanson Jarrett died on 11 April 1891 and was buried in Saugor New Cemetery, Madhya Pradesh, India, Grave 210 (his headstone may now be missing). His VC is not publicly held.

Henry Evelyn WOOD, Sindwaho and Sindhora, 19 October & 29 December 1858

Evelyn (as he would be known) Wood was born on 9 February 1838 at Cressing, near Braintree in Essex, the son of Sir John Page Wood (chaplain and private secretary to Queen Caroline) and Emma Caroline (née Mitchell). At the age of 9, Wood was sent to the newly founded public school Marlborough College. A near-starvation diet and a brutal headmaster led to a mutiny among the pupils. Wood pleaded with his parents to take him away from this school and he applied to join the Royal Navy. At the age of 14, he passed his entrance test and joined HMS *Queen*. This was the start

Henry Evelyn Wood.

of a successful but rather short naval career. In 1853, his uncle, Captain Frederick Mitchell, took command of the ship and Wood graduated to midshipman at the end of the year.

When war with Russia was declared in March 1854, HMS *Queen* was part of the fleet that bombarded Sebastopol during the long siege of the city. After silencing four of their batteries and having survived his first action, Wood was almost killed by one of his own crew. Every evening the twenty-five midshipmen would play 'follow the leader', pursuing each other around the more dangerous parts of the ship. Wood did not enjoy this game, as he suffered from giddiness when high up in the rigging. One evening in July, Wood had crawled from the main yard to the brace, where he was resting, when a shipmate opened the quarter-gallery window and so startled him that he fell over 40 feet into the water. His head narrowly missed an open gun port, which would have undoubtedly killed him if he had hit it. Shocked, he had some difficulty swimming back to the ship and climbing aboard.

Having survived this tomfoolery, Wood, with the rest of the ship's company, now faced an even greater danger: cholera had broken out in the British camp in August. The French flagship saw the first sign of it among the fleet and she lost 140 men. The British flagship *Britannia* lost 10 per cent of her crew. Only two ships were not affected: the *London* and the *Queen*. Within days, many ships had insufficient men fit to work the sails. The 16-year-old Wood was sent to HMS *Britannia* to assist in running the ship, but was soon involved in burying the dead, which went on for days.

In September 1854, British and French forces were landed at Kalamita Bay and, by the 19th, were marching off to Sebastopol. The next day saw the Battle of the Alma, which Wood was able to watch from the *Queen*'s top mast (despite the giddiness, no doubt). He later recalled how he thought Lord Raglan had advanced further forward than was safe for a general; something he would face criticism for himself in the Zulu War. After the battle, Wood was sent ashore to view the field and spent the next three days helping to bury the dead.

In October, Wood joined the Naval Brigade, which was sent ashore to help with the bombardment of the Great Redan at Sebastopol. Commanding the 21-gun battery was Captain William Peel, who would also be awarded the VC for his actions in Crimea. Wood and Edward St John Daniel, another midshipman, became devoted to Peel and Wood became his ADC in April the following year. Despite the terrible winter of 1854/55, they were constantly on duty in the trenches. Peel later recalled that Wood did not miss a day's duty in nine months. Sustained exposure to cannon fire during the bombardment undoubtedly contributed to his deafness, which affected him for the rest of his life.

During one artillery exchange on 18 October 1854, while Wood was at lunch, an enemy shell exploded overhead, setting the thatch of a powder magazine on fire. Wood climbed onto the roof and stamped out the fire (Peel would later recommend him for the VC for this act and for bringing up ammunition under fire). Wood and Daniel, the two young midshipmen, seemed to vie with each other in acts of bravery. They would bring up ammunition or repair a damaged parapet under fire. Peel was perplexed by their devotion to him; they were risking their lives just to impress him.

On one occasion, the Russian guns succeeded in bringing down the Union flag that was flying above Peel's battery. Wood jumped up, picked up the flag and remounted it on the parapet. He had just climbed down when another shell hit the staff, so Wood went back up a second and indeed a third time to replace it on the parapet. Finally, with no staff left, Wood spread the flag over the top of the parapet to the cheers of the gunners. All this time he was under fire.

In the following summer of 1855, the allies attempted a number of abortive attacks on the Russian defences. On 18 June, the British made a suicidal assault on the Redan, during which they suffered heavy casualties. The Naval Brigade carried the scaling ladders and the now 17-year-old Wood was the only one to reach the Redan, despite being wounded twice. He was sent home to recuperate and was reflecting on his future. Having tasted the excitement of fighting on land, he decided to resign his commission in the navy and apply to join the army. His outstanding service gained him a cornetcy without purchase in the 13th Light Dragoons.

Upon joining his new regiment, they were promptly sent back to Crimea as reinforcements to fill the losses from the Charge of the Light Brigade. Unfortunately for Wood, he was struck down with both typhoid and pneumonia, spending five months recovering at Scutari. This was just the start of his lifelong battle against sickness and accidents.

During the next fifty years, Wood suffered with malaria, dysentery, sunstroke, blinding headaches, deafness, toothache, stomach and eye problems and, to crown it all, ingrowing toenails.

By the time he had recovered, the war was over and he returned to England. Despite being recommended for the VC and probably earning it four times during the war (although like all the other Crimea VCs, he would only ever have received one), when the VC was introduced in 1856, Wood would miss out on it as he had by then left the navy and joined the army. As each service and regiment was trying to get their 'own man' an award, the navy would not pursue his claim. However, he was awarded a Turkish medal and the Légion d'Honneur.

In 1857, he exchanged into the 17th Lancers, who were being sent to quell the Indian Mutiny. On arrival, he purchased a horse, which he called 'Pig' as it would eat any food within reach. A wealthy uncle had purchased a promotion to lieutenant for him and, as he could read and write, Hindustani Wood was appointed interpreter. This led to secondment to the 3rd Bombay Cavalry.

At some point, while in India, he was challenged to ride a giraffe and ended up on the ground with a bloody nose, cut lips and cheeks, and was unable to work for a week. It is not recorded what his commanding officer thought of this.

By the middle of March 1857, the British force, including Wood's troop of 100 men, were after a group of rebels under the command of Tatya Tope. There followed a period of eleven months of pursuit in the most unforgiving terrain. Many of the men, including Wood, suffered from sunstroke. Then, on 19 October at Sindwaho, he single-handedly attacked and drove off a body of the enemy, for which he was highly praised with a mention in despatches.

In December 1858, a band of rebels captured Chemmun Singh, a pro-British local chief. They took him into the jungle, where they intended to hang him. Wood set out with fifteen men to free him. Intelligence reports put the rebel band at about twenty-five men, so he was confident he could surprise them. They set off at 9 pm and after three hours they could see the light of a campfire. Wood decided to leave three men with the horses and led the rest towards the fire. A slow approach got Wood to within 10 yards of the camp, only to discover that there were seventy to eighty rebels. With these odds, Wood considered retreat but felt this would not only discredit him, but certainly lead to Singh being killed. Thus, he resolved that a surprise attack was the only option.

Wood called his small party together and before they realised the size of the enemy force, ordered them to get ready. But as one of his men cocked the hammer of his rifle, a sentry called out, 'Who is that?' Wood replied, 'We are the Government,' and shouted for his men to charge. Wood led from the front only to trip over a sleeping rebel and fell headlong into a hollow. He was joined by his sergeant and a private, who had fallen over the same man. In the noise and confusion, the rebels awoke and the majority fled thinking they were being attacked by a larger force. Wood got up only to discover that he was being attacked by a rebel. The two men cut and thrust at each other but their sword blows were deflected by the foliage. Finally, by crouching down, Wood was able to wound his man in the thigh; he staggered into the path of Wood's sergeant, who cut at him but also caught his sword in the trees. Wood ran after the two men and fell into a drainage ditch with them. After a few seconds scrabbling around, the sergeant killed the rebel. Wood emerged breathless, muddy and bloody to discover the rebels had gone and the prisoner was alive. The remainder of his men, who had held back until now, joined him. So, with only two men, he had routed a group of seventy to eighty rebels, freed their prisoner and earned himself the Victoria Cross.

The VC was for this action and that on 19 October at Sindwaho. The award itself was something of an anti-climax as it was forwarded to him by registered post and he did not receive it until July 1862, as it had been sent to him in India and Wood had been invalided home by the time it had arrived.

Back in England, Wood exchanged into the infantry, purchasing a captaincy in the 73rd Regiment of Foot, primarily to get into the Staff College at Camberley. During this time he would make many influential contacts, the most notable being Garnet Wolseley, who at first was impressed by Wood's energy, intelligence and infectious good humour but, as time passed, became less so. Wood was also promoted to brevet major at just 24 years of age.

Wood was injured again in 1863 while hunting, when he fell from his horse and was kicked in the head, but was hunting again within three weeks. He graduated at the end of 1864 and was sent to Ireland as ADC to Colonel Napier. However, the Irish climate did not suit him and he spent more time in London due to poor health. In 1866, the 73rd had been sent to Hong Kong and Wood exchanged into the 17th Regiment at Aldershot, where he was responsible for cooking (something he said he know nothing about) and for teaching military drawing (his worst subject at Staff College). Perhaps fortunately for the officers and men, a vacancy for brigade major became available and Wood was accepted for the post.

All through 1868, Wood suffered with stomach pains and, because he was ill for so long, he seriously considered leaving the army and qualifying for the Bar. It was not until he took prescribed doses of opium that he recovered sufficiently to be able to continue with his military duties.

By 1873, Wood was married (he and his wife would have three sons and three daughters, one of whom he called Victoria, the vain Wood naming her either after his queen or his medal). He had also been promoted to brevet lieutenant colonel. He was then chosen by Wolseley to be his transport officer for the Ashanti Campaign of 1873–74, after which both men emerged as public figures. Mentioned in despatches, and with a fresh wound caused by a nail fired from a blunderbuss, Wood was made a Companion of the Bath and brevet colonel. He was so vain, it was said of him that he probably wore his medal ribbons on his pyjamas!

A series of staff appointments led to him being sent to South Africa in 1878 as colonel of the 90th, and he took part in what was soon to be known as the Ninth Frontier War, more a series of skirmishes than a war. During this, Wood failed to hear a challenge from a sentry and was fired on by his own men. Lieutenant Colonel Thesiger (soon to be Lord Chelmsford), commanding for the first time, came to rely on the experienced Wood and the two became friends.

The next perceived conflict was Zululand and Wood persuaded Thesiger that the Field Force should march to Natal rather than attempt the complications of sea transport. The column marched 500 miles over rough terrain and crossed thirty-seven rivers. By the time they reached Pietermaritzburg, the experience had toughened them and they had learned to 'rough it'. Wood summed it up by saying, 'A healthy climate, with proper sanitary arrangements and the absence of public-houses, the young soldiers improved out of all recognition.' Considering Wood's many ailments, it is amazing that he himself made the 500-mile trip.

Before the war even got going, Wood was nearly killed by a runaway wagon, which he jumped onto in an attempt to stop it. After the disaster at iSandlwana in January, and while waiting for reinforcements, Chelmsford bolstered Wood's force with the entire volunteer cavalry. His wish was for Wood's successful raiding to increase in order to divert Zulu attention away from the south, where Chelmsford was about to lead a column to relieve Pearson at Eshowe.

Wood made several raids to harass the Zulus and capture their cattle. It was during this time that the Zulus named him Lakuni, the name of the very hard wood used to make the knobkerrie (a wooden club). In March, Cetshwayo's brother Prince Hamu agreed to come over to Wood with all his warriors and his 300 wives.

On 28 March, Wood led a column to attack the Zulu stronghold at Hlobane. It rose 1,500 feet above the surrounding plain, was 3 miles long and about a mile wide. Narrow tracks led to the summit, which was a plateau littered with boulders and scrub.

It would be hard to find an objective more unsuited for mounted troops, but Wood decided not to take any infantry except for his native irregulars. The debacle that followed left a question mark about Wood's state of mind; he ignored standard military practice and had no control over the fighting. He adopted a floating form of command, which meant he was distant and unable to influence events. Lieutenant Colonel Russell would attack from the west while Lieutenant Colonel Redvers Buller's force would attack from the east.

Wood and his small entourage (three staff officers and eight mounted men from the 90th) made their way leisurely to the base of the mountain with the intention of following Buller's route to the summit. Flattened grass, discarded bits of equipment and the odd dead horse made it an easy trail to follow and soon they heard the sound of gunfire from above. Shortly afterwards they came upon the Border Horse riding towards them claiming to have lost their way. Wood had to forcefully persuade their commander, Lieutenant Colonel Weatherley, to turn about and accompany him to the summit. With Wood and his staff in the lead, they began to climb when a volley of shots rang out from some rocks and caves above them. To Wood's horror, his trusted interpreter and political officer Mr Lloyd had been mortally wounded. Wood had him taken to a nearby kraal, where most of the party had taken cover. Advancing again, Wood's horse was shot from under him, pinning him down. It took him a few minutes to free himself and he ordered Weatherley's men to flush out the Zulus. This they refused to do, so Captain Campbell, together with another staff officer, Lieutenant Henry Lyons, and Private Edmund Fowler of the escort charged in, but Campbell was killed by a direct shot. Lyons and Fowler were awarded the VC for this action.

Wood seems to have had something of a mental breakdown at this point. With an uncontrolled battle raging on the plateau above him and a large Zulu force approaching him, he went into meltdown and ordered his two friends to be buried, and for his bugler Walkinshaw to fetch his bible from his dead horse. With no digging tools, Wood ordered his Zulu irregulars to use their assegais to dig the graves.

Six men from the Border Horse were killed and eight wounded while this was going on. Wood now ordered the Border Horse to join Buller on the summit while he and his escort retraced their steps back down the mountain. Within a short time of the Border Horse reaching the summit, they were all but wiped out.

Wood's small group made their way slowly westwards unaware that 20,000 Zulus were swiftly approaching from the south. Although Buller, on top of the plateau, had observed them for some time, Wood, who was nearer, was completely oblivious to the danger until one of his Zulu scouts spotted them. This galvanised Wood into action and his party swiftly made their way back to the Zunguin Range, running the gauntlet of the Zulu vanguard. From there, Wood sent some of his escort back to Khambula with the news of the approaching Zulus. Wood then watched as Buller's command were decimated as they tried to climb down from Hlobane on the aptly named Devil's Pass. Buller would be awarded the Victoria Cross for his actions that day.

When both Buller and Wood met at Khambula, to his shame, Wood sought to cover up his mistakes by embellishing the deaths of Campbell and Lloyd, both sons of wealthy and influential families. He also unfairly laid blame on Weatherley and the Border Horse, conveniently, most of whom were killed. But luck was on Wood's side. Hlobane was mostly a colonial affair and, as there were no correspondents with him, it did not receive much coverage in the British press. Also, his mishandling of the assault on Hlobane was conveniently overshadowed by the events of the next day.

The Zulus, fired-up by their success at Hlobane, attacked the well-prepared British laager at Khambula. The Zulus suffered the greatest defeat of the war and Wood was justly able to claim great credit for this. If, indeed, he had suffered a breakdown the day before, he had made a remarkable recovery. His handling of the firepower was effective and he timed his counter-attacks to perfection. Typically, he even managed to get involved in the fighting on the front line. He joined in the firing and managed to kill four Zulus, one of them a chief.

Having sent out a series of bayonet charges to clear the Zulus from positions that were close to the laager, Wood felt that the attacks were lessening and ordered Buller's mounted men to charge. Thirsting for revenge, the horsemen chased and killed their opponents until darkness forced them to stop. Khambula was the turning point of the war and it convinced Cetshwayo that he could never win against the firepower of the Martini-Henry rifle, Gatling gun and artillery.

The next two months were spent stockpiling supplies for the second invasion. When, at last, the invasion started, Wood's No. 4 Column was renamed 'The Flying Column', effectively making it an independent command. This created a great deal of resentment among the senior officers. Much of the fighting was done by Wood's column, to the annoyance of those officers looking to advance their careers.

By July, Wood's column found itself at Ulundi and joined with Lord Chelmsford. During the battle, Wood stayed by the side of his general.

Wood rightly believed that the Zulus were reluctantly forced into fighting at Ulundi, saying, 'The Regiments came on in a hurried, disorderly manner, which contrasted strongly with the methodical, steady order in which they advanced at Khambula.'

With Ulundi, the war was over and Wood was looking forward to going home to England. Both Chelmsford and his replacement, Wolseley, were lavish in their praise for Wood and his men. Wolseley went so far as to say, 'You and Buller have been the only bright spots in this miserable war, and all through I have felt proud that I numbered you amongst my friends, and companion-in-arms.'

Once back in England, Wood was made Knight Commander of the Bath for his service. He attended numerous dinners in his honour and was a guest of both the Queen and Disraeli. However, there was no promotion.

Six months later, Wood was on his way back to South Africa as a personal favour for the Queen to take Empress Eugenie on a pilgrimage to see where her son Louis Napoleon had been killed during the second invasion of Zululand. Among the party was Mrs Campbell, the widow of Wood's staff officer and friend. When they arrived at Cape Town, Wood paid a visit to Cetshwayo.

The group left Pietermaritzburg on 29 April 1880 on what was to be a 500-mile round trip. On 21 May, Mrs Campbell was taken to Hlobane, where headstones were placed on the graves of her husband and Llewellyn Lloyd.

Finally, they reached the site where the Prince Imperial had been killed. Another memorial stone was laid and the empress planted cuttings of a tree she had brought from the family estate at Camden Place in Chislehurst. The party returned to England by the end of July.

But Wood was not finished with South Africa just yet, for within six weeks of the start of the First Boer War he was back. Soon after his arrival, in February 1881, General Sir George Colley, the army commander, was killed along with many of his men at Majuba Hill. As a result, Wood was sworn in as Acting Governor of Natal and Administrator of the Transvaal and given the local rank of major general. At the age of 43, he was the youngest person to have attained that rank.

He became unpopular in the colony and among his fellow officers when, under instructions from the British Government, he negotiated peace with the Boers to end the war. This infuriated Wolseley, who not only believed Wood had negotiated the peace on his own initiative, but also that a military victory was possible. This was something that would not prove to be so easy during the Second Boer War.

Wood was offered the governorship of Natal but declined it and, in February 1882, he left South Africa for the last time. Although Wolseley had come to dislike Wood personally, he employed him in the war against Arabi Pasha in 1882, but Wood would never see action under Wolseley. The result of this campaign was the British annexing Egypt and appointing Wood as C-in-C of the new Egyptian Army.

This new service was made attractive to seconded British officers who received higher pay and Egyptian ranks one or two grades higher than British Army rank. This resulted in success with a less corrupt and better disciplined army. Wood also managed to get sunstroke while visiting the pyramids.

Wood's final campaign was the attempted relief of Khartoum in 1884–85, during which the ever accent-prone Wood injured one of his fingers in a folding chair. Although the rest of his career was long and filled with interesting appointments, his days of campaigning were over.

He spent the remainder of his career working on reforms, manly in welfare for military men, permanent barracks, and better sanitary care and food. He believed officers should be trained centrally and not by the regimental colonels. He saw to it that the army took part in large-scale manoeuvres, where the three arms could work together. In fact, we are indebted to him for acquiring Salisbury Plain as a military training area for the army. He also believed in the men doing as much live firing as possible. However, he was not just about spending money; he could save it too. In 1903, Wood was promoted to field marshal, but he retired the following year. In his old age, he wrote books, not least his 1906 autobiography *From Midshipman to Field Marshal*, which was so long that it was published in two volumes and so popular that it had to be reprinted in its first year. Wood delivered eulogies for old comrades whom he outlived. He indulged in his favourite pastime of foxhunting right up until his death. He saw the start and end of the Great War and died, aged 81, at his Essex home on 2 December 1919 during the flu pandemic.

Wood's grave, Aldershot Military Cemetery.

Field Marshal Sir Evelyn Wood, vc, was buried with full military honours at Aldershot Military Cemetery, Hampshire, Section V, Grave 1402. His VC is held by the National Army Museum, London.

Herbert Mackworth CLOGSTOUN, Chichumbah, 15 January 1859

Herbert Clogstoun was born on 13 June 1820 in Port of Spain, Trinidad. Almost nothing is known of his life before he was commissioned into the 19th Madras Native Infantry in January 1838. In 1856, he transferred to the 2nd Cavalry Hyderabad Contingent as second in command.

On 15 January 1859, his regiment was part of Brigadier Hill's Berar Field Force, searching for rebels 35 miles from Hingoli, Maharashtra. They caught up with 400 rebels at Chichumbah. With

Herbert Mackworth Clogstoun.

only eight men, Captain Clogstoun charged the rebels, forcing them into the town and causing them to abandon their plunder. During this action, Clogstoun lost seven of the eight men with him, and he was severely wounded.

He was promoted to major and took command of the regiment. His VC was gazetted on 21 October 1859 and was presented to him on 19 January 1860 at Madras.

Herbert Clogstoun was killed in action at Hingoli on 6 May 1862 and was buried in Madras Cemetery, Tamil Nadu, India. His VC is held by the National Army Museum, London.

Charles Augustus GOODFELLOW, Fort of Beyt, 6 October 1859

Charles Goodfellow was born on 27 November 1836 in Poona, India. He was the son and grandson of two Bombay engineers, both of whom became generals. Young Goodfellow was enlisted into Addiscombe Military Seminary and on passing out in 1857, joined the Bombay Sappers and Miners. He served with General Rose's Central India Field Force during the early part of 1858 against the Waghers, a fanatical community of Hindu people living in the remote area of Kathiawar in western Goojerat.

Charles Augustus Goodfellow.

A second expedition, led by Colonel Edward Donovan of the 33rd (Duke of Wellington's) Regiment against the Waghers' stronghold on the island of Beyt, was undertaken. On 6 October 1859, during the assault on the fort of Beyt, Lieutenant Goodfellow carried off a mortally wounded man of the 28th Regiment under heavy fire and took him to a place of safety. The attack was repulsed, with heavy losses. However, the Waghers abandoned the fort during the night and it was blown up by the engineers the following day.

Goodfellow's VC was gazetted on 16 April 1863 and was presented to him the same year at a parade in Mhow. He served in the expedition to Abyssinia in 1868, where he was mentioned in despatches. After the campaign, he was assigned to conduct an archaeological excavation of Adulis, Eritrea, on behalf of the British Museum.

The remainder of his career was uneventful and Goodfellow retired in 1889 as a lieutenant colonel.

Charles Goodfellow died on 1 September 1915 and was buried in Royal Leamington Spa Cemetery, Warwickshire. His VC is held by the Royal Engineers Museum, Gillingham, Kent.

Goodfellow's grave, Royal Leamington Spa Cemetery.

Chapter 4

Third China War, 1860–62

Chinese resentment of European traders and diplomats had already resulted in the First China War, of 1840–42. An uneasy peace ended when the Chinese executed a French missionary and five Chinese sailors were removed from a British ship and tried for piracy. This led to the Second China War, of 1846–47, which was concluded with the Treaty of Tientsin. When the British and French commissioners set sail up the Pei-ho River to ratify the treaty, they were fired on from the three Taku forts, thus starting the Third China War.

Andrew FITZGIBBON, Taku Forts, 21 August 1860

Andrew Fitzgibbon was born on 13 May 1845 in Petagurh, Goojerat, India, the son of Quartermaster Sergeant William Fitzgibbon. Almost nothing is known about his early life apart from that he joined the Indian Medical Establishment, Indian Army, at the age of 13. In February 1860, he sailed for China attached to the 67th Regiment of Foot.

On 21 August 1860, Hospital Apprentice Fitzgibbon was within 500 yards of the north Taku Fort when he proceeded under heavy fire to attend to a wounded dhooli-bearer and, while the regiment was advancing under the enemy's fire, he ran across open ground to attend to the wounds of Lieutenant Gye. During this act, Fitzgibbon was severely wounded.

He was gazetted, incorrectly as Arthur Fitzgibbon, for the VC on 13 August 1860, but there is no record of it being presented and it may have been posted to him. Fitzgibbon returned to India and became an assistant apothecary 2nd Class in January 1867, and 1st Class in 1872. In May 1869, he married Mary Amelia Coleman and they went on to have two children.

Andrew Fitzgibbon died from a stroke on 7 March 1883 and was buried in an unmarked grave, Old Delhi Military Cemetery (The Nicholson Cemetery), India. His VC is believed to have been buried with him. At just 15 years and 3 months at the time he earned his VC, he is one of the two youngest recipients of the medal, the other being Thomas Flynn, also 15 years and 3 months.

Umbeyla Campaign, 1863

During the late 1850s, the Peshawar District of British-held India came under frequent attack by the Hindustani Pathans based in the nearby Mahabun Mountains. The warlike Pathans were violently opposed to British rule. An expedition in 1858 drove them from their base, but by 1863, they had regrouped around the mountain outpost of Malka, so an expedition was sent to destroy it.

George Vincent FOSBERY, Umbeyla Pass, 30 October 1863

George Fosbery was born on 11 April 1832 in Stert, near Devizes, Wiltshire, one of seven children born to the Reverend Thomas Fosbery. George was educated at Eton in 1846–50. He signed up for the 4th Bengal European Regiment in 1852. In 1858, he married Emmeline Georgiana and they went on to have ten children, many of whom later emigrated to Canada.

In 1863, Neville Bowles Chamberlain commanded an expedition to destroy Malka. Having set up an operational base in the Chamla Valley, his men accessed via the Umbeyla Pass but were soon bogged down by a numerically superior force.

George Vincent Fosbery.

On 30 October, Lieutenant Fosbery led a party of men up one path while Lieutenant Pitcher led a party up another to recapture the Crag

Piquet, after its garrison had been attacked by the enemy. Fosbery led his group to the top of the cliff two abreast and he was the first man to reach the summit. When his commanding officer was wounded, Fosbery led his men in pursuit of the fleeing enemy and inflicted many losses on them.

Fosbery was promoted to captain in 1864 and his VC was gazetted on 7 July 1865, but it is unknown when and where it was presented to him. He was promoted to major in 1868, and lieutenant colonel in 1874. He retired from the army in 1877 and devoted himself to perfecting the machine gun, which he brought to the attention of the British Government. In 1895, he also invented the Webley-Fosbery automatic revolver and the Paradox gun, a shotgun capable of firing both shot and solid projectiles with accuracy. He also introduced the explosive bullet, as a means of establishing range for infantry and mountain guns.

Fosbery's grave, St Mary's Cemetery, Bath.

George Fosbery died on 8 May 1907 and was buried in St Mary's Cemetery (aka Bathwick Cemetery), Bath, Somerset. His VC is in the Lord Ashcroft Gallery, Imperial War Museum, London.

Henry William PITCHER, Umbeyla Pass, 30 October & 16 November 1863

Henry Pitcher was born on 20 December 1841 in Kamptee, Maharashtra, India, the second son of Vincent Pitcher and Rose Mary (née le Geyt). In March 1859, Henry was appointed to the 1st Punjab Native Infantry. He was then seconded as acting adjutant to the 3rd Punjab Native Infantry, and in 1860 to the 4th Punjab Native Infantry. In May 1861, he returned to the 1st Punjab Native Infantry as adjutant.

In 1863, Neville Bowles Chamberlain commanded an expedition to destroy Malka. Having set up an operational base in the Chamla Valley, his men accessed by the Umbeyla Pass but were soon bogged down by a numerically superior force.

On 30 October 1863, Lieutenant Pitcher led a party of men up one path while Lieutenant Fosbery led a party up another to recapture the Crag Piquet after its garrison had been attacked by the enemy. Pitcher led his men up until he was knocked down and stunned by a large stone thrown from above.

On 16 November, he led the first charge during the recapture of the same post, this having again been taken by the enemy. Pitcher was some way ahead of his men during the assault when he was severely wounded and had to be carried back down.

Henry William Pitcher.

His VC was gazetted on 16 July 1864 but, as with Fosbery, there is no record of an investiture and the medal may have been posted to him. Pitcher was later promoted to captain.

Henry Pitcher died from heatstroke on 5 July 1875 and was buried in Dehra Ismail Khan Cemetery, Kohat, India (now Pakistan). His VC is held by the Jersey Museum, St Helier.

Second Maori (Waikato-Haubau) War, 1863–66

The truce that ended the first Maori War of 1861 had dealt only with the immediate territorial problems. By 1863, there was an increasing flow of settlers to New Zealand's North Island and the consequent demand for land was again the cause of more fighting. In July 1863, several regiments of foot, artillery, Bengal infantry, the Auckland Militia and a detachment from HMS *Harrier* launched a massive invasion of the Maori King Tawhiau's home area, the Waikato.

John Carstairs McNEILL, Ohaupo, 30 March 1864

John McNeill was born on 28 March 1831 on the island of Colonsay, Argyllshire, Scotland, the son of Captain Alexander McNeill and Anne

Elizabeth (née Carstairs). He was educated at St Andrews College and at Addiscombe Military Seminary before joining the 12th Bengal Native Infantry. His regiment mutinied in 1857 and McNeill became ADC to General Sir E. Lugard. After the mutiny, McNeill transferred to the 107th Bengal Infantry (later the Royal Sussex Regiment) and was promoted to captain in 1860, to major in 1861, and lieutenant colonel in 1864.

John Carstairs McNeill

On 30 March 1864, at Ohaupo, Waikato, Lieutenant Colonel McNeill was riding with Private Vosper and Private Gibson when they observed a body of the enemy, the Maoris. McNeill sent Gibson to bring up the infantry. McNeill and Vosper then moved to higher ground to observe the enemy whereupon they were surprised by a group of fifty natives. As they turned to gallop back, Vosper's horse fell and threw him. The natives rushed at Vosper but McNeill rode after the horse, caught it and helped Vosper to remount. Although the enemy were very close and firing sharply, by galloping hard they managed to get away.

McNeill's VC was gazetted on 16 August 1864 and he was presented with it on 6 December 1864 by the Governor General of New Zealand, Sir George Grey, in Auckland.

During the Fenian uprising of 1866–67 in Ireland, McNeill commanded the Tipperary Flying Column. He was then appointed military secretary to the Governor General of Canada, Lord Lisgar, a post he held until 1872. On his promotion to colonel, he was appointed second in command of the Ashanti Campaign of 1873, where he was mentioned in despatches and severely wounded.

McNeill was appointed equerry to Queen Victoria and ADC to HRH, The Commander-in-Chief in 1874. He also served in the Egyptian Campaign of 1882 and was promoted to major general. In retirement, he became a Justice of the Peace and Duty Lieutenant for Argyllshire.

John McNeill died on 25 May 1904 and was buried in the family chapel at Oronsay Priory, Isle of Colonsay, Argyllshire. His VC is in the Lord Ashcroft Gallery, Imperial War Museum, London.

Bhutan War, 1864–65

The Indian state of Bhutan lies to the east of Nepal, and in 1864, following a civil war in the region, the victorious leader of the Punakha people had broken with the central administration and set up a rival government. The legitimate governor was deposed, and so Britain, protecting her interests in her Indian Empire, sent a peace mission to restore order. The British mediated, dealing alternately with the supporters of both the deposed and the new government. After the new government rejected all British attempts to broker peace, Britain declared war on the new regime in November 1864.

William Spottiswoode TREVOR, Dewan-Giri, 30 April 1865

William Trevor was born on 9 October 1831 in Calcutta, India, the son of Captain Robert Trevor of the 3rd Bengal Cavalry and Mary (née Spottiswoode). When Captain Robert Trevor was posted to Afghanistan, the whole family accompanied him. In 1842, during the retreat from Kabul in the First Afghan War, Captain Trevor was murdered and the remainder of the family taken hostage. They were rescued nine months later, following General Sir George Pollock's reoccupation of the city.

William Spottiswoode Trevor.

After their release, the family returned to England, where William and his two brothers obtained cadetships at the Addiscombe Military Seminary. On passing out in December 1849, William entered the Bengal Engineers and after training at Chatham, he was posted to India in 1851. He served in the 'Army of Ava' throughout the Second Burmese War under General Godwin, and was mentioned in despatches for his actions in the storming of the White House Stockade at Rangoon on 12 April 1852.

Trevor remained in Burma until he was posted to Bengal in 1857. He constructed barracks on a site at Senchal for European soldiers, and would later join the Darjeeling Field Force under Captain Curzon, which was sent to intercept the mutineers from Decca. In 1861, Trevor was appointed garrison engineer at Fort William in Calcutta. However, he did not see the work completed because, in February 1862, he was appointed superintending engineer of the Northern Circle, and under his supervision completed the Ganges–Darjeeling Road.

Trevor's grave, Kensal Green Cemetery, London.

In February 1865, Trevor was a major attached to the Bhutan Field Force under Major General Tombs, vc, and, on 30 April 1865, at Dewan-Giri, Major Trevor led an attack with Lieutenant Dundas on a blockhouse defended by 200 men. To gain entry, the two men had to climb a 14-foot wall and then enter through a small hole between the wall and the roof. After setting this example, they were followed in by the Sikh soldiers. Both officers were wounded but the blockhouse was taken with sixty prisoners, the rest being killed, fighting to the last.

William Trevor's VC was gazetted on 31 December 1867 and was presented to him on 23 March 1868 by Major General C.F. Fordyce in Calcutta. Trevor was promoted to lieutenant general in 1874 and was made special chief engineer for Famine Relief Works, north of the Ganges, and from December 1875 to 1880, he was the chief engineer in British Burma. In 1880, he succeeded his brother as director general of railways and in February 1882, was appointed secretary to the Government of India in the Public Works Department, a post he held until his retirement in 1887. Following his retirement, he returned to England.

William Trevor died on 2 November 1907 and was buried in Kensal Green Cemetery, London, Square 179/RS, Grave 31775. His VC is held by the Royal Engineers Museum, Gillingham, Kent.

James DUNDAS, Dewan-Giri, 30 April 1865

James Dundas was born on 10 September 1842 in Edinburgh, the son of George Dundas (who adopted the title Lord Manor) and Elizabeth (née MacKenzie). He was educated at Edinburgh Academy, Trinity College Glenalmond and Addiscombe Military Seminary. On passing out of Addiscombe in June 1860 as a lieutenant, he was appointed to the Bengal Engineers.

He sailed to India in March 1862 and on arrival was posted to the Sappers and Miners at Roorkee, Uttarakhand. Dundas was appointed to the Public Works Department in Bengal, and was soon promoted to executive engineer of one of the most responsible divisions in that presidency. In 1865, he was appointed to the Bhutan Field Force.

James Dundas.

On 30 April 1865, at Dewan-Giri, he led an attack with Lieutenant Trevor on a blockhouse defended by 200 men. To gain entry the two men had to climb a 14-foot wall and then enter through a small hole between the wall and the roof. After setting this example, they were followed in by the Sikh soldiers. Both officers were wounded but the blockhouse was taken with sixty prisoners, the rest being killed, fighting to the last.

Dundas's VC was gazetted on 31 December 1867 and was presented to him by Major General C.F. Fordyce at the same time that William Trevor received his, on 23 March 1868 at Calcutta. After the campaign was over, Dundas re-joined the Public Works Department, returning to England on leave in 1870 and 1877, the second time due to the death of his father. Dundas returned to India in 1878 and in the summer of that year, he rescued a native from a burning house in Simla.

In 1879, Lord Roberts, vc, selected him to accompany his Field Force as Commanding Royal Engineer on his advance to Kabul. In the autumn, Dundas was attached to General Macpherson's Field Force to aid in the destruction of the line of forts held by the enemy. It was while carrying out this work on 23 December 1879, at Seah Sang, near Sherpur, that one of the mines exploded prematurely, killing Dundas.

James Dundas was buried in Seah Sang Cemetery, near Sherpur, Afghanistan. His VC is in the Lord Ashcroft Gallery, Imperial War Museum, London. In 2002, the Dundas Bridge, built by the Royal Engineers between Kabul and Bagram in Afghanistan, was named in his honour.

Chapter 5

Third Ashanti War, 1873–74

In 1872, the coastal fort of Elmina in Ashanti (now Ghana) came into British possession. This was the last outlet for trade to the sea for the native Ashanti people and their king, Kofi Karikari, was ready to fight to protect it. In 1873, he mustered a 12,000-strong army and crossed the Pra River and invaded the coastal area. The British Governor and C-in-C Major General Sir Garnet Wolseley issued a warning that he was ready to attack but he also offered an armistice if the Ashanti would retreat from the coast. However, negotiations failed and war became inevitable.

Reginald William SARTORIUS, Abogu, 17 January 1874

Reginald Sartorius was born on 4 May 1841 in Sintra, Portugal, the son of Admiral of the Fleet Sir George Rose Sartorius, GCB. Young Reginald joined the army in January 1858 and in the following May was promoted to lieutenant.

Reginald William Sartorius.

Sartorius fought in the Indian Mutiny, taking part in the relief of Azimghur, where he volunteered to carry despatches through the encircling enemy, during which his cap was shot through and his head grazed, and he was also shot in the heel. In 1864, he served in the Bhutan War, and in 1868, he was promoted to captain.

When, in 1873, a large-scale invasion of the coastal area of the Gold Coast by the Ashanti tribesmen took place, it was deemed necessary to mount a full expedition, which was led by Sir General Garnet Wolseley. By now a major, Sartorius was part of a detached column under the command of Captain Glover on the right flank of the main body. He was later sent out ahead of the column to join up with Wolseley at Kumasi, and moved across the entire war zone with twenty-five men who had only forty rounds of ammunition each.

Sartorius's grave, St Mary's Church, South Baddesley.

On 17 January 1874, while serving in the 6th Bengal Cavalry during the attack on Abogu, Sartorius went to the assistance of a doctor, Sergeant Major Braimah, a Houssa NCO who was lying mortally wounded, and brought him to a place of safety while under heavy fire. Sartorius's VC was gazetted on 26 October 1874 and was presented to him on 30 March 1875 by the Queen at a Windsor Park Review. Sartorius joined the staff of the Prince of Wales (later Edward VII) for his visit during 1876–77. He then saw service in the Afghan War of 1878–79. He was promoted to colonel in 1886, and married Agnes Kemp in 1887. He was promoted to major general in 1895 and retired in 1897, becoming a member of the Royal Yacht Squadron.

Reginald Sartorius died on 8 August 1907 and was buried in St Mary's Churchyard, South Baddesley, Hampshire. His VC is held by the National Army Museum, London. His brother, Euston Sartorius, was also awarded the VC.

Baluchistan, 1877

During the Anglo-Dutch War of 1838–42, Britain had briefly occupied Baluchistan to protect her lines of communication, but they were forced to leave in 1841. However, relations improved with the signing of two treaties, in 1859 and 1876. The treaties strengthened Baluchistan's ties with the British Indian Empire, and in 1876, British forces set up a strongly garrisoned army station at Quetta, in the west of Baluchistan, commanding the Bolan and Khojak passes through the mountains. In July, some officers were attacked by a group of native labourers.

Andrew SCOTT, Quetta, 26 July 1877

Andrew Scott was born on 22 August 1840 in Devon. He joined the army at the age of 20, becoming part of the Bengal Staff Corps. He was promoted to lieutenant in 1862 and captain in 1872.

On 26 July 1877, at Quetta, Captain Scott was on duty on the regimental parade ground when he heard that some British officers were under attack and being killed by native labourers. He immediately went to their assistance. He found Lieutenant Hewson cut down and Lieutenant Kunhardt under assault and wounded, although sepoy Ruchpul Singh was trying to protect him. Scott bayoneted two of the enemy and closed with a third, who fell to the ground and was killed by a sepoy (probably Ruchpul Singh).

Scott's VC was gazetted on 18 January 1878 and was presented to him on 15 April the same year in India. He was later promoted to major in the 4th Sikh Infantry and served in the Afghan War of 1878–79.

Andrew Scott was killed in action at Srinagar, Kashmir, on 5 September 1882 and was buried in Kashmir Cemetery, India. His VC is not publicly held.

Second Afghan War, 1878–80

Britain had been keeping an eye on this important buffer to the north-west of India as part of a 'masterly inactivity' policy. In 1866, the Emir Sher Ali came to power. He was well disposed towards Britain and feared Russian intrusion as much as he feared the British. In 1872, Britain and Russia signed an agreement stating that Russia would respect Afghanistan's northern border, and that there would be no need for the British Government to give any promises of support to Afghanistan. Alarm bells sounded when, in 1876, the Emir reluctantly allowed a Russian mission to Kabul, and then refused to admit the British envoy. This intrusion was too close to British-ruled India to go unopposed. Sher Ali had to go; an ultimatum was sent demanding a British envoy be admitted. When this was ignored, three columns of British soldiers moved in.

Reginald Clare HART, Bazar Valley, 31 January 1879

Reginald Clare Hart.

Reginald Hart was born on 11 June 1848 in Scariff (or Scarriff), County Clare, Ireland, the son of Lieutenant General Henry George Hart and Frances Alicia (née Okes). He was educated at Marlborough and Cheltenham colleges, and represented his college at Rugby Union from 1864 to 1865. Hart entered the Royal Military Academy in June 1866 and passed out as a lieutenant in the Royal Engineers in January 1869.

In July 1869, he was awarded the Royal Humane Society Silver Medal and a French Medal of Honour for saving the life of a drowning man at Boulogne, during which he was injured. He was then present at the siege of Paris in 1871, during the time of the Paris Commune. In 1872, he married Charlotte Augusta, daughter of Mark Seton Synnot, and they went on to have three sons and one daughter.

Later in 1871, Hart sailed to India and on his arrival was posted to the Bengal Sappers and Miners. From September 1874 to March 1878, he was Assistant Garrison Instructor at Umbelya. Hart returned to England briefly in 1878 on sick leave, but was back in December serving with the Khyber Field Force in the Afghan War. Following this, he joined the Second Bazar Valley Expedition against the Zakka Khel Afridis.

On 31 January 1879, in the Bazar Valley, Lieutenant Hart ran 1,200 yards to the assistance of a wounded sowar who was in a riverbed and exposed to enemy fire. He reached the man as the enemy were about to cut him to pieces, drove them off and brought him back to safety with the help of others.

Hart's VC was gazetted on 10 June 1879 and was presented to him on 9 December 1879 by the Queen at Windsor Castle. After his investiture, he served in the 1st Division of the Khyber Field Force, being employed in reconnaissance. In February 1881, he was posted to the West Coast of Africa with Sir Samuel Rowe to the Ashanti War. In 1882, Hart was promoted to brevet major and served in the Egyptian War, being twice mentioned in despatches, and ending the war as brevet lieutenant colonel. In 1884, Hart returned to India and in December of that year was awarded a Silver Clasp (Bar) from the Royal Humane Society for saving the life of a gunner who had fallen into the Ganges from a pontoon bridge.

Hart's grave, St Mary's Church, Netherbury.

In the Tirah Campaign of 1897–98, Hart commanded the 1st Brigade and was twice mentioned in despatches. In 1899, he was given command of the Quetta District with a temporary rank of major general. He then served on the North-West Frontier before returning to England. He commanded the Cape Colony in 1907–09 and was C-in-C South Africa in 1912–14. During the First World War, he was appointed as Lieutenant Governor of Guernsey. After his retirement, he returned to England.

Reginald Hart died on 10 October 1931 and was buried in St Mary's Churchyard, Netherbury, Dorset. His VC is in the Lord Ashcroft Gallery, Imperial War Museum, London.

Edward Pemberton LEACH, Maidanah, 17 March 1879

Edward Leach was born on 2 April 1847 in County Londonderry, Ireland, the second son of Lieutenant Colonel Sir George Archibald Leach and Emily Leigh, daughter of Edward Leigh Pemberton. Young Edward was educated at Highgate School, London, and at the Royal Military Academy, Woolwich. He passed out in October 1866 and sailed for India in 1869.

From March 1869 to February 1870, he commanded a detachment of the Bengal Sappers and Miners at Rawalpindi, and subsequently joined the Public Works Department in Central India. In October 1871, he was appointed to the Indian Survey and served with the Cachar Column of the Lushai Expeditionary Force. In November 1877, Leach went on home leave but was back the following year as private secretary to Sir James Caird, Famine Commissioner. On the outbreak of the Afghan War in 1878, Leach joined the Khyber Survey Party.

Edward Pemberton Leach.

On 17 March 1879, near Maidanah, Afghanistan, Captain Leach was on a survey reconnaissance with detachments of the Guides Cavalry and the 45th Sikh Infantry when his party was attacked by tribesmen. While covering the retreat of the survey escort, who were carrying the mortally wounded Lieutenant Barclay, as the enemy began to press from all sides Leach led a charge of the 45th Sikh Infantry, killing three Afghans single-handedly and receiving a severe wound to his arm. His actions prevented the annihilation of the whole party.

Leach was back in England due to his wounded arm when his VC was gazetted on 9 December 1879 and presented to him three days later by the Queen at Windsor Castle. After his wound had healed, he was back in Afghanistan in March 1880 and joined the Kandahar Field Force under Major General Primrose, for survey work. He was later appointed brigade major, Royal Engineers, and was present at the final defeat of the enemy by Sir Frederick Roberts, vc. Leach was mentioned in despatches four times and ended the war as a brevet lieutenant colonel.

Leach married Elizabeth Mary Bazley in 1883 and they went on to have a son and two daughters. In 1885, he was part of the Suakin Expedition under Major General Sir Gerald Graham, vc, and was twice mentioned in despatches. After a short spell in England, Leach was given command of the 9th Division, 3rd Army Corps in Belfast, before becoming C-in-C in Scotland, a post he held for four years. In 1905, he was promoted to lieutenant general, and in 1910 to general. He retired to Italy in 1912.

Edward Leach died on 27 April 1913 and was buried in Grienze Churchyard, near Cadenabbia, Lombardy, Italy. His VC is held by the Royal Engineers Museum, Gillingham, Kent.

Walter Richard Pollock HAMILTON, Futtehabad, 2 April 1879

Walter Hamilton was born on 18 August 1856 in Inistioge, County Kilkenny, Ireland, the fourth son of Alexander Hamilton JP and Emma (née Pollock). He was educated at Eagle House, Wimbledon, and Felsted School, Essex. In January 1874, he was gazetted into the 70th Regiment of Foot, and embarked for India in October that year.

On being promoted to lieutenant he was offered a commission in the Bengal Staff Corps (Corps of Guides) and within three months had passed the higher standard of examination in languages and was detailed to the cavalry.

Walter Richard Pollock Hamilton.

Hamilton served throughout the Jowaki-Afridi Expedition of 1877–78. He then served as ADC to the commanding officer, General Keyes.

In March 1879, he was present at the operations against the Ranizai village of Skhakat. In October 1879, the Corps of Guides were moved to Jamrud at the mouth of the Khyber Pass and for six weeks were engaged in reconnoitring the mountains. In the first two weeks of the campaign, Hamilton participated throughout with the cavalry and was present at the capture of Ali Musjid. In March, he commanded a troop on escort duty with a surveying party, during which time Captain Leach would earn himself the VC. At the end of March, Hamilton was involved in the advance of General Gough's Brigade towards Futtehabad.

On 2 April 1879, Lieutenant Hamilton led a charge of the Guides cavalry against superior numbers of the enemy. When his commanding officer, Major Wigram Battye, was killed, Hamilton, the only officer left with the regiment, assumed command and cheered the men on to avenge his death. In this charge, seeing that Sowar Dowlut Ram was down, and was entangled with his horse and being attacked by three of the enemy, Hamilton rushed over to him and killed all three of his attackers, thus saving the sowar's life.

Hamilton was recommended for the VC but it was turned down due to his action 'not being covered by the Victoria Cross Warrant'. Shortly afterwards, Hamilton was selected to be part of the seventy-man escort for Sir Louis Cavagnari to Kabul. Walter Hamilton was killed in action on 3 September 1879, leading a charge against a gun as the Residency was being attacked by the enemy. He was buried in an unmarked grave, in a garden near the Residency in Kabul, Afghanistan.

When Lord Cranbrook was reviewing Hamilton's case he noted that the action was similar to that of John Cook and Reginald Hart, both of whom had been awarded the VC. The VC recommendation was sent in again on 28 September, but in order to avoid the precedent of appearing to award a posthumous VC, the submission was backdated to 1 September. Hamilton's award was gazetted on 7 October 1879. The VC medal was passed down through the family and is now in the Lord Ashcroft Gallery, Imperial War Museum, London.

Garrett O'Moore CREAGH, Kam Dakka, 21 April 1879

O'Moore Creagh (as he would be known) was born on 2 April 1848 in Cahirbane County Clare, Ireland, the son of Captain James Creagh RN and Grace Emily (née O'Moore). He was educated at a private school and at the Royal Military Academy Sandhurst. He entered the 95th Regiment of Foot in October 1866 with a purchase as ensign and was posted to India in 1869.

In June 1870, Creagh was promoted to lieutenant and joined the Bombay Staff Corps. He served for a short time with the Marine Battalion and the 25th Bombay

Garrett O'Moore Creagh.

Light Infantry, and was then appointed officiating adjutant to the Deoli Irregular Force, and station staff officer at Deoli. In 1871, he was selected as adjutant to the Merwara Battalion on its transfer to from civil to military establishment. He married Mary Letitia Longfield, but she died two years later.

In 1878, Creagh was promoted to captain and when the Merwara Battalion volunteered for service on the outbreak of the Afghan War, he was the only European officer present. He was second in command during the campaign in the Peshawar Valley Field Force, until March 1879.

O'Moore Creagh's grave, East Sheen Cemetery.

On 21 April 1879, at Kam Dakka, Captain Creagh was ordered to take a detachment of 150 men to protect the village against a threatened incursion of the Mohmands. He had to repel an attack by about 1,500 men; the inhabitants of the village had joined with the Mohmands. Creagh's force was compelled to retire, so he took up a position in the cemetery and held it, repulsing repeated attacks with the bayonet until the 10th Bengal Lancers arrived, charged the enemy, and routed them.

Creagh's VC was gazetted on 17 November 1879, but there is no record of an investiture. Following his award, he was appointed deputy assistant quartermaster general to the Kurram Field Force, and served with them until November 1880. He then served in the Zaimusht and Cham Kanni expeditions. On his promotion to brigade major, he returned to the Merwara Battalion. From 1882 to 1886, he was in command of the 44th Merwara Infantry, at which time he was given command of the 2nd Baluchis.

Creagh married Lilah Read in 1891 and they went on to have a son and a daughter. In 1895 he was appointed adjutant general of his division and in 1896, assistant quartermaster, Bombay Command. From 1898 to 1900, Creagh was political resident commanding in Aden. From 1900 to 1903, he commanded the China Field Force, after which he was given command of the 129th Baluchis. In 1907, he was made secretary to the Military

Department at the Indian Office. Promoted to general in 1907, Creagh was C-in-C India until 1914, and then ADC to King Edward VII.

Following his retirement, Creagh was editing *The Victoria Cross 1856–1920*, although sadly he did not live to see it completed.

O'Moore Creagh died on 9 August 1923 and was buried in East Sheen Cemetery, Surrey, Section B, Grave 193. His VC is held by the National Army Museum, London, England.

James William ADAMS, Killa Kazi, 11 December 1879

James Adams was born on 24 November 1839 in Cork, Ireland, the only son of Thomas O'Brien Adams, JP, and Elizabeth (née Williams). He was educated at Hamblin and Porter's Grammar School, Cork, and at Trinity College, Dublin, where he took his Bachelor of Arts degree. Adams was a keen sportsman in athletics and gymnastics; he was also a fine horseman.

James William Adams.

Adams was ordained as a deacon in 1863 and a priest in the following year, and was curate to the Reverend Warren at Hyde, Hampshire, until 1866. He wanted to travel to India, where, in October 1866, he became a chaplain in the Bengal Ecclesiastical Establishment, under Bishop Robert Milman, based in Calcutta. Shortly afterwards, Adams contracted a fever and was sent to Ceylon to recuperate. On his recovery, he was posted to Peshawar, and began to work with the troops stationed there. He did a great deal of work during the cholera outbreaks that regularly occurred in the camps. In 1870, he transferred to Allahabad, and was sent on special duty to Kashmir in 1874.

In January 1876, Adams was appointed to Meerut and in December given charge of the Cavalry and Artillery Camp for the Delhi Durbar assemblage, on the occasion of the Prince of Wales's visit. Then, in November 1877, he was summoned to join the Kurram Field Force, and accompanied the Kabul Field Force under Sir Donald Stewart and Sir

Frederick Roberts, vc, taking part in the march to Kandahar, and was present at a number of engagements.

At Killa Kazi, on 11 December 1879, some of the men from the 9th Lancers had fallen from their mounts into a wide ditch and were trapped underneath their horses. Well aware from the shouting and firing that the enemy were nearly upon them, Reverend Adams jumped into the water, pulled the men clear of their horses and escaped on foot. He was known by the men as the 'Fighting Parson'.

Lord Roberts recommended Adams for the VC, but was told it could not be given to him as the award was only for the army and navy. However, in 1881, the Queen signed an amendment to the Royal Warrant allowing members of the ecclesiastical establishment to be eligible for the award and Adams's VC was gazetted on 24 August 1881. It was presented to him on 1 December that year by the Queen at Windsor Castle.

Adams was married to Alice Mary (née Willshire) in August 1881 and they went on to have one daughter. In February 1883, he was sent to Naini Tal, Uttarakhand, on a two-year appointment, after which he was requested by Lord Roberts VC to accompany the Burma Field Force. In 1886, after twenty years' service in India, Adams returned to England and became the rector of Postwick, near Norwich, remaining there until 1894 due to ill health. He spent two years in Jersey, and some time working in Wimbotsham, Norfolk. In May 1900, he was appointed honorary chaplain to the Prince of Wales and, following the prince's accession as Edward VII, Adams was confirmed as honorary chaplain to the King. In 1902, Adams resigned and moved to Ashwell in Rutland.

James Adams died from acute neuritis on 24 October 1903 and was buried in St Mary's Churchyard, Ashwell. His VC is not publicly held. A brass plaque was dedicated in his honour by Sir Thomas Hare at the church in Stow Bardolph, Norfolk, where he lived for a time. Adams is one of only five civilians to have been awarded the VC, the others being William McDonell, Thomas Kavanagh, Ross Lowis Mangles and George Chicken.

Adams's grave, St Mary's Church, Ashwell.

Arthur George HAMMOND, Asmai Heights, 14 December 1879

Arthur Hammond was born on 28 September 1843 in Dawlish, Devon, the fifth son of Major Thomas John Hammond and Anne (née Warren). He was educated at King Edward VII School, Sherborne, Dorset, and entered the Addiscombe Military Seminary in February 1861. In June of the same year, Hammond was commissioned and was posted to India. On his arrival in Calcutta in December, he was attached to the 82nd Regiment of Foot.

In October 1862, Hammond joined the 12th Native Infantry and, following a successful examination in Hindustani, was posted to the Corps of Guides in September 1863. He was then involved in the Umbeyla Campaign, during which

Arthur George Hammond.

he commanded a detachment and held the fort at Mardan in the Valley of Peshawar. In May 1864, he was made quartermaster of his regiment and in June 1867, joined the Bengal Staff Corps. Having passed Military Surveying and Field Engineering at Roorkee College, he served in the Jowaki Campaign of 1877–78, and was mentioned in despatches.

During the Afghan War, he took part in the storming of Takht-i-Shah on 13 December and the Asmai Heights on 14 December 1879. Then Captain Hammond defended the top of the hill, single-handedly, with only a rifle and fixed bayonet against large numbers of Afghans, allowing the 72nd Highlanders and Guides to retire. On his retreat down the hill, he stopped to help carry a wounded sepoy when the Afghans were only 60 yards away and firing heavily all the time.

Hammond's VC was gazetted on 18 October 1881 and was presented to him on 1 December that year by the Queen at Windsor Castle. In June 1886, he married Edith Jane Wright and they went on to have three children. Hammond commanded the 3rd Sikhs during the Hazara Campaign of 1888 and was mentioned in despatches. On 12 April 1889, he was awarded the DSO for his actions on the North-West Frontier. He was appointed ADC to the Queen in 1890. Then he became commandant of the Queen's Own Corps of Guides, a post he held from 1891 to 1985.

In 1897, he was appointed brigadier general of the Assam Brigade, and commanded the Peshawar Column, and later the 3rd Brigade, Khyber Field Force, in the Tirah Campaign of 1897–98.

Arthur Hammond died on 20 April 1919 and was buried in St Michael's Churchyard, Camberley, Surrey. His VC is in the Lord Ashcroft Gallery, Imperial War Museum, London.

Hammond's grave, St Michael's Church, Camberley.

William John VOUSDEN, Asmai Heights, 14 December 1879

William Vousden was born on 20 September 1845 in Perth, Scotland, the son of Captain Thomas Vousden, late of the 51st Fusiliers, and Catherine (née Horrigan). He was educated at Hill's Establishment at Woolwich, and King's School, Canterbury. He entered the army as an ensign in January 1864, joining the 35th Regiment of Foot. In October 1867, he was promoted to lieutenant and transferred to the 5th Punjab Cavalry, and in due course was entered into the Bengal Staff Corps.

Vousden was promoted to captain in January 1876 and served in the two Afridi campaigns on the staff, and during the Afghan War with his regiment. He was present in the Khort Valley Expedition in January 1879,

William John Vousden.

and took part in the second campaign with Sir Frederick Roberts VC on the advance to Kabul.

On 14 December 1879, at the Asmai Heights, Captain Vousden charged with a small party into the centre of the retreating Kohistani force, who outnumbered them greatly. After rapidly charging through, backwards and forwards, cutting down thirty, five of whom he killed himself, Vousden and his party then swept off round the opposite side of a village and joined the rest of the troops.

Vousden was mentioned in despatches three times during the Afghan War and was promoted to brevet major. His VC was gazetted on 18 October 1881 and was presented to him on 24 May 1882 by the Lieutenant Governor of Bengal, the Honourable A.R. Thompson.

Vousden saw service in the Miranzai Expedition, the Tochi Field Force, the Tirah Campaign and on the North-West Frontier, during all of which he was mentioned in despatches.

William Vousden was married in 1891 to the daughter of Major General Drummond. In 1901, now a major general, he was given command of the Punjab Frontier Force and district. He died from dysentery on 12 November 1902 and was buried in Lahore Cemetery (now in Pakistan). His VC is not publicly held. His nephew, Arthur Borton, was also awarded the VC.

William St Lucien CHASE, Deh Khoja, 16 August 1880

William Chase was born on 2 July 1856 on the island of St Lucia, in the West Indies, the eldest son of Captain R.H. Chase, Commissary of Ordnance, and Susan (née Hill). He was educated privately, and entered the army in 1875, joining the 15th Regiment of Foot.

Chase was posted to India, where he served with the regimental HQ for two years and, on passing his exams with distinction, was admitted into the Bombay Staff Corps. He did his duty

William St Lucien Chase.

successfully at Poona, Ahmadabad, Baroda and Surat. During the Afghan War, he served with the 28th Bombay Native Infantry and accompanied the HQ of his regiment as part of the Kandahar Field Force.

He was present throughout the defence of Kandahar, and took part in the ill-fated sortie to Deh Khoja on 16 August 1880, when Lieutenant Colonel Newport and fifty men were killed or wounded. Lieutenant Chase, with Private Thomas Ashford (of the Royal Fusiliers), went to the aid of Private Massey, who had taken cover in a blockhouse and was wounded. Chase and Ashford carried Massey for over 200 yards. Bullets were raising dust all around them and they fell three times, but they eventually reached safety.

For this action, both Chase and Ashford were awarded the Victoria Cross. After Chase's regiment left Kandahar, he was given command of the Killa Abdulla post, until he was relieved in November 1880. Then he was sent to command the post of Gatai, on the lines of communication, remaining there until all the troops of the Kandahar Evacuating Force had passed through en route to India.

Chase's VC was gazetted on 7 October 1881 and was presented to him on 23 January 1882 by the GOC, Bombay, at Poona. In 1884, he served in the Zhob Campaign, in the Chin Lushai Expedition, and the advance on Fort Haka. In 1893, he took part in the Naga Hills Campaign and Manipur, in the 1897 Mohmand Expedition, the Tirah campaigns of 1897 and 1898, and was present at the actions of the Sampagha Pass, the occupation of Maiden and Bagh Valley, and operations in the Dwatoi Defile, Rejghul Valley and Bara Valley, being mentioned in despatches numerous times. He later commanded the 28th Bombay Pioneers and was made brevet colonel.

William Chase died on 24 June 1908 and was buried in the English Cemetery, Quetta, Pakistan. His VC is held by the Army Museum of Western Australia, Fremantle.

Karen-Ni Expedition, 1888–89

Following the British victory in the Third Anglo-Burmese War, many of the natives refused to accept the authority of the occupying British Army and resorted to guerrilla action. They were led mainly by former officers of the disbanded Burmese Royal Army, village headmen, and even some Royal princes. Two punitive expeditions were needed to crush the rebels.

John CRIMMIN, Lwekaw, 1 January 1889

John Crimmin was born on 19 March 1859 in Dublin. He studied medicine, becoming Licentiate of the Royal College of Physicians, Licentiate of the Royal College of Surgeons, and Doctor of Public Health in Ireland, before entering the Bombay Medical Service in 1882. He served in Burma from 1886 to 1889 with the Karen Field Force as senior medical officer.

On 1 January 1889, at Lwekaw, Lieutenant Tighe and four men charged into a large body of the enemy who were moving off from the Karen left flank, and two men were wounded. Surgeon Crimmin ran out to attend to the wounded men, in the midst of a skirmish with bullets flying all around him. Crimmin then joined the firing line, which had by then come up. Then, shortly afterwards, they were engaged in driving the bandits away from small clumps of trees in which the enemy took shelter. Crimmin was attending to a wounded man near one of these clumps of trees when several bandits attacked him. Crimmin jumped to his feet, ran his sword through one of the assailants and engaged boldly with another, causing them to flee into the bush.

John Crimmin.

His VC was gazetted on 17 September 1889 and was presented to him later that year by the Commander-in-Chief, Bombay, the Duke of Connaught, in India. Crimmin was promoted to major in 1894, and lieutenant colonel in 1902. He was appointed Civil Surgeon at Rutnagberry and Health Officer for the Port of Bombay. In October 1913, he was promoted to colonel.

John Crimmin died on 20 February 1945 and was buried in Wells Cemetery, Somerset, Section F-D-3, Grave 274. His VC is not publicly held.

Chapter 6

Hunza-Nagar Campaign, India 1891–92

In 1891, following tribal unrest in the Hunza-Nagar District, an expedition was sent to the mountain region to storm the fort at Nilt.

Fenton John AYLMER, Nilt Fort, 2 December 1891

Fenton Aylmer was born on 5 April 1862 in Hastings, Sussex, the second son of Captain Fenton John Aylmer (of the 97th Regiment) and Isabella Eleanor (née Darling). His father was killed in action on 9 April 1862, soon after his second son's birth. Fenton was educated privately, joined the Royal Engineers as a Gentleman Cadet in 1880 and was promoted to lieutenant in July. He served in both the Burma Expedition of 1885–87 and the Hazara Expedition of 1891, and was mentioned in despatches during both.

Fenton John Aylmer.

On 2 December 1891, at the Nilt Fort, Captain Aylmer was serving in the Corps of Royal Engineers (attached to the Bengal Sappers and Miners) when, during the assault, he forced open the Inner Gate with guncotton. Aylmer was shot in the leg and hit on the hand by a rock dropped from above. However, he dashed through the gate and engaged the enemy hand-to-hand, firing nineteen rounds with his revolver, killing several of the enemy, until he collapsed from loss of blood.

His VC was gazetted on 12 July 1892 and was presented to him on 28 October the same year by the GOC, Rawalpindi. Following his promotion to major, Aylmer served in the Isazai Expedition of 1892 and the Chitral Expedition of 1895, again being mentioned in despatches, and was made a brevet colonel. By the outbreak of the First World War, he had been promoted to lieutenant colonel.

Aylmer was put in charge of the Tigris Corps, tasked with ending the siege of Kut in Mesopotamia. With 20,000 men, he left Basra in late December 1915 and arrived at Sheikh Sa'ad on 3 January 1916. After two days of fighting, the Ottoman Army withdrew. British casualties were about 4,000. On 13 January at the Battle of Wadi, the British suffered 1,600 casualties but carried the position.

Having received reinforcements, Aylmer passed on to Hanna and on 21 January assaulted the position without success, suffering a further 2,700 casualties. Following this, he was reinforced again and spent much of February resting his men. Then, with time running out for the garrison at Kut, he lunched a two-pronged attack at the Sinn Abtar Redoubt and the Dujaila Redoubt on 7 March. Both assaults ended in failure, with his force suffering another 4,000 casualties. Shortly after this, Aylmer was replaced; he would not command in battle again.

Aylmer married Lady Risley (born Elsie Julie Oppermann), with whom he had had a long-running affair, which was well known within Indian society at the time.

Fenton Aylmer retired from the army in 1919, although from 1922 until his death on 3 September 1935, he was Commandant of the Royal Engineers. His ashes were scattered at Golders Green Crematorium, London. His VC is held by the Royal Engineers Museum, Gillingham, Kent.

North-West Frontier, 1895

In 1889, the British entered the Chitral District of India (now Pakistan) and established an agency, to which the local tribesmen were very hostile. In 1895, the Chitral chief was murdered. This signalled the start of fighting among local tribes. When Umrah Khan, ruler of the Narai District, invaded Chitral, Britain sent in 400 men to restore order.

Harry Frederick WHITCHURCH, Chitral Fort, 3 March 1895

Harry Whitchurch was born on 22 September 1866 in London, the son of Frederick Whitchurch. Educated in London, France and Germany, he entered a medical career in St Bartholomew's Hospital, London, in 1883. Whitchurch served in the 1892 Expedition to Lushai.

On 3 March 1895, Surgeon Captain Whitchurch was serving in the Indian Medical Service when, during a sortie from Fort Chitral, he went out to the assistance of Captain Baird (of the 24th Bengal Infantry) who was lying wounded 1½ miles from the fort. The wounded man was placed in a dhooli, but on the return journey three of the bearers were killed and the fourth wounded, so Whitchurch took the wounded man on his back and carried him for some distance. They were fired on incessantly the whole way, but he eventually succeeded in getting them back to the fort, although they were nearly all wounded and Baird died.

Harry Frederick Whitchurch.

Whitchurch's VC was gazetted on 16 July 1895 and was presented to him on 27 July that same year by the Queen at Osborne House, Isle of Wight. During 1897–98, Whitchurch took part in the defence of the Malakand and the relief of Chakdara, as well as the engagement at Landakai on the North-West Frontier. In 1901, he was in China and took part in the relief of the Chinese Legation during the Boxer Rebellion, following which he was posted to India, where he served with the 1st Gurkha Rifles.

Harry Whitchurch died from enteric fever on 16 August 1907 and was buried in Dharamsala Churchyard, Punjab. His VC is in the Lord Ashcroft Gallery, Imperial War Museum, London.

Chapter 6

Malakand Frontier War, 1897–98

In 1894, the new frontier between India and Afghanistan was finalised by Colonel Sir Mortimer Durand's commission, bringing many tribes under Britain's influence. These tribes were extremely hostile to this annexation and widespread unrest followed. In 1897, the Amir of Afghanistan published a fiercely anti-Christian work in his assumed capacity as the King of Islam. This incited uprisings against the British garrisons all along the frontier.

Edmond William COSTELLO, Malakand, 26 July 1897

Edmond Costello was born on 7 August 1873 in Sheikhbudia, on the North-West Frontier of India, the son of Colonel C.P. Costello (of the Indian Medical Service) and Mrs Costello (née Harkan). He was educated at Beaumont College, Stonyhurst College and the Royal Military College Sandhurst. In 1892, Costello was commissioned into the West Yorkshire Regiment, but transferred to the Indian Army in 1894, being posted to the 22nd Punjab Infantry.

On 26 July 1897, at Malakand, Lieutenant Costello went out from the hospital enclosure and, with the help of two sepoys, brought in a wounded lance havildar lying some 60 yards away on a football field. The field was overrun with the swordsmen and was being raked with fire from both sides.

Edmond William Costello.

Costello's VC was gazetted on 9 November 1897 and was presented to him on 2 December 1897 by the Queen at Windsor Castle. In 1900, Costello was appointed adjutant of his regiment and promoted to captain the following year. He worked as a recruiting officer until 1908, when he served in the Mohmand operation. He was promoted to major in 1910, and in 1913 entered the Indian Staff College at Quetta, graduating just prior to the start of the First World War.

In 1914, he re-joined his regiment as second in command and was posted to Mesopotamia as part of the 17th Indian Infantry Brigade, where he served throughout the war. Costello was promoted to brevet colonel in 1916 and was awarded the DSO in 1917. In May 1918, he took command of the 12th Indian Infantry Brigade with the rank of lieutenant colonel. He was mentioned five times in despatches and was also awarded the French Croix de Guerre.

In 1919, Costello was promoted to brevet colonel and joint commander of the Indian contingent at the Peace March in London. He was promoted to colonel in March 1920, although he had held the acting rank of brigadier general since 1918. He was appointed Commander of the Royal Victorian Order in the 1920 New Year Honours. In March 1921, he was posted to Palestine as temporary commander of the Palestine Defence Force, and remained there to command a brigade in 1922. Costello retired the following year and became Director of Military Studies at the University of Cambridge.

Edmond Costellow died on 7 June 1949 and was buried in St Mark's Parish Churchyard, Hadlow Down, Sussex. His VC is held by the National Army Museum, London.

Costello's grave, St Mark's Parish Church, Hadlow Down.

Tirah Campaign, 1897–98

In a spate of individual uprisings by Afghans against the British, fighting broke out in the Tirah region. This was put down by General Sir William Lockhart's punitive expedition.

Robert Bellew ADAMS, Nawa Kili, 17 August 1897

Robert Adams was born on 26 July 1856 in Muree, India, the son of Major Robert Roy Adams (of the Bengal Staff Corps) and Frances

Charlotte (née Bellow). Major Adams was murdered by a fanatic in Peshawar in 1865, when his son was just 9 years old. Young Robert was educated privately before attending the Forest School, Walthamstow, London.

Adams was commissioned a sub lieutenant in the 12th Regiment of Foot in September 1876 and served in India until 1879, when he was promoted to lieutenant. He transferred into the 3rd Punjab Cavalry and served with the Queen's Own Corps of Guides during the Afghan War of 1879–80. He marched with the corps to Kabul, and was present at all the subsequent operations. Adams was appointed the officiating adjutant of the corps in July 1880 and was mentioned in despatches. He was promoted to captain in 1887.

Robert Bellew Adams.

In 1895, Adams served with the Chitral Relief Force in command of the Guides Cavalry and, following the death in action of Lieutenant Colonel Battye, commanded the Corps of Guides Infantry. He was present at the storming of the Malakand Pass, the action near Khar, at the passage of the Swat River, and at Mamugai. Adams was mentioned in despatches twice and was given the brevet rank of lieutenant colonel with the substantive rank of major in September 1896.

On 17 August 1897, at Nawa Kili, while serving with the Malakand Force, Brevet Lieutenant Colonel Adams, with the help of Lieutenant Viscount Alexander Fincastle, Lieutenant Hector MacLean and five guides, went to the assistance of Lieutenant Greaves (correspondent for *The Times* of India), who had fallen wounded from his horse and had been set upon by the enemy with tulwars and knives. The enemy were driven away and Adams held them off while Fincastle and MacLean attempted to move Greaves, but he was shot and killed. MacLean was mortally wounded. Along with Robert Adams, Fincastle and MacLean were also awarded the VC for this action.

Adams's VC was gazetted on 9 November 1897 and was presented to him on 9 July 1898 by the Queen at Windsor Castle, following which he returned to India and took part in the Buner Field Force, being mentioned in despatches. In April 1899, Adams was appointed commander of the Queen's Own Corps of Guides, and in September 1901 he was appointed ADC to the King. He was promoted to major general in 1906, but an illness brought on by an accident in 1908 forced him to retire in 1911.

Robert Adams died on 13 February 1928 and his ashes are interred in Tomnahurich Cemetery, Inverness. His VC is not publicly held. His second cousin, Edward Bellew, was also awarded the VC.

Alexander Edward Murray Viscount FINCASTLE, Nawa Kili, 17 August 1897

Alexander Edward Murray was born on 22 April 1871 in London, the son of Charles, 7th Duke of Dunmore, and Lady Gertrude (née Coke). Alexander immediately took the title of Viscount Fincastle. He was educated privately, including at Eton prior to joining the army in 1891, and was promoted to lieutenant in 1894.

Fincastle was posted to India and became ADC to the Viceroy of India between 1895 and 1897. He served in the Dongola Expedition in 1896, and the Malakand Frontier War, during which his horse was shot from under him.

Alexander Edward Murray Viscount Fincastle.

On 17 August 1897, at Nawa Kili, Lieutenant Fincastle was serving in the Corps of Guides Cavalry when he, along with Brevet Lieutenant Colonel Robert Adams, Lieutenant Hector MacLean and five guides, went to the assistance of Lieutenant Greaves (correspondent for *The Times* of India), who had fallen wounded from his horse and had been set upon by the enemy with tulwars and knives. The enemy were driven away and Adams held them off while Fincastle and MacLean attempted to move Greaves, but he was shot and killed. MacLean was also mortally wounded during this action.

Fincastle's VC was gazetted on 9 November 1897 (the same day as Adams's) and was presented to him on 28 February 1898 by the Queen at Windsor Castle. He was promoted to captain in 1899 and served on the staff throughout the Second Boer War with the 6th (Inniskilling) Dragoons and 16th Lancers, and was mentioned in despatches. He commanded the Imperial Yeomanry in the immediate aftermath of the war.

In January 1904, Fincastle married Lucinda Dorothea Kemble and they went on to have one son and two daughters. He succeeded his father, becoming the 8th Earl of Dunmore in 1907. As Lord Dunmore, he served in the First World War, was wounded, awarded the DSO and mentioned in despatches four times. After the war, he commanded the 16th Lancers with the rank of lieutenant colonel.

Alexander Fincastle died on 29 January 1962 and was cremated under the name Murray. His ashes were scattered at Golders Green Crematorium, Section 4-C, Garden of Remembrance, Hoop Lane, London. His VC is not publicly held.

Hector Lachlan Stewart MacLEAN, Nawa Kili, 17 August 1897

Hector MacLean was born on 13 September 1870 in Bannu, on the North-West Frontier of India (now Pakistan), the oldest son of Major General Charles Smith MacLean and Margaret MacQueen (née Bairnsfather). He was educated at Fettes College, in Edinburgh, before joining the Northumberland Fusiliers as a second lieutenant in April 1889.

Posted to India, MacLean became Probationer for the Indian Staff Corps in 1891, and in March joined the Corps of Guides. He took part in the Hazara Expedition of 1891 and the Chitral Expedition of 1895, and was appointed adjutant to the Corps of Guides in 1896.

Hector Lachlan Stewart MacLean.

On 17 August 1897, at Nawa Kili, Lieutenant Maclean, with Brevet Lieutenant Colonel Robert Adams, Lieutenant Alexander Fincastle and five guides, went to the assistance of Lieutenant Greaves (correspondent for *The Times* of India) who had fallen from his horse and was set upon by the enemy with tulwars and knives. The enemy were driven away and Adams held them off while Fincastle and MacLean attempted to move Greaves, but he was shot and killed.

Hector MacLean was also mortally wounded during this action and was buried in the Guides Cemetery, St Alban's Churchyard, Mardan, now in Pakistan. He was recommended for the VC but it was not awarded posthumously at that time (although there is nothing in the Royal Warrant to this effect, but it had been practice not to do so). Once a change of policy came into effect (after the posthumous award to Lord Roberts in 1900), MacLean's VC was gazetted on 15 January 1907, along with a number of other backdated awards. His VC is in the Lord Ashcroft Gallery, Imperial War Museum, London.

Mohmand Campaign India 1897–98

On 8 August 1897, Mohmand tribesmen raided Shabkadar, near Peshawar, but the means to crush this uprising were already in the region. Two divisions of Sir Bindon Blood's expedition had advanced from Malakand and it would be these men who would do the work.

Thomas Colclough WATSON, Mohmand Valley, 16/17 September 1897

Thomas Colclough Watson was born on 11 April 1867 in Velsen, in the Netherlands, the son of Thomas Colclough Watson and Eliza Holmes Watson (née Reed). He was educated at King Edward VI Grammar School in Louth, Lincolnshire, and abroad. He entered the Royal Engineers in February 1888 and was posted to India. In January 1892, he married Edythe Welchman in Meerut and they had

Thomas Colclough Watson.

one son, born in 1892. Edythe was awarded the Royal Red Cross for her actions during the Black Mountains Expedition in 1888. (The only other British officer who was awarded the VC (in 1858) and his spouse the RRC were Lord Frederick Sleigh Roberts and his wife Nora Henrietta (née Bews).)

On the night of 16/17 September 1897 in the Mohmand Valley, Lieutenant Watson was in command of the 4th Bengal Sappers and Miners when he led a party of volunteers, including Lieutenant James Colvin and Corporal James Smith of the East Kent Regiment (The Buffs), in a bayonet charge on the burning village of Bilot to try to dislodge the enemy, who were inflicting losses on British troops. After Watson was wounded in the hand, he made two more attempts to take the village. He did not desist in his efforts until he was more severely wounded and had to be carried back. Colvin then made a further two attempts on the village. Corporal Smith, although injured, assisted in removing the wounded to shelter. Smith was also awarded the VC for this action.

Watson's VC was gazetted on 20 May 1898 and was presented to him on 23 June 1898 by the Queen at Windsor Castle. He remained in the Royal Engineers and served during the First World War in Mesopotamia, with the rank of lieutenant colonel. In June 1915, he became ill and was invalided home. He never fully recovered and died on 15 June 1917.

Thomas Watson was cremated and his ashes interred at Golders Green Crematorium, London, Niche 1153. His VC is in the Lord Ashcroft Gallery, Imperial War Museum, London.

Watson's ashes, Golders Green Crematorium, London.

James Morris Colquhoun COLVIN, Mohmand Valley, 16/17 September 1897

James Colvin was born on 26 August 1870 in Bijnor, India, the son of James Colquhoun Colvin (of the Bengal Civil Service) and Camilla Fanny Marie (née Morris). He was educated at Charterhouse School in Surrey and the Royal Military Academy, Woolwich. He entered the Royal Engineers in July 1889 and, after being posted to India, joined the Bengal Sappers and Miners, and took part in the Chitral Expedition of 1895.

On the night of 16/17 September 1897 in the Mohmand Valley, Lieutenant Colvin was in a party of volunteers, including Lieutenant Thomas Watson and Corporal James Smith of the East Kent Regiment (The Buffs), in a bayonet charge on the burning village of Bilot to try to dislodge the enemy, who were inflicting losses on British troops. After Watson was wounded in the hand, he made two more attempts to take the village. He did not desist in his efforts until severely wounded and had to be carried back. Colvin then made a further two attempts on the village. Corporal Smith, although injured, assisted in removing the wounded to shelter. Smith was also awarded the VC.

James Morris Colquhoun Colvin.

Colvin's VC was gazetted on 20 May 1898 and was presented to him on 19 July that year by the Queen at Windsor Castle. He served in the Boer War as a Special Service Officer and on the staff; he was also given the brevet rank of major. In January 1904, he married Katherine Way and they went on to have three children. In 1909, Colvin passed out of the Staff College in Camberley, and was a general staff officer at Quetta from 1911 to 1915. He was promoted to lieutenant colonel in 1917 and became commandant to the 3rd Sappers and Miners in Kirkee, India. He retired from the army as a colonel and returned to England.

James Colvin died on 7 December 1945 and his ashes were scattered at Ipswich Crematorium, Suffolk, December Section, Old Garden of Rest. His VC is held by his family.

Chapter 7

Second Boer War, 1899–02

Having subjugated the southern African tribes to create the colonies of Natal and Cape Colony, Britain now wanted to bring together her colonies and Boer republics, the Orange Free State and the Transvaal into one British-dominated South African Federation.

The Dutch-speaking Boers, whose population was now in the majority, had already suffered incursions from outsiders, mostly Britain. After gold was discovered in the Transvaal in 1886, the Boers were unwilling to lose their independence.

Francis 'Frank' Aylmer MAXWELL, Korn Spruit, 31 March 1900

Francis Maxwell was born on 7 September 1871 in Guildford, Surrey, the son of Surgeon Major Thomas Maxwell. He joined the Royal Essex Regiment in November 1893 but transferred to the Indian Staff Corps in December. Two years later, he served in the Waziristan and Chitral expeditions of 1894–95, where he displayed great gallantry in the recovery of the body of Lieutenant Colonel F.D. Battye of the Corps of Guides, under fire, for which, although recommended, he received no award. Maxwell also served in the Tirah Expedition 1897–98, for which he was awarded the DSO.

Francis 'Frank' Aylmer Maxwell.

In 1900, he volunteered to take remounts to South Africa, and not long after became attached to Roberts's Light Horse.

On 31 March 1900, 'Q' and 'U' batteries were ambushed by the Boers, with the loss of most of the baggage and five guns of the leading battery. When the alarm was given, 'Q' Battery went into action under Major Phipps-Hornby until he ordered the guns to retire. Maxwell volunteered to help the men to save the guns. Five times he went out under a hail of bullets, bringing in two guns and three limbers, one of which was dragged back by hand.

Maxwell's grave, Ypres Reservoir Cemetery, Belgium.

He was one of those trying to bring in the last gun until the attempt had to be abandoned.

Maxwell's VC was gazetted on 6 March 1900 and was presented to him on 14 August 1901 by the Duke of Cornwall & York (later George V) at Pietermaritzburg. Maxwell was appointed ADC to Lord Kitchener, Chief-of-Staff, South Africa, on 1 November 1900. Kitchener liked his outspokenness and dubbed him 'The Brat', but the two got on very well together. After the war Maxwell returned to England on board the SS *Orotava* with Kitchener. In November 1902, the now Captain Maxwell was again appointed ADC to Kitchener and sailed with him to India. In 1905, he attended the Staff College at Camberley. In 1906, he married Charlotte Alice Hamilton and they went on to have two daughters. In 1910–16, Major Maxwell was military secretary to Lord Hardinge, Governor General of India. During the First World War, he commanded the 12th Battalion of the Middlesex Regiment and was awarded a Bar to his DSO.

On 21 September 1917, Brigadier General Frank Maxwell was commanding the 27th Infantry Brigade, 9th Scottish Division, when he was shot and killed by a sniper near Ypres. He was one of the most senior officers to be KIA. He was buried in Ypres Reservoir Cemetery, North Ypres, Belgium, Plot I, Row A, Grave 37. His VC is in the Lord Ashcroft Gallery, Imperial War Museum, London.

Fifth Ashanti War 1900–01

Being first suppressed in 1874, the Ashanti people of Gambia had risen again in 1895. This was crushed and a resentful peace followed until 1900, when the British decided to capture the symbolic 'Golden Stool' – the royal throne of the kings of the Ashanti people and their ultimate symbol of power in Ashanti.

Charles John MELLISS, Obassa, 30 September 1900

Charles Melliss was born on 12 September 1862 in Mhow, Madhya Pradesh, India, the son of Lieutenant General George Julius Melliss of the Indian Staff Corps. Charles was educated at Wellington College, Berkshire, and the Royal Military Academy Sandhurst, before joining the East Yorkshire Regiment in 1882. He was posted to India, where he joined the Indian Staff Corps in 1884, and served in East Africa against the Mazrui tribesmen in 1896.

In 1897–98, Melliss served on the North-West Frontier, being present during the operations in the Kurram Valley in August and September 1897. He also served in the Tirah Campaign of 1897–98, taking part in the action at Dargai and in the operations in the Bara Valley. Promoted to captain, he served with the Northern Nigeria Regiment with the West African Frontier Force from 1898–1902.

Charles John Melliss.

On 30 September 1900, at Obassa, Captain Melliss collected as many men as he could and led a charge through the bush. Although wounded, he fought hand-to-hand, during which he grappled with one of the enemy before running him through with his sword. His bold rush caused panic among the enemy, who were pursued by the Sikhs as they fled.

Melliss's VC was gazetted on 15 January 1901 and was presented to him on 12 October 1901 by Edward VII at St James's Palace, London. Earlier that year he was married to Kathleen Walter. From 1902–04, Melliss served in East Africa, taking part in operations in Somaliland, and was mentioned in despatches. At some time in 1903 he was attacked by a lion while hunting, almost losing an arm. From 1906–10, he commanded the 53rd Sikh Frontier Force, and from 1907–12 was ADC to Edward VII.

In 1914, Melliss was attached to the 6th (Poona) Division as it moved into the Ottoman province of Basra, in southern Iraq. In April 1915, he was instrumental in the victory at Shaiba, and also fought at Ctesiphon, the furthest his division would advance. After Ctesiphon, General Townsend ordered a retreat, pursued by the Ottomans until they reached Kut-al-Amara, where the 6th was ordered to dig in and await relief. Melliss fell ill during the siege and was still in hospital when Townsend surrendered on 29 April 1916.

Transported upriver by steamship, Melliss remained in hospital and was unable to travel as the survivors were marched north towards Anatolia. When Melliss was well enough to follow, he was allowed an escort and better supplies because he was a senior officer. Along the way, they encountered sick and dying men. Melliss took any survivors he found with him; at each stop, he insisted that these men, both British and Indian, be admitted to hospital.

Melliss spent two and a half years in Turkish prisons. For his services during the war, he was mentioned in despatches five times, and was knighted in 1915. After his release, he returned to England and rose to the rank of major general before his retirement.

Charles Melliss died on 6 June 1936 and was buried in St Peter's Churchyard, Frimley, Surrey. His VC is held by Wellington College, Crowthorne, Berkshire.

Melliss's grave, St Peter's Church, Frimley.

Second Somaliland Expedition, 1902

Since the mid-nineteenth century, Britain had been securing territory in Somaliland and defining its borders with France, Italy and Abyssinia. The majority of local tribal chiefs accepted Britain's protection, but the most belligerent chief was Mohammed bin Abdullah, dubbed the 'Mad Mullah'. He mustered an army of 15,000 dervishes. In 1899, bin Abdullah declared himself Mahdi and launched attacks on pro-British tribes. These tribes asked for British protection and Colonel E.J. Swayne was sent to help with an army of Somali levies.

Alexander Stanhope COBBE, Erego, 6 October 1902

Alexander Cobbe was born on 5 June 1870 in Naini Tal, India, one of seven children of Lieutenant Colonel Sir Alexander Hugh Cobbe and Emily Barbara (née Jones). He was educated at Eagle House School, Wimbledon, Wellington College in Crowthorne, Berkshire, and the Royal Military Academy Sandhurst, from where he passed out in 1889. At 19, Cobbe was commissioned a lieutenant in the South Wales Borderers (formerly the 24th Regiment of Foot). He was promoted to lieutenant in 1892 and joined the Indian Staff Corps.

Alexander Stanhope Cobbe.

He took part in the Chitral Expedition of 1895 and in July 1900 was commanding the Central African Regiment with the brevet rank of major. He took part in the Third Ashanti War and in January 1902 was given the brevet rank of lieutenant colonel and appointed commandant of the 1st (Central Africa) Battalion, the King's Rifles.

On 6 October 1902, at Erego, when some of the companies had retired, Captain Cobbe was left alone in front of the line with a maxim gun. Without any assistance, he brought in the gun and used it most effectively at a most critical time. He then went out under heavy fire and carried back a wounded orderly who was lying 20 yards from the enemy.

Cobbe's VC was gazetted on 20 January 1903 and was presented to him on 22 February that year by Major General William Manning (also spelt Mannering) at Obbia, Somaliland. He married Winifred Ada Bowen in 1910 and they went on to have two daughters. Serving primarily in staff positions in India, Cobbe was promoted to major, and returned to the War Office in London in 1912.

Cobbe's grave, St Peter's Church, Sharnbrook.

In 1914, Cobbe was appointed to serve with the BEF in 1914, and was then sent back to India. Reaching the rank of major general, he served thereafter in Mesopotamia under Sir Frederick Maude. With the III (Indian) Corps, he saw a run of success at Kut-al-Amara in February 1917, and the capture of Baghdad the following month. He played a notable role in the success at Samarrah in April and, at Ramadi in September 1917. Cobbe also helped to defeat a Turkish force at Sharqat in October 1918. He was appointed military secretary at the India Office after the war and was promoted to full general in 1924. From 1926 to 1930, he was in charge of the Northern Command in India, but returned to the India Office in 1930.

Alexander Cobbe died on 29 June 1931. He was buried in St Peter's Churchyard, Sharnbrook, Bedfordshire. His VC is held by the Royal Welsh Regimental Museum in Brecon, Powys.

Third Somaliland Expedition, 1903–04

As the Mullah retreated, it became apparent that the Somali levies were not seasoned enough to deal with the threat he posed, so a much bigger force was sent to the region.

George Murray ROLLAND, Daratoleh, 22 April 1903

George Rolland was born on 12 May 1869 in Wellington, Tamil Nadu, India, the son of Major Patrick Rolland RA and Albinia (née Crofton), a successful novelist. George was educated at Harrow and the Royal Military Academy Sandhurst, and on passing out in November 1889, was commissioned a second lieutenant in the Bedfordshire Regiment. He was promoted to lieutenant in 1891 and to captain in November 1900.

George Murray Rolland.

Rolland was adjutant of the 1st Bombay Grenadiers from 1894 to 1901, and in August he joined the Indian Army. He served with the Somaliland Field Force from October 1902 to June 1903, acting as intelligence officer to the Berbera Bohottle Flying Column and staff officer to the column under command of Major John Gough VC.

On 22 April 1903, at Daratoleh, Captain Rolland, along with Captain Walker and four others, was in the rearguard under heavy fire from the pursuing enemy. When Captain Bruce was shot through the body, Rolland ran 500 yards to fetch help, while Walker kept up a desperate fire to keep the enemy at bay. When Rolland returned with the column commander, Major John Gough (of the Rifle Brigade), they helped lift Bruce onto a camel. The enemy remained in close pursuit for a further three hours, during which time Bruce was wounded again and died. Gough was also awarded the VC for this action.

Rolland's VC was gazetted on 7 August 1903 and was presented to him on 30 November 1903 by the officer commanding at Dehra Dun, India. In 1906, he joined the Nagpur Volunteer Rifles as adjutant and was promoted to major the following year.

George Rolland died on 8 July 1910 from a fractured skull following a fall. He was buried in Takli Cemetery, C of E Section, Nagpur, India. His VC is in the Lord Ashcroft Gallery, Imperial War Museum, London.

Fourth Somaliland Expedition, 1903–04

In an effect to destroy the Mullah's power once and for all, some 8,000 British troops under Major General C. Egerton were sent to the region.

Herbert Augustine CARTER, Jidballi, 19 December 1903

Herbert Carter was born on 26 May 1874 in Exeter, Devon, second son of the Reverend Conway R.D. Carter. He was educated privately, and was commissioned into the Duke of Cornwall's Light Infantry in May 1897. He served throughout the Tirah Campaign of 1897–98 under General Sir William Lockhart. In 1899, he was transferred to the Indian Army, joining the Indian Staff Corps.

In 1901, Carter was seconded for active service in Somaliland with the King's African Rifles. On 19 December 1903, at Jidballi, during a reconnaissance when two sections were falling back, Lieutenant Carter rode back 400 yards towards a large force of dervishes to assist Private Jai Singh, who had lost his horse. The private was so badly wounded it took Carter three attempts to lift him onto his horse. Without Carter's help, Private Singh almost certainly would have been killed.

Herbert Augustine Carter.

Carter's VC was gazetted on 9 December 1904 and was presented to him on 31 January 1905 by Major R.W. Falcon in Wadamago, Somaliland. In 1908, Carter was appointed Officer Commanding, Indian Contingent, King's African Rifles and proceeded to India to raise a new contingent. He returned to Somaliland in 1909 and served throughout the East Africa Campaign under Colonel John Gough, vc. In 1910, he was appointed to the Egyptian Army, attached to the 15th Sudanese, and was posted to the Blue Nile District as commandant.

Carter returned to England to marry Helen Lillian Wilmot Ware in February 1911, following which he resigned his appointment in the

Egyptian Army and joined the 101st Grenadiers for duty in Bangalore, Karnataka. In 1913, he was appointed attaché to the Army Headquarters Staff, Simla, in the state of Himachal Pradesh.

Carter was on home leave in 1914 when the First World War broke out and he served with the 10th and 16th Service battalions, Durham Light Infantry. In 1915, he joined the Indian Expeditionary Force and went with them to British East Africa. Arriving in Mombasa, Kenya, Carter contracted a fever, but took command of the 40th Pathans and was soon marching with them to the relief of Mwelo Mdogo. Tragically, the fever worsened and, as a result, Carter died on 13 January 1916. He was returned to England and buried in the churchyard of St Ercus, St Erth, Cornwall. His VC is held by the Duke of Cornwall's Light Infantry Museum, Bodmin, Cornwall.

Carter's grave, St Ercus Church, St Erth.

First World War, 1914–18

The causes of the First World War are well known. The Austro-Hungarian Archduke Ferdinand was assassinated in Sarajevo, in Bosnia and Herzegovina, on 28 June 1914. Austria-Hungary turned to Germany, which, on 6 July, confirmed that it would back Austria-Hungary in reprisals against the Serbs. The war might have ended as a local Balkan skirmish if it were not for a series of complex treaties that locked countries together.

On 30 July, Austria-Hungary declared war on Serbia. Russia and France, linked by treaty, began to mobilise. Germany presented ultimatums to Russia and France, threatening war if they did not demobilise. On 1 August, Germany declared war on Russia and the next day entered Luxembourg. On 3 August, Germany declared war on France, and a day later, German troops entered neutral Belgium. Britain, who had promised to protect Belgium's neutrality, declared war on Germany. Austria-Hungary declared war on Russia the same day. Five days later, France declared war on Austria-Hungary.

KHUDADAD KHAN, Hollebeke, Belgium, 31 October 1914

Khudadad Khan was born on 20 October 1888 in Dab Village, Chakwal, India (now Pakistan). Almost nothing is known about his family or early life. Although he served in a Baluchi regiment, he was a Pathan. Very few Baluchi served in the Indian Army and the Balochistan regiments were made up of men from various tribes from within the India frontier. Khudadad Khan was mobilised in August 1914 at Ferozepore in the Punjab.

In October 1914, the Germans launched a major offensive in order to capture the vital port of Nieuport in

Khudadad Khan.

northern Belgium in what became known as the First Battle of Ypres. Khudadad Khan's regiment, the 129th Duke of Connaught's Own Baluchi, were rushed to the front to support the hard-pressed British.

On 31 October 1914, at Hollebeke, after two companies of the 129th were overwhelmed, suffering heavy casualties, Sepoy Khudadad Khan's machine-gun team, along with one other, kept up a steady fire all day, preventing the German breakthrough. Eventually, the other machine gun was disabled by a shell but Khudadad Khan kept on firing his gun until all his comrades were killed. Badly wounded himself, he was left for dead by the Germans but managed to crawl back to his unit.

Khan's VC was gazetted on 7 December 1914, making him the first native Indian to be awarded the medal. He was presented with his VC on 26 January 1915 by George V, most probably while still in hospital in England.

Khan served on the North-West Frontier of India in 1919 and received a Viceroy's Commission to Subedar in 1929. He attended the VC centenary at Hyde Park, London, on 26 June 1956, as well as the first VC Association Reunion at the Café Royal, London, on 24 July 1958. He also became a committee member of the VC and GC Association.

Khudadad Khan died on 8 March 1971 and was buried in Rukhan Village Cemetery, near Chakwal, Pakistan. His VC is in the Lord Ashcroft Gallery, Imperial War Museum, London.

DARWAN SINGH NEGI, Festubert, France, 23/24 November 1914

Darwan Singh Negi.

Darwan Singh Negi was born on 4 March 1883 (although some say November 1881) in Kabartir Village, Garhwal, India, the son of Kalam Singh Negi, a landowner and farmer. He was educated at a local regimental school and in February 1900 married the daughter of Ratan Singh Rawat and they went on to have one son. Before enlisting into the 39th Garhwal Rifles in March 1902, he worked as a goat herder for his father.

Negi's regiment was mobilised in August 1914 and arrived in Marseilles, in southern France, as part of the Indian Expeditionary Force in October that year. They travelled to Lillers, in the Pas-de-Calais department, and arrangements were made for them to take over the trenches of the British II Corps.

On the night of 23/24 November 1914, near Festubert, when this regiment was engaged in retaking and clearing the enemy out of the British trenches, Naik Darwan Singh Negi was always either first or among the first to push around every traverse. He did not even report that he had been wounded in the head and arm until the fighting had ceased, by which time over thirty Germans had been killed and over 100 captured.

Negi was presented with his VC on 5 December 1914 (two days before it was gazetted) by George V at St Omer, France. Although he was not the first native Indian to earn the VC, he was the first to be presented with it.

Negi was commissioned jemadar, which was backdated to 23 November 1914, and he returned to India on recruiting duties in January 1915. He was promoted to subedar in August 1915 and transferred into the 18th Garhwal Rifles, seeing active service in Iraq and Kurdistan. Negi retired in February 1920 and was granted land by Lord Gort vc. In recognition of his work on behalf of wounded soldiers and war widows, he was honoured with the title of bahadur in 1926.

Darwan Singh Negi died on 24 June 1950 and was cremated at Kabartir Village, Chamoli Garwhal District, United Provinces, and his ashes were scattered in the Ganges River. His VC is held by the Garhwal Rifles Museum, Lansdowne, Uttarakhand.

Frank Alexander de PASS, Festubert, France, 24 November 1914

Frank de Pass was born on 26 April 1887 in London, the son of Sir Eliot Arthur de Pass and Beatrice (known as Trixie) (née de Mercado). He was educated at Abbey School, Beckenham, Kent, and Rugby School, Warwickshire, which he entered in 1901. He entered the Royal Military Academy, Woolwich in 1904, having been placed 3rd on a list of successful candidates. De Pass was commissioned into the Royal Field Artillery in December 1906 and posted to India.

Promoted to lieutenant in March 1909, he was transferred into the 34th Prince Albert Victor's Own Poona Horse. He

Frank Alexander de Pass.

learned to speak Hindustani in just six months and, subsequently, Persian. In 1913, de Pass was appointed orderly officer to Sir Percy Lake, Chief of the General Staff in India. On the outbreak of the First World War, de Pass re-joined his regiment and arrived in Marseilles as part of the Indian Expeditionary Force in October 1914. The regiment saw its first action in November at Neuve-Chapelle and for the next few weeks served dismounted, providing work parties and acting as a mobile reserve.

On 24 November 1914, near Festubert, Lieutenant de Pass entered an enemy sap and crawled along it until he reached a traverse from which the enemy had been lobbing bombs into the British trench. He placed a charge into the loophole and fired it, destroying the traverse. Later, he carried a wounded sepoy to safety under heavy fire.

Frank de Pass was killed in action the next day in a second attempt to capture the sap, which had been re-occupied by the Germans. His VC was gazetted on 18 February 1915 and was posted to his father, who was too ill to attend the investiture. De Pass was buried in Béthune Town Cemetery, Pas-de-Calais, France, Plot I, Row A, Grave 24. His VC is held by the National Army Museum, London. He was the first Jewish VC recipient of the war.

William Arthur McCrae BRUCE, Givenchy, France, 19 December 1914

William Bruce was born on 15 June 1890 in Edinburgh, the son of Colonel Andrew Murison McCrae Bruce and Margaret Hay. After his father retired, the family settled in the Channel Islands. Bruce was educated at Victoria College, St Helier, Jersey, from 1904 to 1908. He entered the Royal Military Academy Sandhurst (King's Indian Cadet) in 1908 and was passed out with a commission in the Northumberland Fusiliers in 1910, and was posted to India.

Bruce learned to speak Urdu. In March 1911, he was transferred into the 59th Scinde Rifles and promoted to lieutenant the following year. When the First World War broke out, Bruce was on leave in England. He started back to India immediately but was ordered to Egypt to re-join his regiment, which had sailed to Cairo. The regiment then sailed for Marseilles, southern France, arriving in September. Its first action was at La Bassée, northern France, in late October 1914.

William Arthur McCrae Bruce.

On 19 December 1914, near Givenchy, Pas-de-Calais, Lieutenant Bruce was commanding a small party that captured an enemy trench. In spite of the pain from a severe neck wound, he paced up and down for several hours, urging his men to hold the trench against repeated German counter-attacks. It was largely due to his example and encouragement that the position was held until dusk, when it was finally retaken by the enemy and he was killed.

Bruce's VC was not gazetted until 4 September 1919, when captured British officers who had been released recommended him for the award. His father was too ill to attend an investiture in England and the medal was presented to his mother by the Lieutenant Governor of Jersey, Major General Sir Alexander Wilson.

William Bruce has no known grave; he is named on the Neuve-Chapelle Memorial to the missing, Pas-de-Calais. His VC is held by Victoria College, St Helier, Jersey, but is on display at the Jersey Museum.

Eustace JOTHAM, Spina Khaisora, India, 7 January 1915

Eustace Jotham was born on 28 November 1883 in Kidderminster, Worcestershire, the son of Frederick Charles Jotham and Mary C.A. (née Laxton). He was educated initially at Lucton Boarding School in Herefordshire as a day boy, and then at Bromsgrove School, Worcestershire, to be prepared for the Royal Military Academy Sandhurst, which he entered in 1902.

Jotham was commissioned a second lieutenant in the Prince of Wales's (North Staffordshire) Regiment in April 1903 and sailed with the 1st Battalion to

Eustace Jotham.

India in September. In June 1905, he was seconded to the Indian Army, and promoted to lieutenant in July. He then became a member of the 102nd King Edward's Own Grenadiers. In 1908, Jotham transferred to the 51st Sikhs (Frontier Force), whose role it was to guard the North-

West Frontier on the border with Afghanistan. In 1912, he was promoted to captain.

While on home leave in 1913, Jotham was returning home from Scotland when, on the leg of the journey from Carlisle to St Pancras, his train was involved in a collision, which became known as the Ais Gill rail accident. He was seen to rescue at least four people from the burning wreckage and was also a witness at the inquiry immediately afterwards.

In November 1914, the 51st Sikhs were ordered to Egypt to guard the Suez Canal while a number of officers, including Jotham, remained in India. He was attached to the North Waziristan Militia.

On 7 January 1915, at Spina Khaisora, Captain Jotham was commanding a party of twelve when they were attacked in a nullah and almost surrounded by 1,500 Khostwal tribesmen. He gave the order to retire, and could have escaped himself, but he turned back to save one of the sowars who had been knocked off his horse. Jotham killed seven of the enemy before he himself was killed.

Eustace Jotham was buried in Miranshah Cemetery, North Waziristan, India (now Pakistan), Plot 4, Grave 45. He is also named on the family grave at St Georges Churchyard, Kidderminster. His VC was gazetted on 24 July 1915 and presented to his father on 29 November 1916 by George V at Buckingham Palace. His VC is held by Bromsgrove School, Worcestershire.

The following is one of many letters received by his father:

Chief Commissioner's Camp, N.W. Frontier Provinces,
1 August, 1915

DEAR MR JOTHAM,
I hope you will excuse my writing to you to tell you how glad I am that your son's services have been recognized by the grant of the VC. No VC can have been more nobly won. Your son having miraculously cut his way through hundreds of fanatical tribesmen, deliberately turned back and went in again to save one of his sowars who was down in the melee, although he knew that he was practically certainly sacrificing his life. He killed seven of the enemy before his death, and his gallantry has made a deep impression, not only on the men of the North Waziristan Militia, but even on the enemy. We are

all proud of him, and grateful to him for setting such a magnificent example, which is specially valuable in a critical time like the present one.

Believe me,
Yours very truly,
G. Roos-Keppel

GABAR SINGH NEGI, Neuve-Chapelle, France, 10 March 1915

Gabar Singh Negi was born on 21 April 1895 (although it has also been recorded as 7 October 1893 and 19 October 1894) in Manjood or Manjaur Village, near Chamba, India, the son of Badri Singh Negi. Very little is known about his life before enlisting into the 2nd Battalion, 39th Garhwal Rifles, on 19 October 1912 other than that he was married to Satoori Devi and they had a number of children.

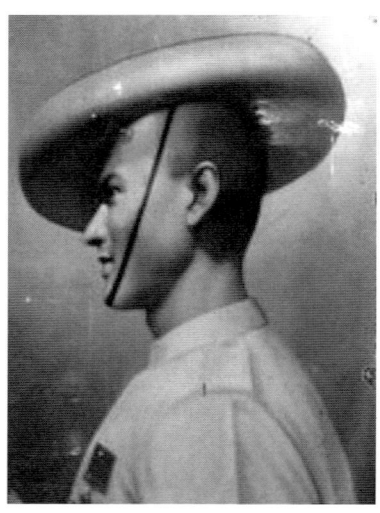

Gabar Singh Negi.

On the outbreak of the First World War, Negi's regiment was sent to France. On 10 March 1914, at Neuve-Chapelle, Rifleman Negi was part of a bombing party during an attack on the German trenches. Resistance was heavy but he was the first man to go round each traverse. He killed several Germans and forced the remainder back until they surrendered. He was killed during this action and his body was not recovered. He is, however, named (as Gobar Sing Negi) on the Neuve-Chapelle Memorial to the missing, Panel 32–33.

Gabar Singh Negi's VC was gazetted on 28 April 1915, and was sent to his widow. However, after this its whereabouts becomes unclear. It is said that it passed to his regiment, who in turn gave his widow a replica, which she wore for the remainder of her life. The location of the original is unknown.

MIR DAST, Wieltje, Belgium, 26 April 1915

Mir Dast was born on 3 December 1874 in the Maidan valley, Tirah, India (now Pakistan), the son of Mir Madha. He enlisted into the 1st Regiment of Infantry, Punjab Frontier Force, and served on the North-West Frontier 1897–98. His regiment became the 1st Punjab Infantry in 1901, and Mir Dast was promoted to naik in September the same year. His regiment became the 55th Coke's Rifles (Frontier Force) in 1903, named after a former commander.

Mir Dast.

Mir Dast was promoted to havildar in September 1904 and served on the North-West Frontier until 1908. On 18 May 1908, he was in action as part of the Mohmand Field Force at Khan Khor Beg. With two other men, he was close to a group of the enemy who were holding a position behind a low wall. Mir Dast and his colleagues rushed forward and took the position, killing three of the enemy. During the attack, Mir Dast was severely wound in the right thigh. For this action, he was awarded the Indian Order of Merit, 3rd Class.

In March 1908 he was promoted to jemadar and was one of only twelve men from his regiment to attend the Coronation Durbar for the proclamation of King George V as Emperor of India in 1911.

When the First World War broke out, Mir Dast's regiment remained in India. Eight officers and nearly 400 men were utilised to supply reinforcements to the front, including Mir Dast, who was attached to the 57th Wilde's Rifles (Frontier Force), seeing action in January 1915 at Neuve-Chapelle.

On 26 April 1915, at Wieltje, Jemadar Mir Dast led his platoon with great gallantry during an attack and later, when no British officers were left, he collected various groups of men together and kept them under his command until the order to retreat was given. He subsequently helped to carry eight wounded officers to safety while exposed to heavy fire.

Mir Dast was promoted to subedar the day after his VC action and was gazetted for the award on 29 June 1915. He was gassed, but continued to perform his duties until wounded in June 1915. He was evacuated to England and was visited by Lord Kitchener in July while at the Royal Pavilion Hospital, Brighton. On 25 August 1915, his VC was presented to him by George V while still in hospital, making him the first Indian officer to be awarded the medal.

Due to the effects of the gas and being no longer fit for active duty, he was sent back to India in October and re-joined his regiment. He once remarked, 'The gas has done for me … I had rather not have been gassed than get the VC.' He never really recovered from the gas and was moved to the Indian Army Reserve with a pension in September 1917.

Mir Dast died on 19 January 1945 and was buried in an unmarked grave (probably), Warsak Road Cemetery, Shagi Landi Kyan, Tehsil District, Peshawar, Pakistan. His VC is not publicly held.

John 'Jackie' George SMYTH, Richebourg-l'Aouvé, France, 18 May 1915

John Smyth was born on 24 October 1893 in Teignmouth, Devon, the son of William John Smyth and Lilian May (née Clifford). He hardly knew his father, who was abroad for much of his childhood and died in Burma while in the Indian Civil Service. John was raised by his mother and a family friend, Mr Hapgood, who became a second father to him.

Smyth was educated at Dragon Preparatory School, Oxford, from 1901 to 1907. He became ill with dropsy and Bright's disease, and took two years to recover. Later, he excelled at sports and went to Repton School, Derbyshire, from 1907 to 1911 and the Royal Military Academy Sandhurst from 1911 to 1912, where he played hockey and football, and also earned a 'Blue' in pistol shooting.

John 'Jackie' George Smyth.

Smyth passed out of Sandhurst with a commission as second lieutenant in August 1912 and was posted to India in September, being attached to the 1st Yorkshire Regiment. He transferred to the 15th Ludhiana Sikhs in November 1913 at Loralai, Balochistan.

When the First World War broke out, Smyth's regiment sailed to Europe, arriving in Marseilles, southern France, in September 1914. He was promoted to lieutenant in November and he trained with his battalion before moving up to the front at Richebourg, Pas-de-Calais. He lived something of a charmed life; he was buried alive by a shell but was dug out, although he was left with a hearing problem that affected him for the rest of his life. He also had a cigarette shot from out of his mouth at Windy Corner, near Cuinchy, and also had his neck cut by a piece of shrapnel.

Early in 1915, he was appointed ADC to Brigadier General Strickland, commanding the Jullundur Brigade, but returned to his battalion when its adjutant became a casualty and so he took over the role.

On 18 May 1915, at Richebourg-l'Aouvé, after two earlier attempts had failed, Lieutenant Smyth, with a bombing party of ten men, volunteered to take supplies to two companies that were holding a captured German trench. They worked their way forward 300 yards from the British lines and crossed a stream through the heaviest machine-gun and rifle fire. Only Smyth and two of his party reached the two companies holding the captured German trench.

Smyth's VC was gazetted on 29 June 1915 and was presented to him on 12 July that year by George V at Buckingham Palace. His battalion was moved to Egypt in August, and in November took part in the Senussi Campaign, after which it returned to India in February 1916 and Smyth was promoted to captain. He took part in the Mohmand Blockade on the North-West Frontier from October to December 1916. In January 1918, he passed out of the Staff School at Saugor and was appointed acting major and brigade major of the Bombay-Deolali Brigade in June. Later, he was appointed brigade major to the 43rd Indian Brigade at Lahore.

On 21 October 1919, at Khajuri, Tochi Valley, during the Waziristan Campaign, a convoy was attacked by Mahsud tribesmen. Smyth set off with 300 men and two armoured cars, arriving at the scene within two hours. He sent the infantry around the enemy to cut off their retreat and charged straight at them with the armoured cars. For this action he was awarded the MC, which was gazetted on 27 September 1920 but had already been presented to him on 21 July that year by the Duke of York at Buckingham Palace. Smyth's brother, Herbert, received the MC the same day.

Smyth married Margaret Dundas the day after his investiture and they would go on to have four children, one of whom was KIA at Kohima in 1944. Smyth returned to India, but was soon posted to Mesopotamia to help put down the Arab revolt there, arriving in August 1920, after which he again returned to India. In 1930, he was sent to Peshawar to put down the riots there, and was appointed City Commandant. In May 1903, he narrowly escaped death when an accidental discharge saw a bullet miss his head. In October 1930, he was posted to England to become an instructor at the Staff College in Camberley.

Smyth was promoted to brevet lieutenant colonel in 1933 and returned to India as second in command of the 3rd Battalion, 11th Sikhs, under Lieutenant Colonel Hyde-Cates at Rawalpindi. He then took part in the Mohmand operations on the North-West Frontier as temporary CO. He was promoted to lieutenant colonel in July 1936 and took command of the 3rd Battalion, 11th Sikhs. Towards the end of the year, he joined the Chitral Relief Force. He was posted to Allahabad in October 1938. By this time, his marriage was failing and he met Frances Mary Blair Read (née Chambers), whom he would marry in May 1940, after his divorce.

Smyth returned to England in July 1939 and served in France prior to the Dunkirk evacuation, after which he was posted back to India to command 36th Indian Brigade near Quetta, Balochistan. He was appointed acting major general in October 1941 and commander of the 19th Indian Division. When the Japanese invaded Burma, General Wavell gave him command of the 17th Indian Division, but Smyth was blamed for the retreat over the Sitting River and was sacked, even though he was suffering from malaria at the time. Due to his malaria, Smyth retired in November 1942 and became a military correspondent.

In 1945, he stood for Parliament in Wandsworth Central but was defeated by Ernest Bevin. He was elected to Parliament for Norwood in 1950, a seat he held until 1966. He served as Parliamentary Secretary to the Minister of Pensions and National Insurance in 1951–53 and was created 1st Baronet Teignmouth in January 1956. Smyth was the founder of the VC and GC Association and its first chairman (1956–71) and life president (1971–83). His VC and MC medals were stolen while he was serving in India; official replacements were issued.

He is author of *The Story of the George Cross*, *The Story of the Victoria Cross*, and *Great Stories of the Victoria Cross*, amongst other books.

John Smyth suffered a fall, breaking two ribs, and died on 26 April 1983. His ashes were scattered at Golders Green Crematorium, London, Section 2-L. His VC is in the Lord Ashcroft Gallery, Imperial War Museum, London.

CHATTA SINGH, River Wadi, Mesopotamia, 13 January 1916

Chatta Singh was born in 1886 in Tilsanda, Cawnpore, India, the son of Ishu Singh. Little is known of his early life prior to him joining the 9th Bhopal Infantry in July 1911. In early 1916, his regiment was posted to Mesopotamia.

On 13 January 1916, at the Wadi River, when after a failed attack Sepoy Chatta Singh went out into the open to the assistance of his commanding officer, Colonel Thomas, who was lying wounded in the open, he tended to his wounds and dug cover for him with his entrenching tool. For five hours, he remained with Thomas under heavy fire until dark, shielding him with his body. Then he went back to get help and brought Thomas to safety. Unfortunately, Colonel Thomas subsequently died.

Chatta Singh.

Singh's VC was gazetted on 21 June 1916, the medal being posted to the India Office five days later. Chatta Singh is believed to have been presented with it in July 1916 by Captain Ralston, Indian Army, at OC Depot, Fyzabad, India.

Chatta Singh transferred into the 16th Punjab Regiment and retired from the army with the rank of havildar. He died on 28 March 1961 and was cremated in Tilsara Village, Kanpur, Uttar Pradesh. His VC is not publicly held.

John Alexander SINTON, Orah Ruins, Mesopotamia, 21 January 1916

John Alexander Sinton.

John Sinton was born on 2 December 1884 in Victoria, Canada, the third of seven children born to Walter Lyon Sinton and Isabella Mary (née Pringle). In 1890, the family moved to Ulster, where John was educated at Nicholson Memorial School, Lisburn, and later at the Royal Belfast Academical Institution, 1889–1902. He studied medicine at Queen's College, Belfast, graduating with MB, BCh, BAO with first class honours in medicine, second class honours with exhibition in surgery and first class honours with exhibition in midwifery and gynaecology. He took up various medical posts in Belfast until July 1911, when he was commissioned a lieutenant in the Indian Medical Service.

On his arrival in India, Sinton was appointed as regimental medical officer to the 31st Duke of Connaught's Own Lancers on the North-West Frontier. In October 1915, he was appointed regimental medical officer to the 37th Donga Regiment and posted to Mesopotamia.

On 21 January 1916, at Orah Ruins, after his regiment had suffered over 340 casualties, Captain Sinton showed the most conspicuous bravery and devotion to duty. Although shot through both arms and the side, he refused to go to the hospital, and remained as long as daylight lasted, attending to his duties under very heavy fire. In three previous actions, Sinton also displayed the utmost bravery.

His VC was gazetted on 21 June 1916 and was presented to him on 31 January 1918 by Lord Chelmsford, Viceroy of India, at New Delhi. After his leave, he returned to active service commanding Cavalry Field Ambulances. From August 1918 to April 1919, he was senior medical officer to the Turkish Military Mission, with the rank of lieutenant colonel.

In 1921, Sinton was attached to the Pasteur Institute of India, based at Kasauli in north-western India. He was soon transferred from there to become the director of the Malaria Survey of India. While there, he published over 200 papers on malariology, chemotherapy, parasitology, immunology, and laboratory and survey techniques, as well as thirty-six papers on Indian species of Phlebotomus, on which he was the leading authority. He retired in 1936 having established a reputation of international standing.

In 1940, Sinton was appointed malariologist to the East Africa Force but was transferred to the Middle East Command in 1941 in the same role. He briefly retired in 1943 with the rank of honorary brigadier, but only for two weeks as he was re-employed by the War Office as a consultant malariologist to advise on malaria in the Far East.

Sinton retired again at the end of the war and settled in Northern Ireland. Instead of his scientific work, he busied himself with civic and public affairs, particularly at Queen's University (as his old college was now called). Sinton was appointed to the senate in 1948, pro-chancellor in 1952, president of the Queen's University Association in 1953 and president of the Queen's University Services Club. He held senior office in the Belfast Old Instonians Association (the organisation of former pupils of his old school, the Royal Belfast Academical Institution), and was also a JP, a high sheriff in 1953 and deputy lieutenant in 1954.

His long list of honours and distinctions is headed by his election as Fellow of the Royal Society in 1946 for his outstanding work on malaria and leishmaniasis. In 1946, he was the Robert Campbell Orator and Medallist of the Ulster Medical Society. Queen's University awarded him a DSc in 1927, and he was awarded the Chalmers Memorial Medal of the Royal Society of Tropical Medicine and Hygiene in 1929, and their highest award, the Manson Medal. He was made an Honorary Member of the National Malaria Society of the USA in 1930. From 1937 to 1946, he was a member of the Malaria Commission of the League of Nations, and from 1943 to 1946, a member of the Malaria Commission of the Medical Research Council. The Egyptian Government awarded him the Anti-Gambia Memorial Medal for his services in a malaria epidemic in 1950.

John Sinton died on 25 March 1956 and was buried with full military honours in the churchyard of Claggan Presbyterian Church, County Tyrone (now Ulster), Northern Ireland. His VC is held by the Museum of Military Medicine, Aldershot, Surrey.

LALA, El Orah, Mesopotamia, 21 January 1916

Lala was born on 20 April 1876 in Parol village, Punjab, India, the son of Dhinga. Lala had no schooling but could read and write Hindi. He joined the 41st Dogra Regiment in February 1901.

In 1914, his regiment was sent to guard the Suez Canal and later went to the Western Front, where Lara was wounded. On his recovery, he re-joined his regiment in Mesopotamia to take part in the relief of Kut.

On 21 January 1916, British/Indian forces attacked the Turkish position at El Orah but were beaten back with heavy losses. Lance Naik Lala dragged a wounded British officer to a temporary shelter, where he had already bandaged the wounds of four other men. Then, hearing the cries of his adjutant, Lieutenant A.H.E. Lindop, who was also lying wounded only 100 yards from the enemy, Lala crawled to him, staying with him until nightfall, using his own clothes to keep him warm. After dark, he carried the wounded men, one by one, to safety.

Lala.

Lala's VC was gazetted on 13 May 1916, but there is no record of an investiture. He later transferred to the 17th Dogra Regiment and took part in the Third Afghan War in 1919, ending his army career with the rank of jemadar. His original VC was lost and an official replacement issued to him in 1924.

Lala died from complications caused by polio on 23 March 1927, and his ashes were scattered at Parol, Kangra District, Punjab, India. His last words were: 'We fought true.' His replacement VC is not publicly held.

SHAHAMAD KHAN, Beit Ayeesa, Mesopotamia, 12–13 April 1916

Shahamad Khan was born on 1 July 1879 in Rawalpindi, Punjab, India (now Pakistan). He joined the army in December 1904 and served in the 89th Punjab Regiment. He served in many theatres during the First World War, including Egypt, Turkey, France and Mesopotamia.

On 12–13 April 1916, at Beit Ayeesa, Naik Shahamad Khan was in charge of a machine gun covering a gap in the British lines, within 150 yards from the enemy. He beat off three counter-attacks and worked his gun single-handedly after all except two belt feeders had become casualties. For three hours, he held the gap under very heavy fire, and when his gun was put out of action, he and his two belt feeders held on with rifles until ordered to withdraw. With help, he then brought back his gun and a severely wounded man, as well as, eventually, all remaining arms and equipment. But for his action, the line would have undoubtedly been overrun by the enemy.

Shahamad Khan.

Khan's VC was gazetted on 26 September 1916 and was presented to him on 13 November by George V at Buckingham Palace. In January 1919, he was promoted to jemadar. Very little is known of the rest of his life, other than that his VC was either lost or stolen, as an official replacement was issued to him.

Shahamad Khan died on 28 July 1947 and was buried in Takhti Village Cemetery, near Rawalpindi, Pakistan. His official replacement VC is in the Lord Ashcroft Gallery, Imperial War Museum, London.

GOBIND (spelt GOVIND on later records) **SINGH**, Pozières, France, 1 December 1917

Gobind Singh was born on 7 December 1887 in Damoi, in the Nagaur District of Rajasthan, India. He joined the Jodhpur Lancers, but was transferred to the 28th Light Cavalry with the rank of lance daffadar, was posted to France, and was later attached to the 2nd Lancers (Gardner's Horse).

On 1 December 1917, near Pozières, when his regiment was surrounded by the enemy, a message had to be sent to HQ. Lance Daffadar Gobind Singh volunteered to carry the message from his regiment to brigade HQ, a distance of 2 miles. His horse was shot from under him and he continued on foot. Having got through, he then had to return with a message for his CO. Given another horse, he started back, and this horse was also shot from under him and once again, he continued on foot.

Gobind Singh.

When a third message needed to be sent, Gobind Singh, although exhausted and wounded, immediately volunteered to take it. At first, his request was turned down, but he insisted as he knew the terrain better than anyone else. During this journey, his horse was killed by a shell, but he nevertheless continued on foot and again reached the HQ.

Gobind Singh's VC was gazetted on 11 January 1918 and was presented to him on 6 February 1918 by George V at Buckingham Palace. At a special reception held in his honour, he was presented with a gold watch and a silver plate. The event was attended by General Sir O'Moore Creagh, vc, and Lieutenant General Maharajah Sir Pertab Singhji.

Gobind Singh stayed on in the army after the war, retiring with the rank of jemadar in 1934. He died on 9 December 1943 and was cremated at Damoe Village, Jodhpur, India. His VC is held by the 2nd Lancers (Gardner's Horse), Indian Army.

BADLU SINGH, Jordan River, Palestine, 23 September 1918

Badlu Singh was born in November (some sources say 13 January) 1876 in Dhakla Village, Punjab, India. He enlisted into the 14th (Murray's Jat) Lancers in September 1895. The regiment was raised by General Murray and made up entirely of Hindu Jats. Badlu Singh was promoted to lance daffadar in October 1908, and daffadar in August 1909.

In January 1915, Badlu Singh was promoted to jemadar, and served on the North-West Frontier from September to October that year. Then his regiment was posted to France, serving there from May 1916 until March 1918, during which time he was promoted to ressaidar in January 1917.

He was posted to Palestine, and by now attached to the 29th Lancers (Deccan Horse), when, on 23 September 1918 at the Jordan River, his squadron was charging a strong enemy position. Ressaidar Badlu Singh realised that heavy casualties were being inflicted on his unit from a small hill that was occupied by 200 men with machine guns. Without hesitation, he collected six men, and with utter disregard of the danger, he charged and captured the position. Singh was mortally wounded on the very top of the hill while attempting to capture one of the machine guns single-handedly, but all the guns and men had surrendered to him before he died sometime later.

Badlu Singh.

In accordance with Hindu beliefs, Badlu Singh was cremated immediately. His VC was gazetted on 27 November 1918 and presented to his son, Chotan Singh, in 1919 in India, possibly by the Viceroy of India. His VC is in the Lord Ashcroft Gallery, Imperial War Museum, London.

Waziristan Campaign, 1919–20

British-occupied towns and military posts on India's North-West Frontier had come under continual attack by Mahsud tribesmen. A force of 63,000 was mustered to put down the growing insurrection.

Henry John ANDREWS, Khajuri, 22 October 1919

Harry (as he would be known) Andrews was born on 23 March 1871 in London. Both his parents were members of The Salvation Army, and it was his dying mother's wish that he be brought up by the First Chief of Staff and Second General (or head) of The Salvation Army, Bramwell Booth. This wish was granted and Booth's sister, Emma, helped care for Andrews, who was educated by The Salvation Army at Clapton, London.

At 15, Andrews accompanied Emma to India with her new husband, where he was destined to become The Salvation Army's first 'medical man' in India,

Henry John Andrews.

serving there for thirty years. His work there started almost immediately when a chance meeting with an Indian boy with acute toothache led him to reading a dental manual and he then used sterilised forceps to remove the tooth. The grateful boy dubbed him 'The Little Doctor' and word spread that he was willing to help those in need.

At 17, he became an officer in The Salvation Army, and as his amateur medical workload increased, he eventually received formal training as a pharmacist. During a cholera outbreak in 1893, he was appointed to assist Major William Stevens at The Salvation Army's Indian HQ. Andrews returned to England in 1896 and had more formal training in dressing injuries and wounds.

However, he was keen to get back to his adopted country of India to assist in establishing the Catherine Booth Hospital in Nagercoil. Four years later, he transferred to Anand in Goojerat, where he helped establish the Emery Hospital. In October 1899, he married Gena Smith, whom he had met at his childhood nursery in Clapton. Andrews went to the USA for more medical training, graduating in 1910, and returned to India in 1912, where he was based at Moradabad.

On the outbreak of the First World War, The Salvation Army placed the hospital at Moradabad under the jurisdiction of the government together with Doctor Andrews and the staff. Once the war had begun, Andrews, now a lieutenant colonel in The Salvation Army, volunteered for active service, but was turned down due to his work at the hospital. However, in 1917 he was finally commissioned as a lieutenant in the Indian Medical Service and was promoted to temporary captain the following year.

In June 1918, he was awarded the MBE, and soon afterwards was allowed to give up his hospital post in order to head for the North-West Frontier serving in the Indian Medical Service.

On 22 October 1919, at Khajuri, Temporary Captain Andrews heard that a convoy had been attacked nearby and he went out to tend to the wounded. He set up an aid post, which offered some protection to those who were injured, but none for himself. He was compelled to move the aid post, but continued to attend to the men. Finally, when a van was available, he collected the wounded and under fire loaded them into it. He was killed just as he was stepping into the van, having completed his task.

Henry Andrews was buried in Bannu Cemetery, south of Peshawar, Pakistan, Grave 160 (the headstone may still exist). His VC was gazetted on 9 September 1920 and presented to his widow on 2 November that year by George V at Buckingham Palace. His VC is in the Lord Ashcroft Gallery, Imperial War Museum, London.

William David KENNY, Kot Kai, 2 January 1920

William Kenny was born on 1 February 1899 in Saintfield, County Down, Ireland, the eldest child of John Joseph Kenny and Miriam Martha (née Newton). He was commissioned a second lieutenant into the Indian Army in August 1918 and posted to the 4th Battalion, 39th Garhwal Rifles, and was promoted to lieutenant the following year.

On 2 January 1920, at Kot Kai in Waziristan, Lieutenant Kenny was in command of a company holding an

William David Kenny.

advanced position that was attacked three times by the Mahsuds in greatly superior numbers. He held them for four hours, being foremost in the hand-to-hand fighting that took place. In the subsequent withdrawal, when he led a counter-attack with a small party to allow the wounded to be reovered, his party was overcome and he was seen fighting to the last.

William Kenny was buried in Jandola Cemetery, North-West Frontier, India (now Pakistan), Grave 5. (It is unclear whether his headstone still exists.) His VC was gazetted on 9 September 1920 and the medal was presented to his parents on 2 November that year by George V at Buckingham Palace.

The medal is in the Lord Ashcroft Gallery, Imperial War Museum, London.

ISHAR SINGH, Haidari Kach, 10 April 1921

Ishar Singh was born on 30 December 1895 in Nanwan, Punjab, India. Little is known about his life prior to enlisting upon the outbreak of the First World War, throughout which he served.

On 10 April 1921, at Haidari Kach on the North-West Frontier, Sepoy Ishar Singh was serving in the 28th Punjab Regiment when he received a very severe wound to the chest and fell beside his Lewis gun. Hand-to-hand fighting having commenced, all the officers and NCOs were ether killed or wounded, and Singh's Lewis gun was taken by the enemy. Calling to two other men, he got up and charged the enemy, recovering the gun and, although bleeding profusely, again got the weapon into action. When his jemadar arrived, he took the Lewis gun from Singh and ordered him to go to get his wound dressed. Instead, he went to the medical officer and was of great assistance in pointing out where other wounded men were lying, and in carrying water to them. He made many trips to the river for this purpose. On one

Ishar Singh.

occasion, when the enemy fire was very heavy, he took a wounded man's rifle and opened fire on the enemy. On another occasion, he stood in front of the medical officer who was dressing a wounded man, thus shielding him with his body. It was over three hours before he finally submitted to being evacuated, by now too weak from loss of blood to object.

Singh's VC was gazetted on 25 November 1921 and was presented to him in March 1922 by The Prince of Wales (later Edward VIII) in Rawalpindi. He attended the 1929 VC Dinner at the House of Lords. During the Second World War, he served with the rank of subedar and was later promoted to captain.

Ishar Singh died on 2 December 1963 and was cremated at Panam Village, Hoshiarpur District, Punjab, India. His VC is in the Lord Ashcroft Gallery, Imperial War Museum, London.

Second Mohmand Campaign, 1935

After years of unrest, the tribes of India's North-West Frontier battled against British colonial expansion, and continued political pressure eventually achieved the same rights for the people of the North-West Frontier as enjoyed in British India. However, the hill tribes remained fiercely anti-British and embarked on a two-year rampage of robbery and murder, which the Indian Army struggled to contain. Eventually, the Nowshera Brigade was sent to deal with the Mohmand tribesmen.

Godfrey MEYNELL, Mohmand Valley, 29 September 1935
___

Godfrey Meynell was born on 20 May 1904 in Kirk Langley, Derbyshire, the eldest of four children of Godfrey Meynell and Edith Violet (née Cammell). He won a scholarship to Eton, where he bullied fellow pupil Cyril Connolly before establishing a friendship with him. Connolly wrote about their friendship in *Enemies of Promise* (published 1938).

Meynell was sent to the Royal Military Academy Sandhurst, and passed out thirteenth in his class and subsequently volunteered to join the Indian Army, being posted to the 5th Battalion (Corps of Guides), 12th Frontier Force Regiment. In 1933, he was awarded the MC during the Chitral reliefs. He married Sophia Patricia, known as Jill, and they were both fluent in Urdu.

On 29 September 1935, at Mohmand, when in the final phase of an attack, Captain Meynell went to the most forward troops, finding them involved in a struggle against vastly superior numbers. He at once took command and with two Lewis guns and about thirty men maintained a heavy and accurate fire on the advancing enemy, but their numbers nevertheless succeeded in reaching the position and putting the Lewis guns out of action. In the hand-to-hand fighting that followed, Meynell was mortally wounded. However, the heavy losses inflicted on the enemy prevented them from exploiting their success.

Godfrey Maynell.

Godfrey Meynell was buried in Guides Cemetery, St Alban's Churchyard, Mardan, Pakistan. His VC was gazetted on 24 December 1935 and was presented to his widow in July 1936 by Edward VIII (the only VC awarded during his reign). The medal is thought to still be held by his family.

Second World War, 1939–45

The causes of the Second World War are well known: Hitler's rise to power in 1933, reoccupying the Rhineland, annexing Austria and taking over the Sudetenland of Czechoslovakia. Next was the demand to Poland to allow access to Danzig. When this was refused, Germany attacked Poland on 1 September 1939. Britain and France had guaranteed Poland's sovereignty and declared war on Germany two days later. The conflict truly became a world war when Japan attacked the USA on 7 December 1941. The Second World War was the most destructive conflict the world had ever known, resulting in the deaths of about 60 million people worldwide.

PREMINDRA SINGH BHAGAT, Gallabat, Abyssinia, 31 January to 4 February 1941

Premindra Singh Bhagat was born on 14 October 1918 in Gorakhpur, India, the son of Surendra Singh Bhagat. In 1930, he went to the Royal Indian Military College, Dehradun, and in 1937 entered the Indian Military Academy as a gentleman cadet. Bhagat passed out as a second lieutenant in June 1937 and joined the Corps of Indian Engineers, attached to the Royal Bombay Sappers and Miners.

In September 1940, he joined the 21 Field Company of Engineers (he was the only Indian officer in the company), and embarked for East Africa as part of the 10th Indian Brigade, 5th Indian Division, landing in Port Sudan in late October. His first action came on 5 November 1940, when, during the advance on Galabad, his CO, Lieutenant Patterson, was mortally wounded when his Universal Carrier hit a mine. Bhagat then took over the section. The Italians were well dug in and the attack stalled, with some men beginning to retreat. Lieutenant Colonel S.E. Taylor stood upright under fire so his men could see him. He was joined by Bhagat, who noticed Taylor was wounded but was refusing to be bandaged. Bhagat later said he was 'stunned with such cool bravery and total dedication'. This undoubtedly influenced his subsequent actions.

Premindra Singh Bhagat.

The Italians put in a strong counter-attack and forced the brigade to leave Galabad. During the retreat the sappers destroyed as many buildings and stores as they could. The next day, two derelict tanks were packed with explosives and fired to block a culvert, but only one of them detonated. Bhagat went back under heavy fire to reset the detonation; this time the charge went off and the culvert was blocked. For this action, he was recommended the MC, but was only mentioned in despatches.

During the pursuit of the enemy following the capture of Metemma, from 31 January to 4 February 1941, Second Lieutenant Premindra Singh

Bhagat was in command of a section of a field company of sappers and miners, detailed to accompany the leading mobile troops in Universal Carriers to clear the road ahead. During this period, he personally supervised the clearing of fifteen Italian minefields. He covered 55 miles, was twice blown up in his Universal Carrier, each time suffering casualties among his men, and during one ambush his ear drums were punctured. He refused relief of any kind until the task was completed. His actions over ninety-six hours ensured the safety of the column, relying on his speed and effort.

Bhagat's VC was gazetted on 10 June 1941 and he was presented with the ribbon (the medal itself having not arrived in time) the same month by General Wavell at a victory parade in Asmara. Bhagat was sent home and received a hero's welcome. He raised a new company, 48 Field Company, and in February 1942 he married Mohini Bhandari. In mid-1943, he was trained in jungle warfare in Burma, but never actually saw active service for the remainder of the war. In January 1945, he was nominated for the Staff College at Camberley, being one of only two Indian officers to attend college in the UK. He wrote a paper entitled *My Land Divided*, reflecting his hope for a reconciliation between the religious groups, in which he commented: 'What greatness and power there is in store for us, the four hundred million people of India, if only we unite, yet we keep apart.'

Bhagat returned to India in time for independence and the terrible aftermath. He was assigned command of the 165th Infantry Brigade at Ramgarh. The rest of his career can be summarised thus: 1959, Director of Military Intelligence; 1961, National Defence College Course; 1962, Commandant, Indian Military Academy; 1963, Chief of Staff to Army Commander Eastern Command; 1964, GOC 9th Mountain Division; 1966, Commander XI Corps, Western Command; 1970, Army Commander, Central Command; 1972, Army Commander, Northern Command; 1974, retired from the army, appointed Chairman, Damodar Valley Corporation.

During his time with the Central Command in the 1970s, the Gomti River flooded near Lucknow. His personal involvement and energy with which he marshalled all available resources contributed greatly to preventing a total disaster.

Premindra Singh Bhagat died on 23 May 1975 and his ashes were scattered in various rivers in India. His VC is held by the Bombay Engineers Museum, Kirkee, Pune, India.

RICHHPAL (sometimes spelt RICHPAL) RAM, Keren, Eritrea, 7/8 & 12 February 1941

Richhpal Ram was born on 20 August 1899 in Barda, Punjab, India. Nothing much is known about him before he enlisted into the 6th Rajputana Rifles on his twenty-first birthday. Following his enlistment, he married and had two sons and a daughter. Richhpal Ram had reached the rank of subedar by the start of the Second World War, and his regiment was posted to Eritrea.

On the night of 7/8 February 1941 at Keren, during an attack, Subedar Richhpal Ram insisted on accompanying the lead platoon. When his company commander was wounded, Ram took over and led the attack. In the face of heavy fire and with only thirty men, he rushed the objective with the bayonet and captured it. His party were now completely isolated but under his inspiring leadership they beat off six enemy attacks. By now, the ammunition had run out, and Ram extricated his men and fought his way back to the battalion with just a handful of survivors.

Richhpal Ram.

On 12 February that year, Ram led another attack on the same position and pressed on fearlessly in the face of heavy enemy fire until his right foot was blown off. He suffered further wounds, from which he died. His last words were: 'We'll capture this objective.'

Richhpal Ram was cremated near where he fell and is named on Keren Cremation Memorial (column 5), Senafe, Eritrea. His VC was gazetted on 4 July 1941 and presented to his widow in 1942 by the Viceroy of India, Lord Linlithgow. The medal is now on display in the Delhi Cantonment Raj Rifles Officers' Mess Museum, India.

Arthur Edward CUMMING, Kuantan, Malaya, 3 January 1942

Arthur Cumming was born on 18 June 1896 in Karachi, India (now Pakistan), and was educated at Karachi Grammar School. On the outbreak of the First World War, he joined the 58th Vaughan's Rifles, attached to the 53rd Sikh Regiment, and was heavily involved in the fighting in the Middle East/Mesopotamia. He was commissioned a lieutenant in November 1918, mentioned in despatches and awarded the MC. His MC citation reads:

Arthur Edward Cumming.

> For conspicuous gallantry and skilful leadership in an attack on a redoubt.
> He led the advance party round the rear of the redoubt, and engaged the retreating enemy in a hand-to-hand fight, which resulted in half of them being killed or captured.
>   Later, when the enemy counter-attacked, he seized a Lewis gun, and under [a] heavy enemy barrage engaged them in the open. His fine example of courage greatly encouraged his men, who drove back the counter-attack with great loss [to the enemy].

Between the world wars, Cumming remained in the Indian Army and by the time of the Second World War was a lieutenant colonel in the 2nd Battalion, 12th Frontier Force, and was posted to Malaya.

On 3 January 1942, at Kuantan, the Japanese made a furious attack on his battalion and a strong force penetrated the position while the brigade HQ and a battalion were being withdrawn. Lieutenant Colonel Cumming, with a small party of men, immediately led a counter-attack and, although all of the men became casualties and he received two bayonet wounds to the stomach, he managed to restore the situation so that the major parts of the battalion and its vehicles could be withdrawn. Later, he drove in a Universal Carrier under heavy fire, collecting isolated detachments of men, and was again wounded. His gallant actions helped the brigade to withdraw safely.

Cumming was promoted to temporary brigadier after Kuantan and was involved in the defence of Singapore. He was one of a small number of officers and men who were ordered to leave before the surrender on 15 February 1942. He was given command of the 9th Jat Regiment before being promoted to brigadier and command of the 63rd Indian Brigade during the Burma Campaign. From 1944 to 1947, he commanded the Dehradun District in India.

Although Cumming's VC was gazetted on 20 February 1942, he didn't receive his medal until 29 July 1947, when it was presented to him by King George VI at Buckingham Palace. Cumming retired from the army the same year and settled in Scotland.

Arthur Cumming died on 10 April 1971 and his ashes were scattered in the Garden of Remembrance, Warriston Crematorium, Edinburgh. His VC is held by the National Army Museum, London.

PARKASH SINGH, Donbaik, Burma, 6 & 19 January 1943

Parkash Singh was born on 31 March 1913 in Sharikar, Lyallpur District, India. He was an unruly boy at school, and in an attempt to set him on the straight and narrow, his headmaster put him in charge of a group of boys. Contrary to the headmaster's intention, they formed a highly disciplined gang, stealing from local villages.

Singh's behaviour was tolerated due to his cleverness and athletic ability (he held the all-India record for the 800 metres). He managed to enrol into college and his headmaster offered him a scholarship, hoping he would take up

Parkash Singh.

further education. However, he had other ideas. A lack of vacancies meant he was unable to join the police, so in 1936, he enlisted into the 8th Punjab Regiment. He first saw action on the North-West Frontier, when his company was besieged by Pathan tribesmen.

In late 1942, General Slim decided to launch an offensive into the Arakan District of Burma to capture Akyab Island, which had a port and an airfield, both of which were needed as a springboard for further offensives.

On 6 January 1943, near Donbaik, when the Universal Carrier platoon came under a strong attack from Japanese forces and the platoon commander was wounded, Havildar Parkash Singh took over. Noticing that two Universal Carriers had been put out of action, he drove forward in his own vehicle to rescue the two crews under heavy fire. They had used all their ammunition and the enemy were rushing at the disabled carriers on foot. Singh got the men under cover while he provided cover fire. When his gunner was wounded, Singh drove at the enemy, firing the Bren gun with one hand, and threw them out of their positions.

On 19 January, three more carriers were put out of action by anti-tank fire in an exposed area, one of which was carrying the survivors of another carrier as well as its own crew. On seeing what had happened, Singh went out in his own carrier, and with complete disregard for his own personal safety, he rescued the crews from one disabled carrier, together with the weapons from another. He then went out again under heavy anti-tank and machine-gun fire, dismounted and connected a towing chain to a disabled carrier with two wounded men in it, and towed it back to safety.

Singh's VC was gazetted over two years later, on 1 May 1945, and was presented to him by the Viceroy of India, Lord Linlithgow, at the Red Fort in New Delhi. In August, he was promoted to jemadar, and later to subedar. He married and went on to have four children, all girls. He was also given 64 acres of land. In the Partition of India, he and the other Sikhs in his regiment went to Pakistan, and Singh was put in charge of the wives and children on their difficult journey to Jalandhar. Once there, he was given land to compensate for the land he left behind.

Singh retired from the army in 1968 with the rank of major and took up farming. In 1985, he appeared in a TV programme entitled *For Valour*, in which he made a very good impression.

Parkash Singh died on 23 March 1991, following an operation, and his ashes were returned to his home village near Jullundur (now Jalandhar), Punjab, India. His VC is on long-term loan from his family to the Lord Ashcroft Gallery, Imperial War Museum, London.

CHHELU RAM, Djebel Garci, Tunisia, 19/20 April 1943

Chhelu Ram was born on 10 May 1905 in Dhenod, Punjab, India. Little is known of his life prior to enlisting into the 4th Battalion, 6th Rajputana Rifles before the First World War.

On the night of 19/20 April 1943, Company Havildar Major Ram was part of an attack on Djebel Garci. While advancing on their second objective, his company was held up by enemy machine-gun and mortar fire from high ground. Armed with a tommy gun, Ram immediately rushed forward through intense fire and killed three or four of the enemy single-handedly, which enabled

Chhelu Ram.

the advance to continue. When approaching the next objective the enemy brought down heavy fire, which mortally wounded the company commander. Ram went over to him and attended to his wounds, but was himself wounded. He then took command of the remnants of two companies, reorganising them. Almost immediately, the enemy counter-attacked and his men ran short of ammunition. During the fierce hand-to-hand fighting that followed, Ram's bravery and determination were beyond praise. He rushed to wherever the fighting was heaviest, rallying the men and driving the enemy back with cries of 'Jats and Mohammedans, there must be no withdrawal! We will advance! Advance!' He then led a counter-attack with the bayonet, and his men, inspired by his example, again drove the enemy back. Ram was mortally wounded during this attack but refused to be carried back, and continued to command until he died.

Chhelu Ram was buried in Sfax War Cemetery, Tunisia, Plot H, Row C, Grave 5. His VC was gazetted on 27 July 1943 and was presented to his window by the Viceroy, Lord Wavell, at the Red Fort, New Delhi. Ram's medal is not publicly held.

NAND SINGH, Arakan, Burma, 11–12 March 1944

Nand Singh.

Nand Singh was born on 24 September 1914 in Bhatinda, Punjab, India. Little is known about him until he enlisted into the 1st Battalion, 11th Sikh Regiment in 1933. On the outbreak of the Second World War, his regiment was heavily involved in action in South East Asia, and by 1944, the Burma Campaign.

On 11–12 March 1944, at Arakan, on the Maungdaw–Buthidaung Road, Acting Naik Nand Singh was ordered to recapture a position called India Hill, the only approach being along a steep knife-edge ridge. Almost immediately, his platoon came under heavy fire, killing or wounding many of his men. Singh moved forward alone, even though he was wounded in the thigh, and he captured the first trench. He crawled further forward and was wounded again, in the face and shoulder. He nevertheless captured the second and third trenches single-handedly.

Singh's VC was gazetted on 6 June 1944 and was presented to him on 24 October 1944 by the Viceroy, Lord Wavell, at the Red Fort, New Delhi.

After the war, Singh stayed in the Indian Army and took part in the Indo-Pakistani War. On 12 December 1947, he led his platoon in a desperate but successful attack to extricate his battalion from an ambush in the hills of south-eastern Uri, Kashmir. He was mortally wounded by a close-range burst of machine-gun fire.

Unfortunately, he was recognised by his VC ribbon and his body was paraded through the streets of Muzaffarabad, with proclamations that this would be the fate of every Indian VC recipient. His body was later thrown into a rubbish dump and not recovered. Nand Singh was posthumously awarded the MVC, the second-highest Indian decoration for gallantry. This makes him unique in the annals of the VC.

Singh's VC is not publicly held, but a replica is on display at the Sikh Regiment Centre, Ramgarh, Bihar, India. He is also the only VC recipient to have been killed in a post-Second World War conflict.

ABDUL HAFIZ, Imphal, India, 6 April 1944

Abdul Hafiz was born on 4 September 1925 in Kalanaur, Punjab, India. Not much is known of him prior to his enlistment into the 9th Jat Regiment and service on the North-West Frontier before the outbreak of the Second World War.

In early 1944, the Japanese attempted to break out of Burma and sought to destroy the Allied forces at Imphal; at one point, the city was almost entirely surrounded. In April 1944, the 9th Jat Regiment were holding a hill 10 miles north of Imphal, and on 6 April, Jemadar Abdul Hafiz was ordered to attack with two sections a position believed to be held by forty Japanese. Before the attack, he told his men they were invincible, and

Abdul Hafiz.

that all of the enemy would be killed or routed. He so inspired his men that the attack proceeded with great dash, and they charged up the slope with no cover into machine-gun fire and grenades. On reaching the crest, Hafiz was wounded in the leg, but seeing a machine gun firing from the flank, he immediately rushed it and grabbed the barrel while another man killed the gunner. He then took a Bren gun and advanced on the enemy, firing as he went, killing several of them. So fierce did his men fight that the enemy, who were still in considerable numbers, fled. As they were pursued, Hafiz was hit in the chest by machine-gun fire from another position. Collapsing, he still tried to fire the Bren gun, shouting: 'Reorganise on the position and I will give covering fire.'

Abdul Hafiz died shortly afterwards and was buried in Imphal Indian Army War Cemetery, Manipur, India, Plot III, Row Q, Grave 2. His VC is in the Lord Ashcroft Gallery, Imperial War Museum, London.

KAMAL RAM, Gari River, Italy, 12 May 1944

Kamal Ram was born on 17 December 1924 in Bholupura, India, the son of Shiv Chand Harsana. Little is known of his early life prior to enlisting into the 3rd Battalion, 8th Punjab Regiment, in 1943. He was posted to Italy with his regiment by 1944.

On 12 May 1944, after crossing the Gari River, his company was held up by heavy machine-gun fire from four posts to the front and flanks. Sepoy Kamal Ram volunteered to try to get around the rear of the post on the right. Crawling forward through wire, he attacked the post single-handedly and shot the

Kamal Ram.

gunner. Another German tried to seize the weapon but Ram killed him with the bayonet and, when an officer appeared from a trench, he shot him too. Still alone, he went on to the next post, shot the gunner and threw in a grenade, and the remaining enemy surrendered. With the help of a havildar, he destroyed the third post. When a platoon pushed further forward to widen the position, Kamal Ram dashed towards a house, shot one German in a slit trench and captured two more. By his courage, initiative and disregard for personal safety he enabled his company to secure the ground vital to establishing the bridgehead.

His VC was gazetted on 27 July 1944 and he was presented with the ribbon the day before it was gazetted, by George VI while still in Italy. The medal itself was presented to him on 24 October that year by the Viceroy, Lord Wavell, at the Red Fort, New Delhi. He was also promoted to subedar. Following the war he returned to India. He attended the 1956 Centenary Celebrations in England and many of the VC/GC Association reunions. He remained in the Indian Army after independence and retired in 1972 with the rank of honorary lieutenant.

Kamal Ram died on 1 July 1982 and was cremated at Sawai Madhopur, Rajasthan, India. His VC is in the Lord Ashcroft Gallery, Imperial War Museum, London.

John Keefer MAHONY, Melfa River, Italy, 24 May 1944

John Mahony was born on 30 June 1911 in New Westminster, British Columbia, Canada. He was educated at the Duke of Connaught High School in New Westminster. Mahony became a journalist and reporter with the Vancouver *Province*, but was also a member of the Westminster Militia Regiment. On the outbreak of the Second World War he was among the first to enlist, joining the Westminster Regiment (Motor), Canadian Infantry Corps, and was quickly promoted to major.

John Keefer Mahony.

On 24 May 1944, Major Mahony was ordered to establish a bridgehead across the Melfa River. He led his men across and directed each section into position. From 15:30 until 20:30, the company came under enemy attack. Shortly after the bridgehead was established, the enemy counter-attacked with tanks, SPGs and infantry. The attack was beaten off by PIATs, 2-inch mortars and grenades. Mahony directed the fire of the PIATs throughout this action, encouraging and inspiring his men. By now, the company strength was reduced to sixty men, and most of the officers were wounded. An hour later, enemy tanks and infantry formed up and launched another attack. Determined to hold at all costs, Mahony went from section to section with words of encouragement, personally directing their fire. At one point, a section was pinned down by accurate and intense machine-gun fire. Mahony crawled forward to its position and, by throwing smoke grenades, succeeded in extricating the section with the loss of only one man. This attack was beaten off with the destruction of three SPGs and a tank. During the action, Mahony was wounded in the head and twice in the leg, but refused medical aid. It was only when the remaining companies had crossed to support him did he allow his wounds to be dressed, but he still refused to be evacuated.

Mahony's VC was gazetted on 13 July 1944 and he was presented with the ribbon on 26 July 1944 by King George VI in Italy, and with the medal itself on 3 December that year, again by George VI at Buckingham

Palace. After the war, Mahony stayed on in the army, serving successively until 1964 as Commandant Cadet Officer of the Western Command, Director of Publications for the Canadian Army and Assistant Adjutant and Quartermaster General of the Western Ontario Area.

John Mahony died on 16 December 1990, after a long battle with Parkinson's disease, and was cremated at Mount Pleasant Crematorium, London, Ontario. His VC is held by the Canadian War Museum, Ottawa, Ontario.

YESHWANT GHADGE, Upper Tiber Valley, Italy, 10 July 1944

Yeshwant Ghadge was born on 16 November 1921 in Palasgaon, Bombay, India. Little is known of his early life prior to his enlistment into the 5th Maratha Light Infantry on the outbreak of the Second World War. Sepoy Yeshwant Ghadge was serving in the Middle East where, in 1941, he was mentioned in despatches for his bravery. By 1944, he had been promoted to naik.

On 10 July 1944, in the Upper Tiber Valley, Naik Yeshwant Ghadge's rifle section came under heavy machine-gun fire at close range, which killed or wounded everyone except the commander. Without hesitation, Ghadge rushed the gun position, first throwing a grenade, which knocked out the gun and gunner, and then shooting one of the crew. Finally, having no time to change his magazine, he killed the two remaining crew members in hand-to-hand combat. Almost immediately, he was shot dead by sniper fire.

Yeshwant Ghadge.

Yeshwant Ghadge has no known grave, but he is listed on the memorial to the missing at Cassino War Memorial, Italy, Panel 17. His VC was gazetted on 2 November 1944 and his medal is not publicly held.

RAM SARUP SINGH, Kennedy Peak, Tiddim, Burma, 25 October 1944

Ram Sarup Singh was born on 13 April 1919 in Kheri, Haryana, India. Nothing much is known about his life prior to him enlisting into the 2nd Battalion, 1st Punjab Regiment on the outbreak of the Second World War. He was promoted to jemadar and by late 1944, was an acting subedar.

On 25 October 1944, at Kennedy Park in the Tiddim area of Burma, Acting Subedar Ram Sarup Singh's section, along with another, was ordered to attack the flank of an enemy position, which

Ram Sarup Singh.

was well defended with machine guns sited in bunkers. The attack was so sudden that the enemy were bewildered and fled from their posts. Singh was wounded in both legs but took no notice of his injuries. While consolidating the position the enemy counter-attacked in three waves. It seemed that the position would be overrun, but Singh got a machine gun in place and then led a charge into the advancing enemy, bayoneting four men himself. Although badly wounded in the thigh, he again went for the enemy, all the time shouting encouragement to his men. He bayoneted one and shot another, but was mortally wounded by a burst of machine-gun fire to the neck and chest.

Ram Sarup Singh has no known grave, but he is named on the memorial to the missing at the Rangoon Memorial, Burma, Face 30. His VC was gazetted on 8 February 1945 and his medal is now in the Lord Ashcroft Gallery, Imperial War Museum, London.

BHANDARI RAM, East Mayu, Arakan, Burma, 22 November 1944

Bhandari Ram was born on 24 July 1919 in Pargna Gugeda, Bilaspur, Himachal Pradesh, India. He was a farmer before joining the 16th Battalion, 10th Baluch Regiment on his birthday in 1941.

On 22 November 1944, at East Mayu, Sepoy Bhandari Ram's platoon was climbing a precipitous slope. As they neared the top, they came under heavy machine-gun fire from a strongly held bunker position. Ram was wounded in the shoulder and leg. The platoon was now pinned down, and Ram crawled forward to within 15 yards of a machine-gun post. The enemy threw grenades at him, seriously wounding him in the face and chest. Undeterred, he crawled to within 5 yards and threw a grenade, killing three crew. Inspired by his example, the platoon rushed forward and captured the position. It was only then that Ram allowed his wounds to be dressed.

Bhandari Ram.

His VC was gazetted on 8 February 1945 and was presented to him on 3 March that year by Lord Wavell, at the Red Fort in New Delhi. Ram stayed on in the Indian Army after independence and took part in the wars over Kashmir, often fighting against old comrades. He left the army in 1969 and married Champa Devi, and they went on to have five children.

In a 1999 interview, Ram explained his action thus: 'It was all to do with wanting to please [the] commanding officer by doing a good job.' He attended many of the VC/GC reunions.

Bhandari Ram died on 19 May 2002 and was cremated at Auhur, Himachal Pradesh, India. His medal is not publicly held.

UMRAO SINGH, Kaladan Valley, Burma, 15/16 December 1944

Umrao Singh was born on 21 November 1920 in Palra, Punjab, India, the son of Mohar Singh. He attended school locally and joined the Royal Indian Artillery two months after the start of the Second World War. He was promoted to havildar in 1942.

On the night of 15/16 December 1944, in the Kaladan Valley, Havildar Umrao Singh was in charge of one gun when his battery was in an advanced position. They came under a ninety-minute sustained bombardment from the Japanese, and his position was attacked by at least two companies of enemy infantry. He directed the rifle fire of his gunners, holding off the assault, during which he was twice wounded by grenades.

A second wave of attackers was also beaten off; at one point, he used a Bren gun, firing over the shield of his artillery piece. His men only had a few bullets remaining and these were rapidly used in the initial stages of the third wave of attacks. Undaunted, Singh picked up a 'gun bearer' and used that as a weapon in hand-to-hand fighting. During the final attack, all but Umrao Singh and two of his men were killed. He was seen to strike down three enemy infantrymen before succumbing to a rain of blows.

Umrao Singh.

Six hours later, after a counter-attack, Singh was found alive but unconscious near to his gun, almost unrecognisable from a head injury, still clutching his gun bearer. Ten Japanese soldiers lay dead nearby. Singh's field gun was back in action later that day.

Singh's VC was gazetted on 31 May 1945 and was presented to him on 15 October that year by George VI at Buckingham Palace. He retired from the army in 1946 and joined the independent Indian Army in 1948, becoming a subedar major, retiring as an honorary captain in 1970. He took up farming and was known as VC Singh in his village. He married and had three children.

At the celebrations of the fiftieth anniversary of VE Day in London in 1995, Singh was almost turned away from the VIP tent because his name was not on the right list, but Brigadier Tom Longland, who organised the event, saw his VC and gave orders to admit him. After the event, Singh complained to Prime Minister John Major about the meagre pension of £100 per year paid to the then ten living Indian VC holders. The amount had been fixed since 1959, but John Major subsequently arranged for the pension to be raised to £1,000 per year.

In spite of personal hardship and receiving substantial offers, Singh refused to sell his medal during his lifetime, saying that selling it would 'stain the honour of those who fell in battle'.

Umrao Singh died on 21 November 2005 (his eighty-fifth birthday) and was cremated in Palra, Punjab, India. His medal is not publicly held.

SHER SHAH AWAN, Kyeyebyin, Burma, 19/20 January 1945

Sher Shah Awan was born on 14 February 1917 in Chakrala, Punjab, India (now Pakistan), the son of Syed Barkhurdar Shah and Makda Bibi. All that is known of his early life is that he was married and a farmer. On the outbreak of the Second World War, he enlisted into the 7th Battalion, 16th Punjab Regiment, and rose to the rank of lance naik.

On the night of 19/20 January 1945, at Kyeyebyin, Burma, Lance Naik Sher Shah Awan was in command of the left forward section of his platoon. At 19:30, an enemy platoon attacked his position. Realising that the enemy would overrun and destroy his section, he crawled forward alone and fired into the rear of the Japanese, breaking up their attack. He killed the platoon commander and six men, and after the remainder withdrew, he crawled back to his post. At 00:15, the Japanese, now reinforced with a company, started to form up for another attack. Awan heard their officers giving orders and bayonets being fixed prior to the assault. Again, he crawled forward alone, and could see the officers and men grouped together. He fired into this group at close range and they ran in disorder. While on his way back, he was hit by a mortar bomb, which shattered his right leg. He made it back to his section and, propping himself against the side of a trench, continued firing and encouraging his men. When asked if he was hurt, he replied that it was only slight. Sometime afterwards, it was discovered that his leg was missing. The Japanese again started forming up for another attack. In spite of his severe wounds and considerable loss of blood, Awan once again crawled forward, firing into them at point-blank range. He continued firing until the attack was broken up, then was shot in the head, from which he subsequently died. Twenty-three dead and four wounded men, including an officer, were found at daybreak immediately in front of his position. His indomitable courage undoubtedly saved his platoon from being overrun, and was the deciding factor in defeating the Japanese attacks.

Sher Shah Awan's VC was gazetted on 8 May 1945 and was presented to his widow. Awan has no known grave but is named on the memorial to the missing, Rangoon Memorial, Burma, Face 48. His battalion, 7/16th Punjab Regiment, now part of the Pakistan Army, is proudly known as the 'Sher Shah Battalion'. Awan's VC medal was sold at auction in 2002 for a hammer price of £85,000 to an unknown buyer.

PRAKASH SINGH CHIB, Kanlan Ywathit, Burma, 16/17 February 1945

Prakash Singh Chib was born on 1 April 1913 in the Jammu and Kashmir region of India. Little is known of his early life prior to him enlisting into the 4th Battalion, 13th Frontier Force Rifles during the early part of the Second World War.

On the night of 16/17 February 1945, at Kanlan Ywathit, Burma, Jemadar Prakash Singh Chib was commanding his platoon when it was attacked by overwhelming numbers. The enemy were supported by artillery, mortars and machine guns. Chib was wounded in both ankles early in the attack, so his

Prakash Singh Chib.

company commander relieved him of command and brought him back to the company HQ. When his second in command was also wounded, Chib crawled back to his platoon and again took command. He was propped up by his batman, who had also been wounded, firing a 2-inch mortar. Chib was shouting encouragement to his men and directing the fire of his platoon. Having fired off all his mortar ammunition, he crawled around collecting ammunition from the dead and wounded, and this he distributed himself. As one section of his platoon had all become casualties, he took over their Bren gun and held the sector alone until reinforcements were rushed forward by the company commander. He fired his Bren gun from a position in the open, as he was unable to stand in the trenches. Again, he was wounded, in both legs above the knees. In spite of his pain, he continued firing his gun and dragging himself from one section to another by the use of his hands, as his legs were now completely smashed. At this time, he continued to encourage and direct his men, regrouping them around him so that they held up a fierce Japanese charge. Being wounded for the third time, again in the leg, he was now unable to move, but he was lying on his side facing the enemy and directing the action of his men. Although it was obvious he was dying, he shouted out the Dogra war cry (*Jwala Mata Ki Jai*, Victory to Goddess Jwala), which was taken up by the whole company. His example and leadership so inspired the company that the enemy were finally driven off, but Chib was wounded for a fourth time, in the chest by a grenade. He died a few minutes later, after telling his company commander not to worry about him for he could look after himself.

Prakash Singh Chib has no known grave but he is named on the memorial to the missing, Rangoon Memorial, Yangon, Myanmar (formerly Burma), Face 43. His VC was gazetted on 1 May 1945 and the medal was presented to his family, who it is thought still hold the medal.

GIAN SINGH, Kamye-Myingyan Road, Burma, 2 March 1945

Gian Singh was born on 5 October 1920 in Sahabpur, Punjab, India. Little is known of him prior to his service in the 15th Punjab Regiment.

On 2 March 1945, on the Kamye-Myingyan Road, Burma, with the Japanese in full retreat, British and Indian forces crossed the Irrawaddy River and advanced on the port of Myingyan. Suddenly, the enemy opened fire with artillery and machine guns. Two companies successfully carried out an encircling movement and established themselves in the rear of the enemy position.

Gian Singh..

They then attacked a village with the aid of tanks, Naik Gian Singh being in command of the leading section. Ordering his Bren gunner to cover him, he rushed forward alone firing his tommy gun. He was met by a hail of bullets and wounded in the arm, but despite this, he continued his advance, throwing grenades and killing several Japanese soldiers. By this time, the tanks had moved up in support and came under fire from a cleverly concealed anti-tank gun. Seeing the danger, Singh again rushed forward alone, killed the crew and captured the gun. His men followed him and he led them down a lane, clearing all the enemy positions. After this action, his company re-formed to take the enemy positions to the rear. He was ordered to the aid post but refused to go, and led his section until the whole action was over. There is no doubt that his acts of gallantry saved the platoon many casualties.

Singh refused to be invalided out of the army and was prominent during the drive on Rangoon, for which he was mentioned in despatches. His VC was gazetted on 22 May 1945 and was presented to him on 16 October 1945 by George VI at Buckingham Palace. His VC was stolen in 1960 and an official replacement was issued the following year. After Indian independence, he saw fighting in the Sino-Indian War of 1962 and in the Indo-Pakistani War of 1965.

After retiring from the army with the honorary rank of captain, he took up farming near Nawabshah, Pakistan. He was married to Hardail Kaur and they had three sons and two daughters. Singh was regular at the VC/GC reunions.

Gian Sing died on 6 October 1996 and was cremated; his ashes were scattered 'to the rivers' in the Northern Punjab, India. His official replacement VC medal is not publicly held.

FAZAL DIN, Meiktila, Burma, 2 March 1945

Fazal Din was born on 1 July 1921 in the village of Hussainpur, Hoshiapur District, Punjab, India, the son of Nur Bakhsh. He passed through school and enlisted into the 7th Battalion, 10th Baluch Regiment in 1939 or 1940, and later served in the Burma Campaign.

On 1 March 1945, the British launched an attack on the town of Meiktila, east of the Irrawaddy River. In a carefully co-ordinated plan, British and Indian forces attacked from the north, east and west.

The next day, Acting Naik Fazal Din was commanding a section of a company during an attack on enemy bunkers when they were held up by machine-gun fire. He rushed the nearest bunker alone and silenced it. Then he led his men against the other bunkers. Suddenly, six men, led by two officers wielding swords, rushed at them. Fazal Din was run through the chest by one of the officers but as the sword was withdrawn, he tore it from the officer's hand and killed him with it. He then attacked another man and killed him. Seeing one of his men struggling with an enemy soldier, he went to his assistance, killing the assailant with the sword. Then, waving the sword in the air, he continued to encourage his men, and then staggered to the platoon HQ to make his report. He collapsed and died soon after reaching the aid post. Almost the entire platoon witnessed this action and were undoubtedly inspired by Din's gallantry; taking advantage of the bewilderment of the enemy, they annihilated the garrison.

Fazal Din.

Fazal Din has no known grave, but he is named on the memorial to the missing at the Rangoon Memorial, Yangon, Myanmar (formerly Burma), Face 39. His VC was gazetted on 24 May 1945 and was presented to his family on 19 December that year by the Viceroy, Lord Wavell, at the Red Fort, New Delhi. The medal is now in the Lord Ashcroft Gallery, Imperial War Museum, London.

KARAMJEET SINGH JUDGE, Meiktila, Burma, 18 March 1945

Karamjeet Singh Judge was born on 25 May 1923 in Kapurthala, India, the son of the city's chief of police. He was a member of the Indian National Congress Party and was studying politics at Lahore College when he decided to enrol for Officer Training School at Bangalore. He opted to join the Pioneer Corps to get nearer the Burma front line. At his brother's (who was serving in the Royal Indian Artillery) written request, Karamjeet Singh Judge was commissioned as subaltern in the 4th Battalion, 15th Punjab Regiment and was posted to Burma in time for the drive on Rangoon.

On 18 March 1945, at Meiktila, Burma, Lieutenant Karamjeet Singh Judge's platoon was leading the attack. Repeatedly, the attack was held up by machine-gun fire from bunkers not seen by the supporting tanks. On each occasion, Singh Judge, with complete disregard for his own safety, went forward to recall the tanks by means of telephone. He pointed out the bunkers to the tanks and then personally led the infantry in to finish them off, being the first to reach each one. On one occasion, as he was going in, two Japanese soldiers suddenly rushed at him and he killed them at a range of only 10 yards. Having cleared some ten bunkers in this fashion, when a nest of three more bunkers were located, he directed a tank to within 20 yards of the first bunker and threw a smoke grenade to help the tank see it. After a few shots he asked the tank to cease their fire and he led a few men in to mop up, when, within 10 yards of the bunker, a machine gun opened fire, mortally wounding him in the chest.

Karamjeet Singh Judge.

Karamjeet Singh Judge has no known grave, but he is named on the memorial to the missing at the Rangoon Memorial, Yangon, Myanmar (formerly Burma), Face 25. His VC was gazetted on 3 July 1945 and presented to his family on 19 December that year by the Viceroy, Lord Wavell, at the Red Fort, New Delhi. His medal is not publicly held.

ALI HAIDAR, Senio River, Italy, 9 April 1945

Ali Haidar was born on 21 August 1913 in Kohat, India (now Pakistan). Little is known of him prior to his VC action with the 6th Battalion, 13th Frontier Force Rifles.

After more than a year of crawling up the Italian peninsula and the stalemate of the Anzio landings, the theatre commander, Field Marshall Sir Harold Alexander, opened an offensive in April 1945 on either side of Bologna with a view to drive the Germans back through the Po Valley.

On 9 April 1945, at the Senio River, Sepoy Ali Haidar's platoon was crossing the river and came under very heavy machine-gun fire from two posts. He was one of only three men to get across.

Ali Haidar.

Leaving the other two men to cover him, he charged the nearest post and threw a grenade into it, at the same time being wounded in the back by a grenade thrown at him by the enemy. The post was destroyed and four Germans surrendered. With complete disregard for his personal safety, Haidar then charged the next post and was again wounded in the right arm and leg. He crawled forward and threw in a grenade and charged, finding two wounded and two men surrendering. The rest of his company were now able to cross the river and establish a bridgehead. Haidar's action undoubtedly saved many lives in his company.

Ali Haidar did not recover fully from his wounds until after the war. His VC was gazetted on 3 July 1945 and was presented to him on 30 October that year by George VI at Buckingham Palace. He returned to his regiment and retired with the rank of jemadar, and took up farming. He married in 1947 but he and his wife Meena had no children. Life was hard as their only real income came from his VC allowance of £100 and his small army pension. However, he did manage to come to London in 1993 to attend the VC/GC reunion, and two years later for the fiftieth anniversary of VE Day, the same year the VC allowance was raised to £1,000 a year.

Ali Haidar died on 15 July 1999 and was buried in Shahu Khel Village, Kohat District, Pakistan. His VC is in the Lord Ashcroft Gallery, Imperial War Museum, London.

NAMDEO JADHAO (also spelt JADAV), Senio River, Italy, 9 April 1945

Namdeo Jadhao was born on 18 November 1921 in Virgaon, India. Little is known of his early life before enlisting into the 1st Battalion, 5th Mahratta Light Infantry and being posted to Italy.

On 9 April 1945, at the Senio River, Sepoy Namdeo Jadhao was crossing the river with his company when they came under fire from three machine-gun posts and his commander was one of several men killed or wounded. He immediately carried one wounded man through deep water and up the precipitous slope on the east bank, and across a mine belt to safety.

Namdeo Jadhao.

He then went back to help another of the wounded men. Both times, he was under heavy fire. He was determined to avenge his dead comrades and eliminate the machine-gun posts that were pinning down the battalion, so, crossing the exposed east bank a third time, he dashed at the nearest enemy post, silencing it with his tommy gun. He was, however, wounded in the hand and unable to use his gun anymore, so he threw it away and resorted to hand grenades. With these, he charged and took out two more enemy posts, one time crawling to the top of the bank to resupply his stock from comrades on the reverse slope. Having silenced all the machine-gun fire from the east bank, he stood in the open shouting the Mahratta war cry – *Bol Shri Chattrapati Shivaji Maharaj ki Jai!* (Cry Victory to King Shivaji!) – and waving the rest of the companies across the river. This sepoy not only saved the lives of the men he rescued, but his outstanding personal bravery enabled the battalion to secure a deeper bridgehead, which in turn led to the collapse of German resistance in the area.

Jadhao's VC was gazetted on 15 June 1945 and presented to him on 20 July that year by George VI at Buckingham Palace. He retired with the rank of havildar.

Namdeo Jadhao died on 2 August 1984 and was cremated at Pune, Maharashtra State, India, where his ashes were scattered. His VC is not publicly held.

Glossary

Addiscombe Military Seminary	Training college for the Honourable East India Company's Army
Assegai	Short Zulu stabbing spear (actually a Portuguese word)
Bahadur	An honorary title originally given to British officers meaning 'a great man'
Bahun	Chaplain
Bashi-bazouk	An irregular or mercenary soldier
Bastion	A projecting part of a fortification
Brevet	Temporary rank
Canister	Also known as grapeshot, fired from a cannon like a giant shotgun against massed infantry
Dervish	A member of a Muslim religious order
Dhooli	A litter or stretcher
Fieldworks	Fortifications made of earth and wood
Guncotton	A replacement for gunpowder as a propellant in firearms
Houssa (also Hausa or Haussa)	A member of a predominantly Muslim ethnic group inhabiting northern Nigeria and southern Niger.
Knobkerrie	Zulu war club
Kukri	Grurkha knife; it is a myth that once drawn, blood must be spilled before it can be sheathed
Levy/levies	Locally raised units of poor training and little fighting value

Lewis gun	Light machine gun
Loophole	Small hole in a defensive wall, for soldiers to fire through
Mahdi	The Guided, or Chosen, One
Nullah	A small river or ravine
Picquet	Sentry duty
Rough rider	Someone who trains horses, either an NCO or a private
Sally	A surprise advance by a body of men
Sap	A covered trench dug to approach enemy fortifications
Slit trench	A narrow trench
Sortie	An attack made by soldiers from a position of defence
Subaltern	An officer of lower rank than a captain, especially a second lieutenant
Tommy gun	Thompson sub-machine gun
Traverse	Perpendicular-dug trench leading into the main trench
Tulwar	Sword
Universal Carrier aka Bren gun carrier	A small, lightly armoured, fully tracked vehicle

Acronyms and Abbreviations

ADC	Aide-de-Camp
CB	Companion of the Bath
C-in-C	Commander-in-Chief
CIC	Canadian Infantry Corps
CO	Commanding Officer
CSI	Order of the Star of India
DSO	Distinguished Service Order
GHQ	General Headquarters
GOC	General Officer Commanding
HEIC	Honourable East India Company
HRH	His Royal Highness
HQ	Headquarters
JP	Justice of the Peace
MBE	Member of the British Empire
MC	Military Cross
MM	Military Medal
MVC	Maha Vir Chakra
NAM	National Army Museum
PIAT	Projectile Infantry Anti-Tank, a spring-loaded, shoulder-fired, anti-tank gun
SPG	Self-propelled gun
RA	Royal Artillery
RAMC	Royal Army Medical Corps
RLC	Royal Logistic Corps
RN	Royal Navy
VJ Day	Victory over Japan Day

Indian Army Ranks

Indian Army	British Army equivalent or role (*in italics*)
Risaldar	Lieutenant
Jemadar	Second Lieutenant
Ressaidar	Platoon commander (same as subedar & Jemadar)
Subedar Major	*Company second in command*
Subedar & Jemadar	Platoon commander
Havildar Major	Company Sergeant Major
Havildar (infantry) or Duffadar (cavalry)	Sergeant
Naik (infantry) or Lance Duffadar (cavalry)	Corporal
Lance Naik (infantry) or Acting Lance Dafadar (cavalry)	Lance Corporal
Sepoy (infantry)	*Rifleman*
Sowar (cavalry)	Trooper

Bibliography

Ashcroft, Michael, *Victoria Cross Heroes*, Headline Publishing, 2006.
Batchelor, Peter F. & Christopher Matson, *VCs of the First World War: The Western Front 1915*, Wrens Park Publishing, 1999.
Best, Brian, *The Victoria Crosses that saved an Empire*, Frontline Books, 2016.
Biggs, Maurice, *The Story of Gurkha VCs*, The Gurkha Museum Publications, 2001.
Brazier, Kevin, *The Complete Victoria Cross*, Pen & Sword, 2020.
Crook, M.J., *The Evolution of the Victoria Cross*, Midas Books, in association with Ogilby Trust, 1975.
Glanfield, John, *Bravest of the Brave: The Story of the Victoria Cross*, Sutton Publishing, 2005.
Gough, General Sir Hugh, *Old Memories*, William Blackwood & Sons, 1897.
Haydon, A.L., *The Book of the VC*, Andrew Melrose, 1906.
Holmes, Richard, *Sahib: The British Soldier in India*, Harper Perennial, 2005.
Leek, Alan, *Frederick Whirlpool VC: The Hidden Victoria Cross*, Pen & Sword, 2018.
Parker, John, *The Gurkhas: The Inside Story of the World's Most Feared Soldiers*, Headline Publishing, 1999.
Rambahadur Limbu, vc, *My Life Story*, Gurkha Welfare Trust, 1978.
Smyth, Sir John, vc, *The Story of the Victoria Cross, 1856–1963*, Frederick Muller, 1963.
Smyth, Sir John, vc, *The Victoria Cross, 1856–1964*, Frederick Muller, 1965.
The Journal of the Victoria Cross Society, Editions 1–12, Brian Best (ed.), The Victoria Cross Society.
The VC and DSO Book: The Victoria Cross 1856–1920, Creagh, Sir O'Moore, vc, & Humphris, E.M. (eds.), The Naval & Military Press.
The Victoria Crosses and George Crosses of the Honourable East India Company & Indian Army 1856–1945, National Army Museum, 1962.

Alphabetical List

ABDUL HAFIZ, 207
ADAMS, James William, 149
ADAMS, Robert Bellew, 160
AGANSING RAI, 29
AIKMAN, Frederick Robertson, 103
AITKEN, Robert Hope Moncrieff, 59
ALI HAIDAR, 219
ALLMAND, Michael, 24
ANDREWS, Henry John, 194
AYLMER, Fenton John, 156

BADLU SINGH, 192
BAKER, Charles George, 114
BHANBHAGTA GURUNG, 34
BHANDARI RAM, 211
BLAKER, Frank Gerald, 31
BLAIR, James, 68
BOISRAGON, Guy Hudleston, 12
BRENNAN, Joseph Charles, 106
BROWN, Francis David Millet, 95
BROWNE, Samuel James, 113
BRUCE, William Arthur McCrae, 179
BUCKLEY, John, 50
BUTLER, Thomas Adair, 104

CADELL, Thomas, 55
CAFE, William Martin, 109
CARTER, Herbert Augustine, 174
CHANNER, George Nicolas, 6
CHASE, William St Lucien, 153
CHATTA SINGH, 187
CHHELU RAM, 205
CHICKEN, George Bell, 115
CLOGSTOUN, Herbert Mackworth, 128
COBBE, Alexander Stanhope, 171
COLVIN, James Morris Colquhoun, 166
CONNOLLY, William, 61
COOK, John, 8
COSTELLO, Edmond William, 159

CREAGH, Garrett O'Moore,	147
CRIMMIN, John,	155
CUBITT, William George,	57
CUMMING, Arthur Edward,	202
DARWAN SINGH NEGI,	177
DAUNT, John Charles Campbell,	84
De PASS, Frank Alexander,	178
DIAMOND, Bernard,	83
DUFFY, Thomas,	81
DUNDAS, James,	138
FAZAL DIN,	217
FINCASTLE, Alexander Edward Murray Viscount,	162
FITZGIBBON, Andrew,	131
FITZGERALD, Richard,	83
FORREST, George,	51
FOSBERY, George Vincent,	132
GAJE GHALE,	23
GANJU LAMA,	25
GIAN SINGH,	216
GILL, Peter,	54
GABAR SINGH NEGI,	182
GOBIND (spelt GOVIND on later records) SINGH,	191
GOODFELLOW, Charles Augustus,	129
GOUGH, Charles John Stanley,	69
GOUGH, Hugh Henry,	89
GRANT, Charles James William,	11
GRANT, John Duncan,	16
HAMILTON, Walter Richard Pollock,	146
HAMMOND, Arthur George,	151
HARINGTON, Hastings Edward,	92
HART, Reginald Clare,	143
HILLS (later HILLS-JOHNES), James,	64
HOME, Duncan Charles,	70
INNES, James John McLeod,	101
ISHAR SINGH,	196
JARRETT, Hanson Chambers Taylor,	117
JENNINGS, Edmond (Edward),	93
JOTHAM, Eustace,	180
KAMAL RAM,	208
KARAMJEET SINGH JUDGE,	218
KARANBAHADUR RANA,	20
KAVANAGH, Thomas Henry,	86

KEATINGE, Richard Harte,	105
KENNY, William David,	195
KHUDADAD KHAN,	176
KULBIR THAPA,	18
LACHHIMAN GURUNG,	35
LALA,	190
LALBAHADUR THAPA,	22
LAUGHNAN, Thomas,	94
LEACH, Edward Pemberton,	144
LISLE-PHILLIPPS, Everard Aloysius,	53
LYSTER, Harry Hammon,	110
McDONELL William Fraser,	66
McGOVERN (aka McGOWAN), John,	56
McGUIRE, James,	75
McINNES, Hugh,	94
McNEILL, John Carstairs,	134
MACINTYRE, Donald,	5
MacLEAN, Hector Lachlan Stewart,	163
MAHONY, John Keefer,	209
MALCOLMSON, John Grant,	46
MANNERS SMITH, John,	13
MANGLES, Ross Lowis,	65
MAXWELL, Francis Aylmer,	167
MAYO, Arthur,	98
MELLISS, Charles John,	169
MEYNELL, Godfrey,	197
MILLER, James William,	85
MIR DAST,	183
MOORE, Arthur Thomas,	47
NAMDEO JADHAO (also spelt JADAV),	221
NAND SINGH,	206
NETRABAHADUR THAPA,	28
OLPHERTS, William,	79
PARK, James,	94
PARKASH SINGH CHIB,	203
PITCHER, Henry William,	133
PRAKASH SINGH CHIB,	215
PREMINDRA SINGH BHAGAT,	199
PRENDERGAST, Harry North Dalrymple,	96
PROBYN, Dighton MacNaghten,	48
RAM SARUP SINGH,	211
RAMBAHADUR LIMBU,	38
RAYNOR, William,	52

RENNY, George Alexander, 77
RICHHPAL (sometimes spelt RICHPAL) RAM, 201
RIDGEWAY, Richard Kirby, 9
ROBERTS, Frederick Sleigh, 99
RODDY, Patrick, 116
ROLLAND, George Murray, 173
ROSAMOND, Matthew, 55
RYAN, Miles, 76
RYAN, John, 81

SALKELD, Philip, 72
SARTORIUS, Reginald William, 140
SCOTT, Andrew, 142
SHAHAMAD KHAN, 190
SHER SHAH AWAN, 214
SHERBAHADUR THAPA, 32
SINTON, John Alexander, 188
SMITH, John Thomas, 96
SMITH, John, 73
SMYTH, John George, 184

THACKERAY, Edward Talbot, 78
THAMAN GURUNG, 33
THOMAS, Jacob, 82
TOMBS, Henry, 62
TRAVERS, James, 60
TREVOR, William Spottiswoode, 136
TULBAHADUR PUN, 26
TYTLER, John Adam, 3

UMRAO SINGH, 212

VOUSDEN, William John, 152

WALLER William Francis Frederick, 112
WALKER, William George, 15
WATSON, John, 90
WATSON, Thomas Colclough, 164
WHIRLPOOL, Frederick, 108
WHITCHURCH, Harry Frederick, 158
WHEELER, George Campbell, 19
WOOD, Henry Evelyn, 118
WOOD, John Augustus, 45

YESHWANT GHADGE, 210